# Whip
# Smart

# Whip
# Smart

*a memoir*

## Melissa Febos

THOMAS DUNNE BOOKS
St. Martin's Press
New York

THOMAS DUNNE BOOKS.
An imprint of St. Martin's Press.

WHIP SMART. Copyright © 2010 by Melissa Febos. All rights reserved.
Printed in the United States of America.
For information, address St. Martin's Press,
175 Fifth Avenue, New York, N.Y. 10010.

www.thomasdunnebooks.com
www.stmartins.com

LIBRARY OF CONGRESS CATALOGING-IN-PUBLICATION DATA

Febos, Melissa.
    Whip smart : a memoir / Melissa Febos.—1st ed.
        p.   cm.
    "Thomas Dunne Books."
    ISBN 978-0-312-56102-4
    1. Febos, Melissa—Sexual behavior.   2. Authors, American—
21st century—Biography.   I. Title.
PS3606.E26Z46   2010
818'.603—dc22
[B]
                                                    2009040282


10   9   8   7   6   5   4   3   2

*For Ariel*

# Author's Note

Everything in this book is true to my memory of it. Most characters' names and many identifying characteristics have been changed. In some instances, time was compressed or altered slightly to facilitate an economical telling of the story. I had to leave a lot out. Transforming actual people into literary characters is unavoidably reductive, and for that I'm sorry.

I am Human, let nothing human be foreign to me.

—MONTAIGNE

I HAVE ALWAYS LOVED SECRETS. Growing up in rural Cape Cod, I used to bury household objects in the woods behind our home, or on the banks of the pond we swam in all summer long. I drew maps with crayons, detailing the locations of my buried toys, or random kitchen utensils, and then cut out the insides of my books to make hiding places for the drawn plots. Those ravaged books on my shelf comforted me. To think of their secret contents, and the hidden knowledge in my own mind, gave me a surge of joy. The point was not that anyone would realize that something had gone missing. What thrilled me was that I was the keeper, I alone possessed the knowledge of a thing that was hidden away. Over time these secrets carved out a space in me—a tiny part of reality over which I had full control. Those parts of me, unknown by other people, felt stronger, safer, removed from the perils of an unpredictable world.

As a teenager, I traded the fantasies of books and daydreams for mind-altering substances and social landscapes as far from my own as I could get. The allure of dark undersides pulled my life toward a future of increasingly fractured extremes. I pursued older lovers, intoxicated by their attentions, and soon found that seduction promised the greatest high of all. I had experienced a happy childhood and I was generally disposed to a calm and gentle demeanor, but underneath I craved the polarities of unmitigated power and total submission. I took drugs to control my world and subjugate my mind. Then I took drugs to escape them. There was no gray area, no middle way; it was always all or nothing.

It made sense that I ended up in New York City, where this story begins, though in the beginning it felt like waking from one dream to another. At twenty-one, I still knew how to be good; I was a college senior with a 3.9 GPA, a prestigious internship—and a new secret life as a professional dominatrix. I was also addicted to drugs, although the craving for that kind of high would prove less tenacious than what I found at the upscale S&M house where I spent the next four years. I walked through the door a self-described cultural anthropologist, and then watched every self-description I'd ever had dissolve.

I was a student of human behavior long before I had the words to articulate what it felt like to be a watcher. For as long as I can remember, I *saw* people, their needs and worries and motives, as people assume children cannot. I thought for a long time that my driving force was my intrinsic curiosity about strangers and all the illicit things that other people do. I thought I sat on the outside, observing, manipulating, and drawing conclusions. I was wrong.

What began as a job became a life, and my most captivating secret of all. Behind that unmarked Midtown door, I uncovered hiding places that I hadn't known existed in me, and whose contents weren't easy to behold. Ultimately, though, when I did, it surprised me to find that my own dark underside wasn't so strange or sick as I feared.

This book is that story.

# Part One

# 1

STEVE KNEW TO BE KNEELING when I walked into the Red Room, his torso bent over his knees, forehead resting on the rug. He knew to be clean. He knew to undress, and to fold his clothes neatly behind the door, so that I walked into an immaculate room, nothing between me and the softly folded fist of his body but anticipation. While desire rose off Steve in fumes, steeping the whole room in its cloying vapor, I reveled in its absence. Just minutes before entering the Red Room, I adjusted my garters before the dressing room mirror, wrapped my fingers in electrical tape, and felt that happy absence, whose vacancy made room for some other, unnamed thing to fill me. I felt it already, the way you can smell autumn coming. Steve was into heavy flogging, and the tape protected the clefts between my index and middle fingers where I would soon clench a flogger handle in each hand.

I had cued the music—which piped from the main office into all twelve rooms of the dungeon—to begin just a few seconds before I walked into the Red Room. The music I sessioned to was all the same; while I preferred angrier music for meaner sessions, all that really mattered was the bass line. I didn't need a plan to have a good session; I needed a pulse.

If that great red-walled room was a womb, I was its heart. I was the moving center, my will a muscular force. There was nowhere I could go, it seemed, that the cushion of my client's longing wouldn't support me. It happened to be 10:45 in the morning, but the only time that mattered in that room was indicated on the wall-mounted timer that I turned a full circle when I walked in. There was only ever one hour in the dungeon.

As I closed the door behind me, the pale stripe of my body shifting on the mirrored walls, I dropped my supply box on the floor by the door. Steve flinched at the sound, as I'd intended. I let my heels fall heavy against the wood floor on my way to a row of hooks lining the wall. Retrieving a smooth length of rope, I draped it around my shoulders. Then, finding Steve's favorite floggers, I held one in each hand, letting their thick tassels swing against my legs as I approached him, knowing the gentle slap of leather against my legs would agitate him. Standing over his curled body from behind, I dropped a flogger to the floor on either side of him and bent over so that only the tips of my hair, and my breath, touched him.

"Get the fuck up," I whispered.

"Yes, Mistress," he exhaled, and hurried to his feet, head still bowed toward his chest. Steve also knew that looking at me was a privilege he had to earn. Pulling his hands behind his back, I slid the rope off my shoulders and looped it around his wrists. With a few quick loops and a single knot, I securely bound his arms from wrists to shoulders. I paused then, giving him a few moments to absorb the warmth of my body so close behind him, and the embrace of the rope, which I knew would only feel tighter as our hour progressed. There were clients I cowed with words, but with Steve his own anticipation was enough to wilt him into submission; I just had to pause and let it accumulate. Slowly dragging the tip of my finger from the base of his spine to the hard vertebral knuckle at the base of his neck, I watched a shudder follow my touch up his body. Pausing again, I let my fingertip rest on him, and knew how the heat of my touch rippled out across his body. No job, indeed, no exercise I've ever done, has been so coldly empathic as this one. I grabbed a handful of hair from the back of Steve's head and pulled hard. Steve yelped, and sank jerkily to his knees. I stepped around in front of him, keeping my handful of hair so that when I crouched down to face him, his head was thrust back to face the ceiling, eyes wide and wild. His mouth trembled with short breaths, lips parted. Pressing a finger against his chin, I gave his hair an extra tug to open his mouth wider.

"Thirsty, Steve?" I asked. He knew I alluded to the golden shower I would end the session with, if he was good. Steve was always good. Between now and then, however, I would tan his ass with those leather tails until he cried for mercy.

Who pays to get peed on before their breakfast has been digested? It's a logical question, and one I've answered after nearly every explanation of my working hours. The day shift began at 10:30 A.M. on weekdays and ended at 5:30 P.M. Often I would arrive at the dungeon at 10:20 and already have a client waiting for me. It didn't take long to figure out that most of the patrons of the dungeon were not, as I had originally suspected, social outcasts who spent their time in basement apartments fondling pet snakes and watching pornography. They were seemingly normal. The majority of them were married fathers, and they were nearly all professionally successful. My client base consisted of stockbrokers, lawyers, doctors, rabbis, grandpas, bus drivers, restauranteurs, and retirees. Getting peed on, spanked, sodomized, or diapered was less often a delicacy than a basic provision to these men. And while the need for it was compulsive, it was also routine; it was an itch that they had been compulsively scratching for many years, and it did not require an atmosphere of nighttime, intoxication, or great fanfare.

The day-shift crowd scheduled their whippings the way they scheduled business luncheons: out of necessity and convenience. En route to the dungeon they dropped off the dry cleaning, or their wives at Macy's. Just as the cafés all over midtown Manhattan had their lunch rushes, so did we.

After Steve's thirst had been quenched and he'd showered and dressed, we exchanged the usual pleasantries: I asked after his wife, and he tipped me a crisp fifty-dollar bill. Leaning my head out the door of the Red Room, I called, "Walking out!"—our practice of warning the occupants of nearby rooms to stay put. Clients could *never* meet in the halls of the dungeon. Then I led Steve down the opulent passageway to the magnetically locked chamber leading to the elevator.

"I'll see you on Friday," I said.

"Thank you, Justine." Steve smiled warmly and adjusted his tie. Before I had even heard the click of the door's lock, I pulled my hair into a bun, kicked off my heels, and headed back to clean the Red Room. I had an exam the next morning to study for.

# 2

Becoming a dominatrix had not been my plan when I moved to New York, though New York had been my plan since childhood; I just knew I would go there for college and stay for life. My ability to identify a Point A and Point B was always well developed; so long as I could figure out the quickest route between where I was and where I wanted to be, I had a deep assuredness that I could get myself there. High school had seemed an impediment to my ambitions; *I* knew better than my teachers what I wanted to learn and how to learn it. At sixteen, after passing the GED, I moved out of my mother's Cape Cod home and into my own Boston apartment and took on a busy schedule of night classes at Harvard, waitressing shifts, and experimental drug use. At nineteen, I didn't bother to research other options, applying only to one school, where I knew I belonged, in the heart of the Village.

In the blistering August of '99, after receiving my acceptance letter from The New School, I moved the crates of books I'd been hoarding all my life up the three flights of stairs of my first New York apartment. My mother had helped me stuff her car with all my crates, and together we trudged up and down the narrow staircase all afternoon. By five o'clock we had finished and sat on the car's rear bumper under the shade of the open hatchback passing a bottle of water between us. My mother speculated as yet another shirtless man with sculpted legs in short shorts walked by.

"He's so handsome as well! Men in New York really take care of themselves. There must be a gym nearby."

I scoffed.

"Mom, this is *Chelsea*. Of course there's a gym nearby, not that that explains the Daisy Dukes."

"*Oh!* Of course." She laughed, and we finished our water. "So Melly, why don't we take showers and then walk down to the West Village and find a little café to grab some dinner in. We should celebrate!"

She turned to me and smiled, her eagerness beaming outward. I squinted ahead, where the sun had sunk behind a row of buildings, crowning their tops with fiery halos.

"You know, you should probably just head back north. You're going to hit traffic, and you won't get home until at least ten, even if you leave right now." I pushed off the car and stretched my arms over my head, blocking her face from view. "I'm exhausted, too. Don't you have work tomorrow morning?"

I didn't turn to see her smile wilt. I knew well the longing I'd see, and the disappointment. I'd seen it when I told her I was leaving the first time, and every time I'd ever spoken with that certainty in my own will, in my own ability to cross the distance between here and there, and to do it with as little help from anyone as I could manage. She knew that to try to stop me would be to risk losing me, a risk she was unwilling to take.

I did struggle those first nine months in New York. It was tougher and lonelier than I'd anticipated, and some of the things I'd thought I could leave behind had followed me. Still, my life gathered speed quickly, and I flourished at The New School. After the first nine months, I moved into an apartment in a Brooklyn neighborhood with three close friends and began to feel as if my life was finally getting started.


We'd been living in a fourth-floor walk-up in Brooklyn's Bedford-Stuyvesant neighborhood for two years when a new tenant moved into the apartment next to us, a young woman. Coming home from class one afternoon, I saw my roommate Rebecca chatting with her in the vestibule of our building. They smiled and parted ways, the new neighbor briefly meeting my eyes as she passed by me on her way out. Rebecca smiled and pulled me inside by the arm.

"You're never going to guess what she does!"

"What? Do you know her?"

"She went to UMass with me, before I transferred to The New School."

"So?"

"She's a professional dominatrix!"

I immediately turned around, hoping I might still see her and be able to apply this new information to the woman who had brushed by me. She was gone, of course, and all I could remember was her steady gaze.

Aside from a few tame experiments with handcuffs, I had no concept of what this meant. What was the job description for a dominatrix? I listened to my neighbor's nocturnal comings and go-ings, and a fascination began to grow in me, unfurling tendrils of curiosity that climbed the wall between our two apartments, where I once pressed my ear to hear her reprimanding someone for not cleaning the toilet properly.

I wanted to talk to her but couldn't stand the thought of sound-ing the neophyte to anyone, about anything, so I conducted some preliminary research. It turned out that every mid-sized newsstand in Manhattan carried S&M periodicals. These publications, which varied from those with glossy, color covers to smaller, black-and-white newsprint weeklies, bore names like *The Vault*, *Dominant*

*Domain*, and *Fetish World*. Underneath these titles posed shapely women with stony eyes and vampish mouths. They glared seductively in nurse costumes, catsuits, and burlesque outfits with riding crops and ropes in their hands, the toes of their heeled boots resting on the parts of other bodies. Though placed in the newsstand near *Playboy*, the fetish magazine models lacked the flirtatious overtures of those neighboring cover girls. Instead of coy compliance they advertised entitlement. *You want me*, these women glared, *ha!*

The contents of these magazines consisted mostly of erotic stories and advertisements for "dungeons." I envisioned literal dungeons: murky, dripping stone caves nestled in some fishy underground nook of Chinatown, or the industrial neighborhoods under the bridges, where you couldn't even hail a cab at night. Still, while some of the "mistresses" featured in the ads seemed to fit that idea, their faces ragged under bad wigs, other models exuded a posh, moneyed glamour. I felt sure they didn't work in dingy cellars.

Some ads also promoted the dominant services of men, or "masters." I found myself giggling nervously while looking at these, as if someone were watching me. I didn't linger over them. Powerful, dominant women were one thing. These men looked silly, I told myself, not threatening. What woman needs to pay to be dominated? Isn't the more common problem finding a man who *doesn't* want to dominate you?

Soon after, I spotted my neighbor loading her whites at the neighborhood Laundromat. I feigned engrossment in the television mounted over her machine, covertly scouring her sweatpants and running sneakers for some sign of her dual life. Did I expect to see a pair of knee-high leather boots emerge from her mesh laundry bag? A whip? Of medium height, with a cascade of dark hair and the kind of face that people call handsome on a woman, she was impenetrable. I would never have pegged her as anything other than another Pratt student.

I had always been fascinated by the ability to appear one thing and to be another and was routinely enthralled by anything taboo: drug culture, deviant sexual practices, the criminal machinations of my hometown's juvenile delinquents. Even as a kid, I'd always found most compelling those stories of underworlds and extremes: Raymond Chandler, Anaïs Nin, *Go Ask Alice*. My interest in this woman, though, was something more specific than the romance of misbehavior.

Though I'd waited tables my first year in New York and had before that been both a chambermaid and boatyard hand on the Cape, my most recent jobs had been in publishing. At the time that I met my new neighbor, I had taken a hiatus from working life—my longest since the age of fourteen—and while I finished college my parents would cover my living expenses. Since childhood I'd never accepted so much help from them, having decided early on that making my own money meant more freedom. Life may have been easier with help, but I could never give in to the pleasure of that ease. I itched for the independence that self-sufficiency lent me, the confidence I found in not needing or owing anyone. Money was security, and I needed my own.

In that August of 2002, circumstances were urging me toward my neighbor's door. Air-conditioning was an unaffordable luxury. I lay draped across our curbside-salvaged couch lacquered in sweat. Feet in a bucket of ice water, I recounted the list of options that awaited me post-graduation, as I had sat and done the day before, and the day before that. I would graduate with a stellar GPA, but what else? A liberal arts degree was indeed a "liberal" qualification to work in the arts; it qualified me to make coffee and answer phones for someone actually doing something related to the arts. I knew I could succeed in a classroom environment, but my stamina for work that I didn't find compelling had never been great. I interviewed well and enjoyed the challenge of playing the right role in order to get a job. It never took long, however, for me to grow bored and simply stop showing up. I couldn't bear office work or ass kissing and had little confidence that my skills—talking about books, writing, and reading people—would translate into employment I could sustain.

I stared at the sneaker trussed to the leg of the couch by a piece of rope, which I used to ferry my recreational drugs up the four stories from my dealer on street level. Thinking of his usual wolf whistle with white knuckles, I watched a water bug brazenly meander across the living room floor. I needed money before I could make that call. In fact, I needed money for more than that. Life in New York cost more than it had in Boston, from subway fares to food. I only accepted the bare minimum from my parents, and too often the utility money ended up in that sneaker.

I heard the choke of pipes in the wall behind me as a toilet flushed next door, where I imagined a life free of these worries. I doubted my neighbor was obsessing about her financial situation right now. She was probably reading the *Times*—or some more exotic fare—in air-conditioned, roachless comfort. Surely she had no need to accept money from her parents, or anyone. That was enough; without knowing what exactly I'd say to her, I stepped out of the bucket into a pair of blackened flip-flops, shuffled into the hallway, heart pounding, and knocked on my neighbor's door.

She opened the door wearing a pink robe, slippers, and a bemused smile, as though she had been expecting me.

"Good morning," she said, raising an oversize mug in cheers.

"Hi," I said, and searched for a good segue. *So I hear you're a dominatrix* wasn't going to cut it.

She raised her brows expectantly. "You're Rebecca's roommate, right? From next door?"

"Yes—Melissa, it's Melissa." I stuck out my hand. She switched her mug to her left hand and shook mine. Did she know why I was there? I felt like an idiot.

"Nice to meet you, Melissa. Do you want some coffee?"

"Sure. Thanks." I followed her into the air-conditioned cool, determined to muster my usual confidence. I had expected to find chains hanging from the ceiling and cages lining the walls—some kind of, well, dungeon. Instead, she had bookshelves lined with the same titles as mine, a Schiele print hanging over the kitchen table, and an assortment of Ikea furniture. After she filled another over-size mug from a French press, we sat at her kitchen table, where there was indeed a "Week in Review."

"So, you went to UMass with Rebecca?" I asked.

"Yeah." She smiled.

"And now you are—"

"In law school," she finished.

"Right." I nodded, suddenly aware of the possibility that she might not want to tell me anything about her work.

"And I work as a domme. But Rebecca probably already told you that." She smiled again, and I relaxed. She went to law school? The polarity of this arrangement appealed to me; what powers of transformation she must have had to be able to exist in such disparate worlds! She looked so *normal*.

After that she answered my questions patiently, if somewhat elliptically:

"So, is there any actual sex involved?"

"No. But it is definitely sexual in nature."

"Is the money good?"

She paused at this, and I worried that I'd crossed a line.

"Yes," she said cautiously, "once you pay your dues. I mean, relatively good. Not compared to other sex industry work." I saw pride flicker across her face with this acknowledgment. The difference between "other sex industry work" and hers clearly went further than money. She shrugged. "Sex sells better than anything, right?"

"Is it hard to get into?" I asked. "I mean, could you help me—"

She shook her head before I'd finished my sentence.

"It's not hard to *get* the job," she said. "There are magazines you can find—even *New York* magazine runs ads. Just call one of the dungeons advertising dommes and ask if they're hiring; they usually are."

"So," I smiled cautiously, "if getting the job is easy, what's the hard part?"

"Keeping it." She smiled. "Domming isn't for everybody." These words rendered it exactly the sort of challenge that screamed out to be marked a Point B.

Nothing she described about the actual sessions frightened me: spanking, bondage, feminization, verbal humiliation, torture, role-play; I didn't know what half of these practices were, but I knew I could master them if I needed to. The vulnerability of stripping had always disturbed me; it seemed too easy to be condescended to, to be humiliated. My need to be in control had always trumped the allure of being so desired. But my neighbor presented the possibility of both. Not to mention the money.

With a stack of books including *The Art of Female Domination* and *Mistress Ruby Ties It Together*, and the unspoken promise that I could one day enlist the services of men who would pay to scrub my toilet, I left her apartment with all I needed to make fast money without taking off my clothes. I was also armed with a kind of certainty; I would become a dominatrix.

# 3

THE AD IN BACK of *The Village Voice* read:

> Attractive young woman wanted for nurse role-play and domination. No experience necessary. Good $$. No sex.

At a loss for how to dress for such an interview, I wore what I did to conventional ones: black pants, button-up shirt, and cardigan. Fighting my way through the congested sidewalks of Herald Square, I dodged tourists outfitted in fanny packs and digital cameras who stopped mid-stride to stare up at the Empire State Building, or the display windows of Macy's. I arrived at my destination unkempt, overwhelmed with sweat and irritation. After ringing the buzzer and riding the elevator to the second floor, I was greeted by a lanky woman in jeans with full lips and bare feet.

"Hi." She sighed, and gave me a blasé smile. "I'm Fiona. I'll give you a tour." I could see I would not wow her with my firm handshake. I gave a feeble wave.

"Hi, Fiona, I'm Melissa."

She gave me a once-over.

"Not for long, you're not."

She led me down hallways of polished wood decorated by ornate rugs, while sconces glowed along the red walls, reflected in mirrors hung in gilt frames. Here, in the sprawling Dungeon of Mistress X, I found what I had expected of my neighbor's apartment, and I was hopelessly impressed. I had nothing to compare it to; it was like a movie set—an atmosphere truly designed for fantasy—more lush than I had even remotely imagined. It occupied the entire floor, comprised of a maze of dark hallways. Along these halls were the polished doors of a highly styled, big-budget dream; think David Lynch. Excitement folded through me in waves. I had to work here.

Behind three of those doors were the official "dungeons": the Red Room, the Black Room, and the Blue Room. Accordingly colored, these rooms were huge—the Blue Room was easily seven hundred square feet—and all with ten-foot ceilings.

"The Red and Blue Rooms have full baths," Fiona explained as she pushed open the bathroom door in the Red Room. She circled the marbled floor, pointing out amenities. "These towel racks are heated, so they need to be unplugged after sessions. All the sinks should have Scope, Dixie cups, and these little packages with disposable toothbrushes and paste." I traced her steps, lingering over the miniature tube of Crest in its sealed package like take-out dinnerware and running my hand along the warm towels as I followed her back out into the Red Room. "That over there is the bondage table," she said, indicating a waist-high bed with leather upholstery and metal rings intermittently hung around its edges. "The top is a lid that opens."

"For storage?" I asked.

"For slaves. It doubles as a coffin."

"A coffin?"

"For clients into sensory deprivation. If you're lucky, you get to tie them up—gag, blindfold, the works—and stick 'em in there for most of the session." She shrugged. "It can get worked into role-play scenes, too."

I nodded, trying to picture myself improvising scenarios that incorporated coffins. She moved on, making her way around the room. "Here you've got the hanging cage, Catherine wheel, candles and clamps and economy-size lube in the wardrobe drawer." She stooped to pull open the drawer. "And it looks like some pornos and panties." I squinted to catch a glimpse as she slid the drawer shut and noticed a straitjacketed dummy propped in the corner behind the wardrobe, thick chains draped around its shoulders, its face hidden under a rubber mask with a zippered mouth. Mounted on the walls were hooks from which hung leather floggers, whips, riding crops, paddles, cuffs, blindfolds, and even a couple of gas masks. Fiona flipped switches, turned on fans, timers, and kicked open a wooden chest filled with muscular coils of rope. "Here are the stocks," she said, pointing to a wooden frame with three holes in its wide horizontal beam: a neck-sized one flanked by two wrist-sized—I'd only ever seen these in period films and maybe at a renaissance faire as a kid. "That," she pointed to a leather riding saddle draped over the stocks, "is the genuine article. Boss man has a thing for equestrian stuff; go figure." As we left the Red Room, I inspected a human-size cage on the floor near the door, complete with a padlocked gate and gleaming dog dish inside.

The other two dungeons proved variations on the first. The Blue Room featured a giant wooden cross instead of a wheel; the Black Room had a leather swing that hung from the ceiling, dangling over a four-poster bondage bed. They all had a throne of some kind and mirrors on most of their walls. I avoided my own reflection in these. Fiona pointed out portable toilets tucked behind the dungeon doors and in the supply closets. Some of these were equipped with wheels and genuine porcelain bowls; some were more closely related to lawn chairs with plastic toilet seats.

Reeling, I wondered how I'd ever remember the names of all this equipment, let alone learn how to use it.

"So, most of this is probably for show, huh?" I asked, hopeful.
Fiona smirked silently.

We then made our way through the three medical rooms: Med 1, Med 2, and Med 3. More pristine than most doctor's offices I had visited, these had adjustable examination tables, mirrored walls and ceilings, and cupboards filled with glinting equipment. There were proctoscopes and stethoscopes, rolling wheels with spikes and pincers. Clamps, syringes, thermometers, tongue depressors, gadgets to peek and pry in ears, eyes, noses, and mouths, and, in Med 2, huge anatomical posters of both the female and male reproductive systems in color.

Down the hall was the Cross-Dressing Room, with a mountainous leather couch and a vanity table whose matching wardrobe was bursting with man-size stilettos, French-maid costumes, and panties big enough to have a picnic on.

"So, the Cross-Dressing Room is just for . . . ," I posited.

"Cross-Dressing is for cross-dressing." Fiona smiled. "Feminization. Usually it's part of a role-play, your slave playing the dirty slut, you with a strap-on, and so forth. Sometimes it's just a game of dress-up, which is easy and fun."

I nodded, aware of how much nodding I was doing.

"Cross-Dressing is also kind of an all-purpose room, for clients who don't want the super dungeony or medical atmosphere. Sometimes they just want to talk about shit in a normal-looking setting." I wanted to ask what kind of shit they liked to talk about but restrained myself.

The kitchen, as well as two dressing rooms, were places for the dommes to hang out in the downtime between sessions. The smallest room so far, the kitchen seemed cozy to me after the daunting enormity of the dungeons; it just looked like a kitchen—something I had a reference for. I didn't realize that feigning placidity for so long had exhausted me until I felt myself relax in seeing something familiar. My default disposition was aloof and knowing, but this place had transcended any previous scenario in shock factor.

"There's usually water and Diet Coke in there," said Fiona, pointing to the refrigerator, "but don't get too used to it. It's supposed to be for the clients, but the girls drink it all, so Remy's going to lock it up sooner or later."

"Remy?"

"He's the boss. He comes in and out, usually at night. Totally harmless, if you stay out of his way."

There was a small counter along the wall, flanked by a pair of stools. The counter bore a half-full ashtray and an empty can of Diet Coke with a lipstick-stained straw. A piece of paper with large black type hung above it, taped to the wall.

It read:

*REMEBER:*

*We think may be not body Understand if we found more of one girl in the Kitchen You have Fine and We discount money from you Paid.*

*We have Camera in Kitchen (everybody Know) this camera is recording 24 hours at day, every week we check that camera and if we found more of one girl in the kitchen we discount from you Paid without Advice.*

*Later no Ask why we discount money from you Paid. We have few reason to not admit more of one Girl in the Kitchen.*

"Um, is that a joke?" I asked.

"Oh no." Fiona waved a hand dismissively. "That's just Remy having a hissy fit. There's always a new note appearing somewhere. Right now he's obsessed with the noise. You're only allowed to eat in the kitchen, so everybody gets dinner delivered, and it gets noisy in here. Sometimes you can hear it in Med Three." She shrugged. "Everybody listens for a little while, because they don't want to get fined, but then things go back to normal."

"So, English is his second language?"

"You could tell?" She cackled.

A small television protruded from another wall, mounted on a metal arm. Below it a large wicker hamper overflowed with laundry, mostly sheets and towels, a few frilly underthings peeking out from the folds.

"Goddamn it," Fiona grumbled, striding over to it. "Nobody's in session, and nobody's doing laundry." Turning her head over her shoulder, she said, "Excuse me while I put a load in."

"Of course!" I was glad for a little time to observe my surroundings without her observing me.

Fiona pulled a pair of latex gloves out of a box sitting on the washer-dryer unit and put them on before loading the machine. Next to the washer-dryer was more countertop that led to a deep metal sink holding a few dishes and something else, which I stared at for a few seconds before recognizing it. A dildo. It was enormous, pink, and sheathed in a condom. As worldly as I considered myself, this was the first actual dildo I had ever seen. I must have inhaled sharply upon recognition, because Fiona turned her head and followed my gaze.

"Oh, for fuck's sake!" She slammed the lid on the washing machine and peeled off one of the gloves, tossing it into a nearby trash can. With her still-gloved hand, she retrieved the dildo from the sink and headed back out into the hallway. "C'mon, I'll introduce you to our illustrious mistresses."

When Fiona pushed open the dressing room door, six pairs of eyes shifted from a wall-mounted television over the door onto us. The shame of being overdressed is a very specific feeling, and I felt it then. They were all wearing sweatpants, jeans, or hot pants. One woman knelt topless in front of the mirrored wall of lockers, a faint smile visible in her reflection as she puckered her lips to apply liner. The others lay draped across a white leather sofa and love seat. They all had a fluidity of body that is particular to those accustomed to being perceived sexually. They slouched over the overstuffed furniture looking bored and normal, some of them heavily tattooed, some fat, many older than me, and a few younger. They could have been friends of mine, schoolmates.

"Who left this in the kitchen sink?" Fiona demanded, dangling the dildo between her thumb and forefinger by its big pink balls.

"I did," volunteered the topless woman, without pausing her lipstick application. "It isn't *used*, obviously."

"It's still not okay, Georgina," Fiona scolded. "Remy would shit if he came in here and found a dick in the sink." Someone giggled from the couch.

"Yeah, yeah," grumbled Georgina, hoisting herself to her feet and breezing by us, breasts bouncing. She grabbed the dildo from Fiona as she passed.

*"Anyway,"* Fiona glanced at me and then pointed with her long finger at each mistress as she said her name, "this is Camille, Autumn, Miss K, Bella, Lena, and that was Georgina." She then motioned to me. "Girls, this is the interview. She doesn't have a name yet." I gave my second feeble wave of the afternoon. They coolly scanned my interview outfit, a few offering lukewarm smiles before their eyes shifted back to another wall-mounted television over my head.

Fiona interviewed me in an office covered with monitors. They revealed any activity in the elevator, the outside stoop, all of the hallways, the entryway, and the stairs. Her desk faced the screens, and on it sat a phone and an open appointment book, crammed with names and notes in various colors of ink. I later learned that each manager, or phone girl as we called them, had a color, so that Remy knew who to give the commission to for every session booked. The phone girls earned an hourly wage between $15 and $20, in addition to a $5 commission per session booked with a repeat client; new clients got them $10. The opposite wall boasted a complicated stereo system and a smaller desk with a computer monitor. At this smaller desk sat the topless Georgina, furiously typing.

"Okay, get out of here so I can interview this nice girl," Fiona demanded after my tour.

"Let me just finish this forum post." Georgina kept typing.

*"Out!"*

The interview lasted about four minutes. I didn't have professional experience, I said, but I did have personal experience. The look on Fiona's face made it immediately clear that this was a common lie. I didn't realize I was hired until she asked me what days I'd like to work the following week. Of our conversation, mainly I remember this: $75 per one hour session, plus tips, which could range anywhere from $5 to $500. I told her I'd be in on Monday, 10:30 A.M.

# 4

I WAS NO STRANGER to what I recognized in the women of that dressing room. All women are used to being perceived sexually to some degree, especially in New York. Still, not all of them acquire that mesmerizing sheen, which is really self-consciousness hammered into a kind of grace. They shone, mirrors of desire, their images pliant, shimmering with mutable fantasy. I wanted that—to effortlessly seduce, to reflect desire rather than emanate it. I'd been practicing for a long time, but my skills were amateur in such company; those women were professionals.

The year I turned eleven, I had transformed from a bookish tomboy into a sex object, at least in the eyes of men. I felt their gaze everywhere: men in cars, men in coveralls, men in suits, men at chalkboards. Men behind desks, men married to my schoolmates' mothers, and the nascent men of my middle school classrooms. At twelve I passed for sixteen; at fourteen, eighteen. I didn't need to be in New York to discover the duality of sex appeal. I had lost the ability to be invisible and the immunities of childhood—but to be seen! I couldn't escape it, and mostly, I didn't want to. Desire intoxicated me. Seduction became my primary pursuit, my first and most compelling drug. In junior high, I filled my diaries with lists of names: conquests and conquered; the daily entries mainly consisted of logs of my progress. It seemed that I could will boys to want me with force of mind, by invisible waves of provocation, a kind of magic, really. My peers proved easy marks, so I collected girlfriends with homes less supervised than mine, girlfriends with older brothers, older brothers with older friends. The thrill of older men, their deep voices and sinewy limbs, was sharper, alluring as only danger can be without any knowledge of consequence. My hunger to be desired was bottomless, consuming. I sensed that it was a thing to hide, and I did so reflexively.

I found that the high of seduction didn't translate to sex, though. Once the chase ended, so did my confidence. I loved the taut line of seduction, but what I reeled in was often unwieldly, a slippery, writhing thing, bigger than me. I hated the child I reverted to in sexual situations—awkward and strangely numb, shy in my body, unable to conceal my innocence. I strategically avoided technical intercourse until the age of seventeen. Nothing else really counted, I thought, and became, in addition to an adept rationalizer, a master of placation, granting lesser acts in place of actual sex. I figured a hand job was worth the pleasure of seduction that preceded it— though the disconnection between the two confused me. By the age of thirteen, I had developed a reputation as a slut. Though I was unsure what I was being punished for, the humiliation drove me away from men for a while.

For the next few years, I experimented with girls instead. They were different, but not that different. I could swoon over them, too, even love them, or as close as I knew to it. But I couldn't stop aligning myself with their desires, and I was disappointed when they didn't intuit mine. What were mine? I didn't have an orgasm with another person until I guided the hand of a girl at summer camp, and suddenly I hated the feeling of being in control. Though addicted to the power of seduction, I didn't want to play the man.

At eighteen, after more than two years of dating women, I thrilled in love with my first real boyfriend. In the year that followed losing my official virginity to this sweet, stoned, boy, the monotony of his sweetness became tedious, his adoration irritating. Out of fear of hurting him, I ended it the most painful way: by slow, unexplained secession. I avoided him, claiming everything was fine. I moved to the other side of the city and stopped answering the phone. He didn't know that we were broken up until he learned I was dating someone else. When I didn't know how to leave gracefully, dropping off the face of the planet was my go-to. I quit jobs, apartments, friendships, and relationships this way for years. My history was scattered with people who hated me for this.

Even my friendships adhered to this model, to some degree. As a kid, rather than groups of friends I'd always had one best girlfriend with whom I was emeshed for a period of time, often years. These girls were my soul mates, for as long as our love, and the insular world we created, could last. A point would always come when they'd tell me their secret histories, the abuses they'd suffered from mothers, stepfathers, brothers, or unknown men. I wondered whether everyone had such hurts or these wounded were simply drawn to me. I felt privileged to be the keeper of secrets, to be so trusted. But inevitably, I'd feel the burden of too much power; like my future lovers, they needed me more than I did them. When I became an adult, my friendships became less dramatic, less fraught with need, but still singular in their intensity. I was never, my entire life, without a best friend. At the time that I started working at the dungeon, my roommate Rebecca was one of these.

By the time I got to New York, I'd fallen in love a few times and had plenty of happy orgasms. But even with long-term lovers, my need was bottomless. They could not want me enough. I always managed to love those who loved me more, but after some months of feverish infatuation I'd grow bored and become repulsed by their desire. Paradoxically the craving to be desired never abated and was only temporarily soothed by the next smoldering gaze.

. . .

What my neighbor had referred to as "paying your dues" meant the apprenticeship that all novice dommes must complete as their training. Being an apprentice entailed sitting around the dressing room for untold (and unpaid) hours until an appointment came in and then asking awkwardly to sit in on the session of a more experienced mistress. The goal of these was not only to pick up what technique I could while trying not to get in the way but also to do more than stare dumbly from behind the door, blushing. Unfortunately, on my first night of "training" I gathered only a small amount of experience witnessing the expertise of Mistress Bella, whose session consisted of putting her potbellied slave into authentic wooden stocks and jerking him off into a Dixie cup. Bella, a thirty-two-year-old Chinese-American woman who could pass for preadolescent, had issued a stream of expletives as she reached around his paunch from behind, her black tresses sweeping across his hairy back in time with the mechanical thrust of her arm. She might have been reading aloud a car manual.

"Just imagine my sranted yerrow pussy under my panties you srobbering pig wouldn't you just rove to fuck my rittle Asian pussy you big perverted cow's ass too bad I've got you stuck in tose tings rike a piece of meat and I'm gonna torture you so bad you won't even be abre to diddre your rittle tiny . . . tat's a good boy. Drink up now."

My lack of interest in her methods aside, Bella had little wisdom to offer on anything except for *The Rules*, a battered copy of which she carried around the dungeon at all times. Perched on a kitchen stool with her dog-eared book and a pack of Virginia Slims, her child's body curled in only a yellow slip, she would meet most addresses with silence. Did her appointment show up? Nothing. Did she want to add anything to the sushi delivery order? A twitch that could be liberally interpreted as a negative. Did she have a light? Nothing. But ask her about *The Rules* and she would go on at such length about the differentiations between first, second, and third date etiquette that you would be forced to walk away from her mid-sentence, at a loss for an appropriate pause. Specterlike, Bella would drift from room to room, spraying Lysol disinfectant in a fog behind her, all the while quietly humming Top 40 radio hits.

Sessions, by definition, are divided into three categories: sensual, corporal, and switch. As Fiona explained on my first shift—stripping the genres of their euphemistic titles—"Just think of them as sexy, mean, and submissive. Well, and medical, but really that could be any of those." The spectrum within and even between each of these was nuanced; usually clients—or slaves, as they were also referred to—wanted a combination of sensual and corporal, with an emphasis on one or the other. Stereotypical dominatrix images: verbal humiliation, bondage, and torture, are straight out of a corporal session. But every domme begins with sensual. Distinguished by their gentle, sexual quality, sensual sessions usually included one or more of the following: light bondage, tickling, light spanking, and nipple play. "Play" in other contexts might refer to electrical torture or piercing, but the "light" always meant caressing, kissing, and other nonviolent forms of titillation. Teasing-and-denial was also featured heavily in sensual sessions. Sometimes that meant what it sounds like: physical teasing (either the domme touching her client or the client touching himself) and then denial of orgasm. But "teasing-and-denial" could also be a euphemism for a hand job. Smothering was similar. In a corporal session, smothering usually included a rubber mask, pillows, a plastic bag, or Saran Wrap—it was a form of torture. In sensual sessions, "smothering" meant rubbing your breasts or ass against your client's face. Role-play—the acting out of specific scenarios, domme and slave playing predefined, usually archetypal, roles—was also frequently requested in sensual sessions, and in these it was usually limited to playing the role of naughty and flirtatious schoolgirl/secretary/girlfriend/babysitter, the only difference be-tween each being a particular costume and pitch of giggling. When someone requested role-play in a sensual session, you knew you weren't going to be playing the part of serial killer or Gestapo in-terrogator.

New hires began with sensual sessions because they didn't re-quire a lot of training; the majority of women in this country have been trained for this their whole lives. New hires were encouraged to start with them quickly, so as not to waste any time not making money on the house's behalf. Sensual sessions didn't require spe-cific and expensive clothing; most of these clients were indifferent to rubber, leather, and corsetry. Their interest lay in that whatever the fabric, it be scant; they preferred lingerie to fetish wear, wanted naughty instead of dangerous or powerful. The sensual mistress's power lay in her inherent feminine sexuality, in her coos and cleav-age, not in her hands or head; her slaves wanted a woman who wasn't quite aware of her strength and who needed the right man to unlock it for her. Like many women, I had been instructed by my culture to play this role since childhood. The catch was that you couldn't get caught playing it; you should act like a tease, a sexpot, and ooze "sensuality" but never let it appear intentional or self-aware, or un*chaste* for goodness' sake. And so, there was certainly a kind of freedom in having that unspoken demand be acknowl-edged, and even having my efforts financially compensated.

It came easily, this cartoonish enactment of the process I'd been practicing since adolescence. Sensual sessions were all soft-core, late-night paid cable channel movie scenes—the "Skinemax" flicks I'd always stayed awake for during sleepover parties at homes that had cable, watching mesmerized with the volume on low while all the other girls slept. In my mind I wanted to cast myself as a cor-poral domme—to ooze the confidence and intimidation of those women on the cover of *The Vault*—but in reality I feared making the transition from the safety of sensual sessions.

In the beginning of my tenure at the Dungeon of Mistress X,

the word "shame" was not one that I'd ever associated with myself. Shame was pathetic, applicable to my clients: people who paid for what hurt them, who had no power over themselves or their environment. Still, I quickly became familiar with a feeling that followed indulging in the roles that sensual sessions featured. I was letting myself act out the paradox that I believed my feminism, my liberal upbringing, and my intelligence should have immunized me to. That feeling was a sister to the exhilaration of secrecy, with an equal sense of groundlessness. It was a spiral, that feeling, a twist of motion that sucked my breath out of me in a murky wisp. In the shower, in the quiet of my still body after those sessions, I felt less a sense of having taken a leap than of having lost my footing.

# 5

THE NIGHT BEFORE my second shift at the dungeon, I arrived home from class to find a message from Fiona on my answering machine.

"Hey, it's Fiona. Make sure you're on time tomorrow. Someone is coming in to see you."

My stomach flipped with anxiety. Sure, I'd complained to her about needing money, but the idea of carrying an entire session myself terrified me. I'd assumed I had a comfortable cushion of time to get used to the idea. What did I have to go on at this point—Bella's example? Emulating that performance was out of the question, but I wasn't equipped to improvise something better. I was going to be revealed as a fraud.

As I sat beside the phone at the kitchen table, trying to muster some confidence, Rebecca wandered in, gnawing on an apple.

"What's up?" she asked.

"Nothing."

"How's work? Any action yet?" My roommates had been updated

at every step along the way, and as far as they knew I was chomping at the bit for my own sessions.

"Oh no, not yet."

"Bummer. You have class tomorrow?"

"No, work."

"Let's make dinner; I'm starved."

I nodded, glad for distraction. She dragged an old radio with a cassette player out of her bedroom, and we blasted a mix tape I'd made of old soul music—our favorite—and chopped vegetables while a pot of rice cooked.

I'd known Rebecca since my years in Boston, where she'd grown up and we'd met through mutual friends. We hadn't become close until I moved to New York, where she was already attending our college. If we hadn't become roommates, we may never have figured out how much we had in common; in all the superficial ways we seemed opposite. Rebecca was as tall and willowy as I was petite and curvy. With her sleepy eyes and close-cropped Jean Seberg haircut, Rebecca had a dreamy way of talking that sometimes belied the sharpness of her observations. She was a spacey, mod beauty, who was always thinking the same thing as me. It was easy between us from the beginning. Mine and Rebecca's conversation vacillated easily between the intellectual and trivial, with equal pleasure. The only thing I ever hid from her was the extent of my drug use.

Our other two roommates came in as I started sautéing garlic and onions.

"Smells good," said Luke, our household's only male member. He leaned over my shoulder and grabbed a slice of pepper from the pile on the cutting board. "Thank god for your Italian mom, Melissa."

"It's no secret, my friend, just garlic and olive oil."

"Can I do something? I have a take-home physics exam to procrastinate."

"Ah, yeah, there's a block of tofu in the fridge. Try and squeeze the water out of it and then cut it up."

We cooked and gossiped and sang along to Otis Redding and Irma Thomas, and for a little while the dungeon seemed farther away than just across the East River. Amidst the warm clamor of familiar voices and cooking my anxiety slipped away and I remembered that I was capable of anything. Dinnertime in my childhood home had often produced the same effect; the crackle and smell of sautéing garlic coupled with the murmur of NPR's "All Things Considered" lulled me into a feeling of safety beyond which my daily worries seemed remote and flimsy. That comfort had always been fleeting, though. That night, as I lay alone in the dark of my bedroom, the world outside loomed again, pregnant with uncertainty.

An hour can be a long time. Hell, a minute can be a long time. The minute before your first kiss with someone is a painstaking collection of seconds, each one more bloated with anticipation than the last. The first minute of a tattoo is a long one as well. Pain has few rivals in its ability to slow time. Fear, excitement, elation—these are kissing cousins, all with the sensorial power to render each second humming with every tick and gasp of our bodies, the whirr of insect wings and distant car engines. Sometimes, I could savor these moments, relish them as opportunities to walk straight into the fact of being alive. In the seconds that crept into the minutes of my very first domination session, I had no idea what I wanted. The $75 certainly, but beyond that? Character-building life experience? I would have confidently named these motives right up until the moment that the door of the Red Room closed behind me. With the clasp of its latch, all bravado and ideology dimmed with the light of the hallway behind. It was only me, a naked old man, and sixty minutes of palpable expectation. An hour alone with a naked man with whom you do not intend to have sex can be a very long time.

On my second shift ever, and after only Mistress Bella's example, I teetered over my first client in a borrowed pair of seven-inch platform stilettos. Anxiety, and a corset that cinched my waist six inches smaller than nature intended, confined my breath to the shallow region of my chest. My bosom literally heaved, straining against its lacy contraption and obstructing my view of the naked man who knelt at my feet. Cold tears ran from my armpits. The darkness smelled of stale incense and the briny tang of bodies past and present. It was hot, and the red walls seemed to breathe slightly, as if I were inside a great belly.

Despite the fact that I was high on heroin, I felt only fear. It snuck up on me as I stepped into the room, and my confidence lifted like a flock of startled birds. I couldn't stop thinking about my mother. What was I, my mother's daughter, doing here? It suddenly didn't make any sense. But that's what the drugs were for: to keep Mom out of moments like this. Narcotics create distance, and I only needed an inch to turn away from that question.

I knew I had to say something. My mouth was gummy with 99-cent lipstick from the all-night drugstore down the block. Opening it, I prayed that the waxy paint would bear some talismanic power and bring the right words to my lips. Instead, I burped.

"Yes, Mistress? Are you all right?"

I felt his breath on my fishnetted knees and fought the urge to back away. "Yeah," I croaked. My gut—displaced by the corset to somewhere near my bladder—clenched in panic. I itched to turn and slam the door behind me on this naked man and the politesse affected to camouflage his entitlement. Everything about him, from his hunched back to the quaver in his voice, was a demand phrased as a question. But I could not fail at this, much as I wanted to flee the shadowy room, my own image in the mirrored walls, and the inquisition-style cage that dangled from the ceiling. My urge to escape was met with an equally familiar will to persist. It was this second urge that had both rescued me from failure and damned me to finish every game in which my hand was called. Language had always saved me: from ever being arrested, attacked, caught in a lie or with my pants down. I would not allow words to fail me now.

"Yes, of course I'm all right. Pig!" I heard my voice echo in the room the way I had on answering machine recordings and home videos, and winced at the wavering childishness of it. In our pre-session consultation, my client had listed verbal humiliation among his requests, and I had nodded knowingly. "Verbal," I'd heard, and assumed it would be easy. Now I was at a loss. Name-calling had always been a last resort, I told myself, something better left to children, drunk people, and those without the capacity for some more sophisticated form of shaming. But it wasn't true. I had always known a lot of words, and how to use them, but never in the service of humiliation. In truth, I didn't know how to be mean. In the past, I had been the one who felt humiliated by my failed attempts at cruelty. I had never sounded more false. I waited for him to scoff and retreat, to call me a phony. My gift for faking it ended here, I thought, where I could not convince even myself. Relief?

Miraculously, no words of reproach were spat against my knees. The old man did not rise from the floor in disgust. When a solid minute had passed with nothing but a vague shifting of limbs below me, I began wracking my brain for follow-up insults. In an adrenaline-fueled excavation of memory, I searched through every television show, movie, and schoolyard scene I could recall for examples of humiliation and struck gold.

"*Stop breathing on my legs, you crust of scum on a rat's cunt!*" Rather than creating the berth I'd intended, my words inspired only a scuttling around my feet. I could feel him nuzzling my toes with little kisses and licks, devotedly pressing his cheek against the patent strap of my shoe. "*Get away from me!*" I shouted.

"Yes, Mistress." Scampering backward, he knelt on all fours and stared at the floor, bald pate gleaming with perspiration. Hands upon hips, I wheezed, the gravity of power alighting on my shoulders once more. Nonetheless, shouting that first insult took all of two seconds. There were 3,598 left. I decided to give him a spanking. He was amenable to the idea, and I was glad to contend with his pasty rear instead of his searching gaze. Eye contact was an intimacy I was determined to avoid for as long as possible.

I ordered him to kneel on all fours facing the wall while I quietly pulled on a latex glove from the box I had been handed on my way in. Whether he would be offended or not at my precaution, I was unsure, but nor was I ready to bare-hand it my first time. In my mind, I was allotting ten or even fifteen minutes to the spanking, ample time to brainstorm my next move. This plan lasted for about three minutes, when my palm began to feel as though a hot iron had been pressed to it, rather than just a saggy butt. I hadn't been warned of this difficulty, nor the nerves that were soaking the borrowed corset with sweat.

In fact, I had been informed of little before entering the Red Room, a practice I would later find was not in keeping with house protocol. It was the resort of office managers sick of cajoling their more experienced dommes into sessioning with undesirable regulars. Toilet Timmy, as they called him, was one of these. He conveniently preferred new hires. I could continue the usual apprenticeship for as long as I wanted, I was told, and certainly shouldn't do anything I didn't feel ready for, but Timmy was sooo easy, and couldn't I use the money? I could. Of course I asked why the moniker.

"Oh, he's just a pee slut, likes it right on his face," offered Mistress Autumn, a cool redhead whose nonchalance was tempered with a warmth that most of the other dommes lacked.

"On his face?"

"Uh-huh. And you might want to try not to get too close. . . ."

"How so?"

"He can be grabby. And he has accidents sometimes."

"Accidents?"

"Don't worry about it; it'll be fine."

Everything did seem almost fine, after I figured out the solution to the eye-contact problem (a blindfold) and found an activity that didn't cause me as much pain as it did Timmy (nipple torture).

"Oh, Mistress!" He squirmed on the bondage table as I pulled on his nipples with my gloved fingers.

"That's right, uh, piggy, you take that!"

"Mistress, Mistress, I am feeling very excited!"

"Well, perhaps I should pinch them harder, eh?" I dug my nails into his fleshy nubs.

"Mistress!" He let out something between a groan and a squeal, and mesmerized as I was by the distortion of his face, the twinkle of his dental fillings, and the excruciating realness of my situation, I felt the warmth of his urine on the back of my gloved hand before I saw it arching up over his belly toward me.

I credit the surge of humiliated anger that rose in me as I beheld his stream of piss for the efficiency of my next move. Stepping back, I reached my gloved hand with little forethought down to his penis, which needed to be raised only a few inches for the stream to reach his yawning mouth. He wasn't nearly so sorry as I would have been to end up with a mouthful of my own pee, but I did feel that the power in the room had shifted. It struck me then, though fleetingly, that Timmy's incontinence might have had less to do with a physical quirk than a passive-aggressive gesture of dominance. Not until I won some power to wield did I realize how unarmed I had been; I had been sweating for the approval of a man who preferred to see dominatrices as inexperienced as me.

As the timer near the door crept closer and closer to its mark, I knew that I would have to initiate the golden shower portion of our session. Taking into account the warning about Timmy's roving hands, and his soon-to-be close vicinity to my privates, I decided it was also time to try my hand at bondage. I was glad to have had the foresight to blindfold him earlier. How could I have forgotten where the ropes in the Red Room were kept?

"What are you doing, Mistress? Am I going to receive your golden nectar soon? I am feeling very thirsty today. . . ."

"Still?" I replied, scouring the room. "Why don't you do your job and let me do mine, piglet?" Where were they? I pulled open drawers and found only clothespins, a few candle stubs, and a single pair of man-size panties with the crotch torn out.

"What's my job, Mistress? Would you like for me to worship your magnificent body?"

"Right now your job is to shut up, piglet, and prepare yourself for just desserts."

"Ooohh, Mistress, I like dessert! You're going to give it to me good, aren't you?"

"Indeed I am."

"I can't wait!"

"Well, you are going to have to, my pet. This isn't, uh, the place for getting what you want, when you want it, is it?"

At last I found them, in a drawer of the leather bondage table not far below the mottled legs of my client. Was it the sock garters that I had forced him to remove earlier that had rubbed his pallid calves hairless? Grotesque or not, unless in the medical or sex industry, one doesn't get much opportunity to unabashedly observe the bodies of other humans, least of all those of elder men. It would take a few months before my slaves' bodies would cease, in a fundamental way, to be so human to me. They would become more akin to dishwashers, vacuums, or any of the other implements I had grown familiar with by virtue of their necessity to whatever job I was performing. But in the beginning, the bodies were spectacular, both hideous and marvelous.

After trussing Timmy to the table with a few square knots— silently thanking the fates for designing me as the daughter of a sea captain—I removed my heels and climbed gingerly over him to stand with a bare foot on either side of his head. Here I was, towering over this wizened body with a handful of toilet paper, in this outfit, in this room.

While certainly there is fear in the alienation from all things familiar, for me it was coupled with exhilaration. I was so distant from everything that had defined me up until then. It was close to the feeling I had gotten in the moment that I first shoplifted a candy bar from the grocery store, lied to my mother about my whereabouts, stepped off the plane alone, or pierced my skin with a needle. How can I explain this kind of weightlessness? It is like stepping off the edge of a cliff that has no bottom. There are a few minutes of complete terror: there is nothing to grab onto, nothing that matches anything in your memory. You are certain that you will perish without the ground, without the reactions that define you. Then you realize that you are still here, you are still a body, still a person, but the reality you have known no longer exists. Of course it is in our nature to settle, wherever we are, to create schemas and repeat reactions, so that we can become something that seems solid. This instinct is part of how we survive. But there is a brief period of time, when the fall has just begun and we are thrust out, when we have no choice but to accept ourselves as utterly strange, bottomless, empty. In this moment you are like a baby: a miraculous hunk of flesh and raw potential. The terror gives way to a tremendous feeling of power.

After a brief moment of vertigo, I reached down and pulled aside my panties.

# 6

WHEN I GOT HOME at 2:00 A.M. after that first session, only Rebecca was awake. She sat at the kitchen table, sleepily bent over Ovid, a pencil tucked behind her ear. She smiled up at me as I dropped my purse on the table and unzipped my jacket.

"I waited up for you," she said. "I've been reading the same verse since midnight." Closing the book, she tilted her head. "So? How was it?"

"Totally bizarre. But great. Really fun, actually. Guess what my first *client*'s nickname is?"

"What?"

"Toilet Timmy."

Her laughter was infectious, and with its first peals all the details of the past eight hours turned hilarious. We laughed at Timmy's "accident," his saggy ass, and every contrived phrase I'd uttered. Rebecca's laughter erased the fear I'd felt, softened the edge that I'd rubbed up against alone in that room. Sharing her laughter, I knew I'd never tell her about the painful uncertainty, the self-loathing I'd felt, about anything that wouldn't elicit the happy ease of her laughter. I wouldn't have even known then how to describe the other side of that fear, the high I'd felt by the end of the session. That feeling seemed even more private than my suffering.

After my inaugural session with Toilet Timmy, I resumed the usual apprenticeship. On my third shift at the dungeon, only three mistresses were working. Fiona manned the silent telephone, alternating between online poker and the chat room on our Web site. I had already spent half a pack of cigarettes and the better part of an hour in the kitchen listening to Bella detail methods of securing a rich husband.

"See, you must not appear to be arr that interested, and you must not sreep with him too soon. The powerful man has to wait for what he wants, or he wirr not want it anymore." I left her humming atop the kitchen hamper and wandered into the dressing room.

Four hours into an eight-hour shift, 9:00 P.M. found me roosting on the couch with the television remote, a stack of books waiting to be read for a Monday class, and a heap of gently heaving blankets nearby that had been referred to as Mistress Autumn. After an attempt at reading while avoiding my own reflection in the wall of mirrored lockers, I had abandoned my highlighter and stretched out, remote in hand. The only evidence of Autumn was a single voluptuous leg thrown over one arm of the overstuffed chair and a few long strands of strawberry blond splayed across the other. For an entire episode of *Law & Order*, I jumped at every sleepy grunt that the heap produced. Folding my legs back under me and adjusting the volume of the television, I didn't want to be caught sprawled across the furniture with such entitlement before I had even qualified for one of those lockers. Finally adjusting to what only sounded like waking, I began to relax and turned up the television's volume loud enough to decipher.

After I flipped through several stations, a sleepy voice commanded that I "go back; that was *COPS!* How can anyone not like *COPS*?" Squinting at me, her green eyes bright with sleep, Mistress Autumn scowled. She had a tousled mane of hair, and a tattoo of a cherry blossom nestled in her cleavage. "Is there anything more pathetic than *COPS*?" She yawned and leaned her head back against the white seat. "I *love* it." My fingers scuttled on the remote, and we caught the rest of the intro. "Thanks."

She turned toward the mirrors and pulled her hair into a haphazard bun with the skill and subtle affectation of someone aware of her physical mien. I tried to watch only peripherally. "I'm Mel—uh, Justine. I'm Justine. You're Autumn?"

"Justine, huh? That's kind of ironic, no? Naming yourself after a famous submissive?"

I couldn't help smiling. I had felt clever adopting the name of the Marquis de Sade's heroine.

"No one else has gotten the reference."

"What'd you expect? These people don't know anything about what they're into, or even why." She reached her arms over her head and pointed her legs out with a groan, languidly arching her back with the stretch. Full and smooth, she had the sort of limbs that would never be skinny but always fill their shape with integrity. I wondered if she was straight. There was a confidence in her movements that I hadn't seen in many women. I wasn't sure yet if I wanted to fuck her or to be her. I was then (and had historically been) easily disarmed by the desire to be liked by someone, and often confused it with the desire to seduce them. I recognized a familiar brand of cultivated sexiness, but either hers was more genuine or she was better at faking it than me. She caught me staring in the mirror and smiled at my reflection.

"I am fucking *starving*. Should we order something disgusting?"

I shrugged affirmatively, despite the homemade tofu salad in my backpack. The trill of the phone sounded from the office and we heard Fiona answer.

"Hello." An answer, not a question, no, *This is the Dungeon of Mistress X. How can I help you?* Just, *Hello.*

"So I don't know what you eat, but you look like a veggie, and there's this place on Ninth Ave. that's veggie, but they sneakily fry everything so it tastes amazing and you get to pretend you're being healthy-"

"Zen Palate!"

"I knew it." Autumn smirked. "Did you convert, or were you raised on Frookies, soy milk, and carob, like me?"

"Frookies! I have nightmares about those things!"

"Did you have a wooden toothbrush?"

"No, but I did get *fruit* in my Easter basket."

Autumn snorted with laughter.

"Don't tell me you're from the Bay Area. . . ."

As I shook my head, Fiona appeared in the open doorway. Craining her neck at the television, she smirked.

"Of course, *COPS*. It must be another bustling Saturday night at the dunge."

Autumn raised her brows in mock indignation. "*COPS* is a *good* show."

"Uh-huh. There's a meet coming up in ten minutes."

"Dom or med?" asked Autumn.

"Dom."

"Newbie or regular?"

"Says he's been here, but I don't know who he's seen. I'm guessing it's yours."

"Unless he's susceptible to our little Asian persuasion, I better get pumped, huh?"

"Superpumped."

Fiona ambled back to the office as Autumn kicked off the hoary blanket with a sigh, revealing a pair of boxer shorts and a wifebeater that read: *Oakland* in black Old English lettering across the chest. "They have such a knack for timing, these pervs. If I get the session you should come in, as long as it's okay with him. It always is. Two for the price of one? They love a bargain like they love a dildo up their ass."

"So, I should go in to meet him, right? That's how it works with new clients?"

"Not just new clients, any client that wants something new. Or just wants to milk his two hundred bucks for some extra time staring at cleavage. But yeah, you should go in for the meet. Ask him if you can sit in."

The process of "meets" entailed each available mistress getting dressed up and conducting a brief interview with the new client or returning clients who simply wasn't sure whom he wanted to see, ostensibly to see if their interests aligned. Since so few of us claimed to have any genuine shared interests with our clients, meets were all about winning the session. I found the overt competition of this setup, and its nod to iconic brothel procedure (everyone lining up and batting their eyes), both anxiety producing and thrilling.

I had been instructed to bring, during my training period, a black dress or slip for domination sessions, a white one for medical, and a pair of heels. For this I was grateful, after a quick Internet survey revealed the price of actual corsets running anywhere between $300 and $3,000: far beyond what I was managing to scrimp for MetroCards and occasional weekend drug binges. Still, dress-up was one of my favorite games as a child and I'd be lying to say that the costumes weren't part of the job's appeal.

To forestall the discomfort of changing into my black slip in front of both Autumn and the wall of mirrors, I knelt with my cosmetic bag on the floor and pulled out my eyeliner. I rubbed at my smeary eyelid, having yet to master the art of makeup application.

When I looked back up at her reflection, she had pulled off the wifebeater and was studying herself in the mirror, from the front, from the side, then sighing. "God, why didn't I get big boobs like yours, Justine? I was meant to have enormous breasts." She unlocked a door from the middle row of lockers that had a Scotch-taped piece of notebook paper stuck to its mirror that read: *CASH*

*COW* in ballpoint pen, accompanied by a crude drawing of a coyly long-lashed cow with a money sign emblazoned on her flank. The overstuffed locker coughed out a garter belt upon opening. The hangers and plastic drawers were burdened by more lingerie than I had ever seen: a mélange of lace, rubber, satin, and leather, with shoes, wigs, hairbrushes, and other unidentifiable articles poking out from the mass.

I have always enjoyed watching women dress. The appeal isn't sexual. Most girls' first glimpse of private female life is watching their mothers dress and put makeup on. It makes sense that we'd find it comforting. Childhood fascinations often crystallize this way. Isn't beauty forever defined, in a sense, by the first things we found beautiful? Surely part of my pleasure results from the inundation of images that we all experience. But I also love ritual, and it is a mesmerizing one. I enjoy the ritual of dressing myself, too. It is a form of basking in a kind of femininity that I am opposed to as an ideal, but for better or worse, I think we all fetishize the female body, and intellectualization doesn't spare anyone the obsession.

Autumn replaced her boxer shorts with a tiny black thong, clipping the garter belt around her waist. Digging into the pocket of a shoe rack hanging from the inside of her locker door, she pulled out and unraveled a pair of stockings, diaphanous and flaccid as the molted reptile skin. Sliding them up her legs, she pinched their edges into the eyelets of the dangling garters and pulled a pair of black lace shorts over the whole contraption. This transformation took about two minutes, and utterly changed the lower half of her body. Hooking a black bra around her waist, she pulled the straps over her shoulders and lifted each breast into the cups, whose lacy seam reached just over her nipples. Kneeling beside me, she dug into a bag of makeup too big to carry onto a plane and pulled out a handful of pencils and brushes. In under five minutes she applied foundation; eye-, brow, and lip liner; mascara; sparkles; and lipstick that matched the walls of the Red Room. Her face had become another, each feature's elegant dimensions as emphasized as those of a comic book heroine. I had never seen anything like it. She looked like a completely new person. My chin must have been hanging, because when she turned away from the mirror to face me, her smile curled with self-satisfaction and an affectionate condescension.

"I'm going to need your help," she said, and stood. Out of the crowded locker she extracted a satin corset the bruised color of plums. Sucking in her stomach, she fastened each of the twentyish hooks that cinched the front of the boned, hourglass brace. "Can you give me a hand with this?"

"Um, sure. How?"

"Just tighten the laces in the back, like a sneaker. You're going to have to pull hard."

"Okay." I tucked my fingertips under the crisscrossed lacing, which looked delicate but could easily have docked a small yacht, and pulled, very much like I was tightening a pair of shoelaces.

"Harder."

"Okay."

I pulled harder and she jerked back toward me slightly, bracing herself on the locker door.

"Harder, Justine; don't be such a girl."

Stepping back with one foot to brace myself, I yanked on the ties with a grunt, my biceps straining. The corset tightened an inch or so, her flesh squeezing out the top in a painful-looking bulge.

"Good." I continued until her already slender waist was narrowed to Betty Boop proportions. "Perfect. Now just tie the ends together."

"*He's here!*" Fiona yelled from the office, where she could see the client at the street level in the little black-and-white screen on her desk.

After stepping into a pair of patent-leather platform stilettos, Autumn appraised herself in the mirror with a sigh and strode out of the dressing room, the staccato tap of her heels fading down the hall toward the kitchen.

Left alone, I sat there on my heels, staring into my own face. It was bland as a hunk of clay after the sight of her, and I found a curious mixture of dejection and curiosity in my own eyes.

Watching Autumn transform herself had awakened a phantom limb of longing. I had always been awed by the transformative power women appeared to have. I also wanted to become something else, to pull that kind of beauty and sexual ease out of myself like a dress from a wardrobe. It must exist in them always, I had thought. It must arrive with the swell of breasts and hips and bellies and thighs, a wisdom and ability like that of survival that blooms in the mind, a kind of built-in manual for use from which mine was missing pages.

"Um, Bella? Could you maybe put some shoes on?" Fiona arched her brows and offered the unshod mistress a managerial smile. Bella responded with a blank stare before sliding into a pair of sandals that could easily have qualified as shower shoes, the sort one might don to take out the trash. As she shuffled down the hallway in her yellow slip, Fiona called after her, "He's in the Black Room, by the way."

"Uh-huh, yeah, okay," Bella muttered under her breath. As she disappeared at the end of the hallway into the Black Room, Fiona turned to Autumn and me.

"Not that it really matters, I guess. If they want an Asian mistress, they want an Asian mistress, shoes or no shoes."

"Or horrific shoes." Autumn cracked her knuckles against the hip of her corset.

A minute later, Bella emerged from the Black Room and shuffled away toward the kitchen.

"You're up, Justine," said Fiona.

"Me?"

"Knock him dead, sister."

I traced Bella's path down the hallway, stumbling only once in my heels. Heart pounding, I opened the door and blinked, my eyes adjusting to lights dimmer than those of the hallway.

"Hello." The man's voice came from the corner of the room. Squinting, I saw that he was seated in a tall wooden chair, adorned on its arms and legs with leather straps.

"Oh, hello." I strode over with what I hoped was an air of blasé confidence and put out my hand. "I'm Justine."

"Hello, Mistress. Nice firm handshake, I like that."

"My father told me never to trust a man with a weak handshake."

"I suppose the same goes for a beautiful woman."

Now, I'm not certain what I had expected. Toilet Timmy had been naked and kneeling during our introduction, as he'd already chosen me, sight unseen, as his mistress. I had figured that this client would be clothed, but also that his sexual druthers would be somehow more apparent. Instantly I felt embarrassed at my own ignorant dilettantism. Had I expected him to be a slobbering, greasy-haired lecher with a permanent hard-on, muttering uncontrollably about enemas and rubber masks? Sort of.

"I'm Roger."

"It's very nice to meet you, Roger." Roger was sporting a well-tailored suit, a full head of not overly gelled hair, and a pleasant, if somewhat unmemorable, face. As we held our smiles and the comfortable pause became an uncomfortable silence, I realized he was waiting for me to speak.

"Well, I'm new."

Roger kept smiling.

"Oh?"

"I mean, I'm still training. So I was wondering if I could, uh, assist on your session."

"Sure. Does that cost me any extra?"

"I don't believe so."

"Well then, count me in." His smile returned, with an added solicitousness that made it obvious that he was now the senior in our exchange. Not that I had known what to do when the upper hand was mine, or even that it was mine, but I felt a twang of defiance at his subtle condescension. "Well, thanks."

"Thank you, Justine."

With nothing left to say, I turned and left the room, aware of his eyes on my back with every step. I had rarely experienced such explicit appraisal. Living as a woman in New York, you get the once-over a few hundred times a day, but not with the same entitlement as of someone who has paid for the pleasure.

Autumn hopped up from the saggy white chair as I entered the dressing room.

"What does he want?"

"I don't know."

"Well, didn't you ask?"

"No, it was weird."

"Yeah, you'll get used to it. Did you ask if you could sit in?"

"Yeah, it's fine with him."

"Great, now let's get this over with."

Autumn strode into the Black Room and strode out thirty seconds later, listing the necessary equipment to Fiona as she stepped into the office.

"Latex enema, colon tube, Bardex, clamps, catheter, piercing needles, leather cuffs, and, um, diapers."

"That it?" Fiona punched the security code into the numbered pad beside her desk, unlocking the door that led to the supply closet where all the valuable equipment was stored. "All that and no dildos?" she asked while sifting through a basket full of rubber bladders.

"And dildos." Handing Autumn a handful of tubes, Fiona knelt in front of a dresser whose drawers had carefully hand-printed signs that read: *small*; *medium*; *large & fists*; *plugs, beads, & vibrating*. A dildo dresser.

After hoisting her assigned box of personal supplies into her arms—each mistress had one whose contents included a box of rubber gloves, a tube of generic lubricant, a box of condoms (for dildos), and a varied assortment of clothespins, clamps, rope, man panties (manties!), and hoarded favorite house supplies—Autumn turned to me.

"Give me ten minutes to get started, then come in and just follow my lead."

"Should I know anything else? What's his fantasy?"

"Don't worry about it; it'll be obvious." I hoped so.

*"Come in!"* After a few moments poised outside the door of the Black Room, listening to the rhythmic slap of what I assumed was her hand on some part of Roger's body, I had given a tentative knock. The lights had been turned up, and this time it was Autumn seated in the pseudoelectrical chair. Roger was bent awkwardly over her knee, his tailored slacks around his ankles, his face flushed. He craned his neck to see me, peering around the slope of her calf. "What the fuck are you looking at, Roggie?" Autumn bellowed, and reached her right hand down to grab a handful of his coiffed hair. "Why don't you keep your goddamn eyes in your head, huh? Your auntie has come over to help me discipline you, you little shit."

I was speechless, awed by the facility with which Autumn's entire personality had shifted, disappearing beneath the sheath of her role. In her domme persona, even the subtle nuances of her personality were absent. The characteristics that almost instantly identify a person, those we like to believe cannot be erased at will, she had erased. The force with which she inhabited her body and the space around her, the way she spoke and gestured, had all been eradicated.

"Noooooo!" Roger whined. "You're not going to tell her what I did, are you?"

"Would you like to hear what sort of trouble this little *asshole* has gone and gotten himself into now, Auntie?" Autumn raised her brows at me and smirked. It was as if she had lifted a veil with that smirk, revealed her personality to me from wherever she had folded it up and tucked it away to. Such is the disconcerting miracle of good acting; at its best it implicitly challenges our faith in who we are, who anyone is.

"Well, I'll tell you what he did, Auntie. This." She whacked his rosy ass cheek for emphasis. "Little." *Whack.* "Creep." *Whack.* "Ate a bunch of garbage." *Whack.* "A bunch of the sugary," *whack,* "salty," *whack, "crap* that he knows is forbidden." Autumn winked at me as Roger flinched in anticipation of the whack that never came. She leaned over his back and hissed, "Don't be such a drama queen, darling; your punishment hasn't even begun yet." Roger moaned, and I felt my lip curl involuntarily. The poised man whom I had introduced myself to a mere fifteen minutes ago had also disappeared, and with him, any advantage he may have held over my inexperience. "Have you ever seen such a despicable excuse for a man, Auntie Justine?"

"I have not." And at that moment, I wasn't sure I had.

"And have you any idea what the punishment for this sort of misbehavior is?"

"Well, I'm guessing it includes a spanking."

"Yes, a spanking, and a great big enema. Little Roger here knows all about his problems with constipation, and yet still, *still* he cannot seem to control his piggy urges."

"No self-control at all, I see."

"None to speak of, Auntie."

"I'm sorry, Mommy! *Please don't give me a great big enema to clean out my bum!*"

How could I not laugh? Instinctively I clapped my hand over my mouth in an effort to stifle the giggle. To my surprise, Autumn's face broke out into a genuine grin, her face shedding its disguise completely as she clutched Roger's back with her gloved hand and dissolved into unaffected laughter of her own. Composing herself, but still smiling, she tilted her head and began.

"Auntie Justine—" She choked on another round of giggles,

raising her brows at me while deepening her tone for an added note of cruelty. "Auntie Justine, it is a truly ridiculous sight, I agree. He is a joke of a man." She abruptly looked down at Roger, wrinkling her nose. "Are you *humping* my leg, Roger, you little scum bucket?" Indeed, he appeared to be slowly grinding his hips against her stockinged thigh.

"I'm sorry, Mommy; I can't help it. You and Auntie were laughing at my dirty bum, and I got too excited."

Autumn sneezed with laughter once again and avoided my gaze to facilitate speaking. "You need to get the fuck off of Mommy now, Roger. If you want to hump my leg like a dirty little dog, that's what we'll have to treat you as." She kicked him onto the floor, where he knelt on all fours, pants still around his knees. His Ralph Lauren boxer briefs remained pulled down just enough to reveal her crimson handprints on his bare behind, an obvious pup tent pitched between his legs. Striding over to the four-poster bed fitted with black leather, a matching hammock swing strung to its posts with heavy chains, Autumn reached into the open box on the bed and pulled out a black dildo the width of my wrist. Lifting the menacing hunk of rubber over her head, she flung it across the room, where it slapped the wall like a fish and bounced crudely onto the Oriental rug. She smiled and turned her gaze to the kneeling Roger. "Fetch, you motherfucker!"

Half an hour later, Autumn walked Roger back out the complicated series of doors leading to the elevator, and I could hear his professions of gratitude as they passed the dressing room door. When she returned, Autumn pulled a crisp fifty-dollar bill out of her bra and handed it to me.

"Here, you earned it just for sitting in that room after he released his enema. I mean, not that it's ever pleasant, but that was exceptional."

"I guess that's good news." I stared at the fifty. "But you don't have to give me that. It's two-thirds of what you're making, and I definitely didn't do two-thirds of the work you did."

"I know I don't have to give it to you; just take it." I took it.

At 1:30 in the morning, after the four of us had cleaned the kitchen, stocked towels in the bathrooms, vacuumed the rugs, and thrown the orphan shoes and articles of clothing behind the couch in the dressing room, we piled into the elevator with the massive black garbage bag from all the day's sessions. Fiona explained that we had to drag the trash around the corner and deposit it on 39th Street, to avoid the suspicious proprietor of the tiny twenty-four-hour deli next door.

"He thinks we're whores," Autumn explained. "Just try getting change for any bill bigger than a twenty. He'll look at you like he can smell the semen in your panties."

Fiona laughed.

"We'll take it, Fiona." Autumn took the garbage bag from her and turned to me. "You're going to the F train with me, right?"

"I am."

Fiona raised her hand and stepped into the street.

"Okay, I'm gonna grab a cab here then. I'll see you ladies to-morrow?"

We nodded and waved as she flagged a cab and headed uptown. As I reached for the knotted neck of the garbage, Autumn shouted to Bella, who was scurrying downtown, the back of her dark head already disappearing into the slippery shadows of the avenue.

*"Bye, Bella!"*

The lift of Bella's hand could have been a wave, a dismissal, or only a change in pace. Autumn shook her head. "It takes all kinds."

Our conversation on the train was easy. Her fresh-scrubbed face seemed already familiar, and I felt myself ease into the comfort of new friendship. I found it difficult to imagine the woman beside me spitting on and slapping the face of a man while he shat, though I had just seen it.

We hugged good-bye at the Union Square station, where she transferred to head to hip Williamsburg and I continued on to Bed-Stuy. Listening to my headphones for the following thirty-minute ride home, I studied my own reflection in the train window and the dark tunnel behind it. I could not have articulated anything other than the glow of hope, throbbing like a vague, sweet ache in my limbs.

# 7

A FTER THOSE FIRST NIGHTS, I mostly worked the day shift. Sensual sessions intimidated me less, and daytime clients wanted them. I adjusted quickly to my new routine. Four mornings a week, I'd pack up my schoolbooks and leave the apartment by 9:00. I loved the subway ride from Bed-Stuy, chicken bones rolling across the subway car's floor as the C train's ungreased wheels shrieked the forty minutes to West 4th Street, where I transferred to the F. Squeezed between the hips and elbows and briefcases of the late-morning crowd on their way to work at 9:30 A.M., I loved passing as one of them while knowing I wasn't. I loved the hard glare of sunlight reflected off car windows and dark sunglasses as the weather grew colder, my cheeks prickling as I climbed up out of the Herald Square train station.

Each of those mornings that I worked was the same: the same train ride, the same crush of grimly purposeful bodies carrying me up the steps to where the cold splashed my face and excitement gently writhed below my diaphragm. They knew me by name (Justine!) at the café where I bought my morning coffee and peach bran muffin. Midtown is lousy with places just like this one: shiny tiled floors and smiling immigrant workers behind polished glass display counters bearing baked goods, create-your-own-salad stations, and hot pressed paninis that look a lot better than they taste. Inevitably you get stuck in line behind the guy who pulls a crumpled envelope out of his paint-splattered pocket that has all the orders for the whole crew of the construction site across the street, or the woman whose latte cannot be got right: it's vanilla when she wanted hazelnut, skim when she wanted soy, foam when she wanted less foam. These assholes I loved, too; they made me privy to the kind of adulthood (sighing, hurrying, heeled) that I admired, in the childish way I still enjoy writing checks and parallel parking, but could not stomach actually experiencing. It was playing at a role that I wasn't sure I believed in and was fairly certain I wasn't qualified for. Passing through the realms of normal folk and clutching a secret. At this I was already an expert.

Coffee and muffin in hand, I would make my way across Sixth Avenue, dodging bike couriers and the less agile café deliverymen on their battered mountain bikes with wide, shallow baskets and naked handlebars. It wasn't uncommon that I'd run into one of my bleary-eyed coworkers as I approached the building whose second floor housed the dungeon. Poking my tongue out at the intercom above the doorbells where the tiny eye of a camera led straight up to Fiona's desk, I would wait for her to buzz us in. Also in our building was a nursing school (a laughable coincidence), a soon-to-fail yoga studio, and sundry other offices, the employees of which were indistinguishable from one another. It was never clear how much the denizens of the other floors actually knew about us. Suspicion was probably as far as their thoughts ever got on the subject, as Remy, the manager of the dungeon, ran a fastidiously tight ship so far as discretion was concerned. If a new domme carelessly happened to fetch her food delivery in a pair of fishnets and a robe, it was the last delivery ever dispatched to us from that place. Still, that suspicion was sometimes apparent when you got stuck on the elevator in mixed company. God forbid you fail to recognize a client and end up sharing the elevator with him.

After Fiona came to retrieve me from the vestibule between the elevator and the first set of doors, we made our way back in through the following two, which magnetically locked. I would follow her into the office to check the appointment book. Then it was a stop in the dressing room to say hello and drop off my belongings; the bathroom to wash my hands and, depending on if I had an appointment or not, pee; and finally the kitchen to stick my lunch in the fridge (I packed it from home regularly in the beginning). I would pick the peaches out of my muffin to eat first and smoke a cigarette with my coffee before putting my makeup on. I loved this routine as well. The morning chitchat in the kitchen, the opening doors, chores, and ringing phones, were all a soothing version of a work ritual that would have been much less enjoyable if they were a preamble to sitting at a desk.

Due to the clients' time constraints and the brisk efficacy with which the day crowd satisfied their perversions, day sessions were more often by individual appointment than the meet-and-greet, mistress-à-la-carte parade. Clients of this particular stripe attracted mistresses of an according one. Businesslike mistresses serviced the businessmen, women who had a straight-job cover to maintain, who took their calls in the bathroom so that their boyfriends wouldn't hear the shouted conversation about dildos and bondage. "Lifestyle" dommes rarely worked the day shift: women who wore their domme personas to nightclubs, kept personal slaves (for bathroom scrubbing, luggage carrying, and other domestic uses), gave public performances, and carried on purportedly congruent personal sex lives. No, the extraordinarily grotesque or obscure fetishist did not excite the day-shifters the way he did the night-, unless he was also an extraordinarily generous tipper.

The day shift paid heed to details like the high volume of thirty-minute sessions during the early afternoon, which, at 50 bucks a pop, paid more for your time and required far less of it endured with a single client. These half-hour sessions were frustrating to lifestyle dommes, who disliked them for the very reasons the others preferred them. It was explained to me early on by Anna, the statuesque Russian veteran (she had been at the dungeon for three years at the time that I started) with the inexorably perky breasts, flat stomach, and husky accent, that if I spent a good long time tying and untying the client and talking a lot, I could easily shave fifteen minutes off of a session. A thirty-minute enema session was Anna's ideal: these clients spent most of it in the bathroom, leaving barely enough time to assume their preferred ejaculation position (legs suspended over head to target mouth and face, crouched over Dixie cup, et cetera), ejaculate (this was never required but more common than not), and run back to the office.

Mistresses like Anna relied on a lot of hand jobs, which were the easiest way to control how quickly your session ended and to ensure that your client would return despite being cheated out of his full time. I didn't see Anna as necessarily lacking the integrity of other dommes, who refused to stoop to hand jobs. It was all the same to her. The difference lay less in boundaries than value systems. To believe that it is a drastically more degrading act to jerk someone off than to shove your arm up his ass is, in a sense, to believe in the entire premise of the thing. It is to believe that subjugation resides in the submissive nature of an act, rather than the sexual. But if the fisted client desires that fist as much as another desires a hand job, how is submitting to one desire any more powerful than the other? And yet most sessions—if not all—were based on such paradigms, so many being a kind of inversion of misogyny, the subjugation of women reenacted by men on themselves. Our clients wanted to be dressed in women's clothing and raped, molested, infantilized, humiliated, and physically abused. Did this kind of mimicry reinforce or subvert the power of these paradigms? The rationales and moral codes of the dungeon were complex beyond my comprehension, though I was promised by those most committed to it that its logic was steady. For a long time,

the apparent inconsistencies did not concern me. I was too infatuated with my new life.

The simplest explanation is that this was the brightest time.
This was the time when it was all too new to be understood, when
its meaning was not yet even suspected, or speculated upon. In that
first fall, I was in the manic flight of a change. Luminous with an
aura of new, my excitement, the *high* of it, was distinctly reminiscent
of countless shifts I had made in the past. I'd brokered deals with
myself to exchange a thing that had lost its power and become banal
or frightening for a newer version. I had traded and abandoned
lovers in this manner, best friends, mood-altering substances. With
each there was always this brightest part: the narrow edge between
the exhilaration of the new and its descent into corruption, mun-
danity, or the sort of wildness that is less likely to sweep you off your
feet than to crush you. Here the comfort of routine that other
people seemed able to sustain was briefly attainable. On this peak,
beyond the reach of both what came before and what was sure to
follow, I was not only happy; I was also invincible.

# Part Two

# 8

I STILL HAVE the first photographs taken of me at the dungeon. My building a clientele depended on publicity, I was told, and pictures were needed for the dungeon's Web site (an impressive spectacle itself). They also ran in the pages of local fetish magazines with our phone number emblazoned below my face. Within my second month of working, before I had even earned enough to purchase my own clothing, Fiona showed up one evening with a bag of cameras and commandeered the Red Room for an hour. At least the cost of her art school education was getting put to use, she claimed, which was more than could be said for most.

The first photo they published was a full body shot, in profile, with my face turned toward the camera. Propped on a large wooden chest, I have one heeled foot on the floor, the other leg dangling over the edge of the chest. Without stockings, my legs are painfully bare. I would not say this while observing a recent, bare-legged photo of myself, but my self-consciousness of that day returns so clearly to me now that I cannot help seeing the picture through the lens of that memory. I might never have felt so naked before. I had to borrow clothing, and the tiny hot pants left the bottom of my ass exposed, while the strapless bustier must have been two cup sizes too small. My mother frequently commented back then that my dyed-black Betty Page haircut looked like a wig, and I agree now more than ever. If I did not remember the night so vividly, I might not recognize myself. My hair is natural now, a brown so light that it shocked me after the years of black, my face leaner, and my eyes open in a way that makes those in that old photo impenetrable by comparison, even in their stark innocence. It was in my innocence that I had so much to hide.

In the grainy version that ran for months in the fetish magazines, you could not make out one detail that I can see now on the disc I have of the whole roll. In the crook of the arm that braces me against the trunk is a shadowy smear. It is of both the mismatched makeup that I used to apply there and the bruise that it was meant to conceal. Perhaps no one noticed on those night shifts my elbow's mismatched inside or that I carried my purse into the bathroom before many sessions and emerged with a voice an octave deeper and the pupils of someone poised beneath a floodlight. I might have been as good at my hiding as I thought I was. But when I think back, it is more likely that I confused ignorance with apathy. I underestimated the wisdom of my witnesses, who could see the futility of intervention, that my course was inobstructible.

If the day shift was the office, with its comforting predictability and gossip traded at the watercooler, then the night shift was a sleepover party, a persona parade under whose playful atmosphere lay a scrupulous network of social politics and pathology. Here were the women for whom the job was not a substitute for an imminent, socially acceptable one. Here were the new girls: the coeds not yet out of their teenage rebellious phase. To them the job was a badge of cool, congruent with their recently acquired taste for nonconformity. They rarely stayed long, usually a maximum of six months. Here were the ex–strippers and escorts, girls from Harlem and the Bronx, neither prepared for nor satisfied with the cut in pay and increase in labor (of a certain kind). The majority of them quit or were bullied out within six months as well. But the demographic that most interested me among the night-shifters was the "lifestyle" dommes. Predominantly college educated, they capitalized all words referring to themselves and other mistresses (She, Me, Mistress, Her, We) and required it from their clients (You). They posted regularly not only from the computer in the office on our Web site's official forum but also on various other S&M community boards, both locally and nationally based. They attended and organized seminars, conferences, parties, and performances, taking pride in their work, so that it became craft. Dominatrices certainly come in the "sluts with whips" variety. This was actually an unfortunate nickname that our dungeon garnered among the serious New York dominatrix community. The name referred to our allegedly liberal hand-job practice, though I doubt we were any more guilty of it than any other dungeon, just looser lipped and less concerned—the day shift at least. The spectrum of domming is broad, with strippers in fishnets at one end and women like Lena at the other.

If anyone was my mentor (Autumn aside, as she and I so quickly became friends and equals), it was Lena. In those first months she was an idol, a larger-than-life symbol of what I thought the job could be; she seemed to exercise real power. My first sight of her was in the dressing room, as I arrived for the night shift. The mountain bike she rode from Sunset Park, Brooklyn, was parked in the hallway, shining beneath the wall sconces, as out of place as a cell phone in a period film. She stood fully nude before the mirrored lockers, dark curls dripping water onto her full breasts and down her tattooed back as she patted handfuls of baby powder between her legs.

"Hey, Ma," she greeted my reflection. "Just shaved. Keeps it dry, no ingrowns. Antiperspirant works, too, but who wants to smear aluminum on their pussy, right?"

I was a goner. Mouth agape, I would watch her verbally humiliate her clients with a semi-automatic mouth, punctuating insults with a hand just as fast across their faces. That first night, I watched her terrorize a man until a pool of urine formed on the floor between his feet. He nearly wept when thanking her as she walked him out to the elevator, tucking two hundreds into her broad hand. She taught me how to chalk the ends of my bullwhips and floggers so that I could practice hitting a mark from three yards away, and tricks such as, when being fellated by a slave, to announce that you're about to come while yanking his head off the strap-on by the hair and spitting in his face. I saw her fuck them like a man. Lena never took her clothes off, or gave hand jobs. She was meticulously clean, exact in all her methods. Each of her sessions was a complete narrative, a performance unto itself; she would no sooner have cut a session short than take one that didn't interest her. Her slaves were utterly devoted, and despite (or perhaps because of) her brutality, there seemed to exist a genuine regard between her and them. I discovered years later that she made $85 a session instead of $75 like the rest of us. She raked in the money, sometimes pulling five or six sessions a shift ($85 × 6 = $510 per day, which doesn't include tips, ranging anywhere between $20 and $500 per session). Lena made her own schedule, and never got any flak from Remy.

As Justine, I still worked hard to hide my insecurity in sessions, sticking to sensual sessions, though their predictable scenarios and the pressure from those clients to give more than I wanted wore on me. Outside of the dungeon, however, I might as well have been Lena.

I had never liked parties. Even as a child, I tended to form intense, one-on-one relationships, rather than groups of friends. Unless there was dancing, I didn't see the point of hanging out in a large group, which made it impossible to connect with any single person and triggered a shyness that I liked to hide. I also typically wanted to get so high that public locations were impractical. At a party, I might have to share my drugs, or talk to someone who'd care that I'd forgotten how my legs worked.

After a few months of working at the dungeon, however, my interest in social events spiked. I now had the power to hijack any conversation, to commandeer the attention of however many people were within earshot at any given moment. As far as I could tell, no one was immune to the curiosity that the phrase "I'm a professional dominatrix" provoked. I lolled happily in the silence that followed uttering it, knowing the torrent of questions that would follow, the shine of eyes that saw me suddenly new. Knowing that I was likely the sole spokesperson for a subculture most people would never experience imbued me with a confidence I otherwise lacked. I was the reigning expert, the beautiful geek, and I loved their shock at how normal I seemed, how unlike what they would have imagined. With this ace in my pocket, parties became fun. Whether I pulled it out or not, I still had its power, and took comfort in worrying it like a lucky stone.

On Halloween, Rebecca and I went to a party in DUMBO—an up-and-coming Brooklyn neighborhood full of industrial lofts and brick streets—where I was supposed to meet a date. With a vile of cocaine, three bags of heroin, and a disposable syringe folded in a sock that I had tucked in an inside pocket of my purse, I convinced my roommate to take a cab, and had her laughing the whole way there. The giddiness of anticipation always made me funny. I had her in stitches with my description of Gene, the "Sweater Man," who brought a duffel bag to the dungeon every week, full of knitted clothing. He liked to be completely swathed in sweaters: sweater socks, sweater underpants, sweater mittens, sweater hats, sweater trousers, sweater masks. When he had nary an inch of naked skin bared, I'd immobilize him with rope bondage. That, really, was it. He liked to be tickled sometimes, while bound and sweater mummified, but really, just being sweaty, sweatered, and bound was enough for him. I could just hang out in the room while he gently writhed and cooed in his fuzzy cocoon. Gene made for an ideal anecdote: ridiculous and benign. I also wanted to distract Rebecca from any nervousness I might exhibit in omitting the fact that I had a purse full of drugs. I had become more comfortable omitting things from her, though I suspected she knew more than I told her. We both felt the distance my lies created, and with increasing frequency I would catch her looking at me with worried eyes. Sometimes I'd meet her gaze, in a fleeting moment of defiance, but more often I'd evade her. She hadn't yet had the courage or the opportunity to voice concern.

I'm not sure I'd ever known a more invincible feeling than that of walking into a party feeling beautiful, with drugs in my purse and a double life that everyone was dying to know about. I've seen the girls who feel this way walking into rooms. Sometimes beauty is enough. They *are* irresistible; one can't help looking at them, their smooth hair and self-conscious hands, their eyes bright with secret joy. But they are so delicate, in their preening and their need. I fear for them, now, knowing what they might do to keep that joy from trickling out of them, as it always does.

"So . . . ," my date said, a few hours later, and I could see him wanting to ask.

"Go ahead." I smiled.

"I'm sorry, I just . . ." He ran his hand through his hair. "I've never known anyone who . . . and you seem so—"

"Normal?"

"I mean, yeah, kind of." He was cute, and I'd already decided to sleep with him. "So, you don't, like—"

"Have sex with them? No." This was everyone's first question. "And I keep my clothes on."

I felt a pang of annoyance at his visible relief. If only people knew how predictable they were.

"So do you do it because you're—"

"Into it? No."

More relief. It was important to defang myself first thing, so that people knew I was safe to question about it, assured that I was just like them, only a little braver. After those two questions were out of the way, they always relaxed and became more eager for details. Were I *into* it, or willing to have sex for money, I would have been less of a curiosity, easily consigned to the diagnosis of broken woman—instantly diminished in intelligence, psychology, morality, or class. I understood this and shared their logic, even as it irritated me in its unexamined narrow-mindedness. The last thing I wanted to be mistaken for was *into it*. The glory lay in my ability to do it *despite* not being into it, in having the balls to choose it based on curiosity rather than compulsion.

"It's an acting job," I said, shrugging. "Probably one of the most reliably paying acting gigs in New York."

He chuckled. They always did at that one. I excused myself to go to the restroom.

There was a line, and I didn't feel like waiting; it had been a couple hours since my last trip to the bathroom, and my mouth felt gummy, eyes glassy. Lately, I couldn't seem to get or stay as high as I wanted. Getting a plastic cup of water from the kitchen sink, I wove through the party and stepped out into the building's hallway. It smelled of sawdust and metal, and I could see my breath— tiny clouds that dispersed quickly in the chilly air. For all the crowd inside the loft, the hall was empty, probably due to the cold. I wandered around the corner, finding a disabled freight elevator and a few empty apartments that were clearly under construction, their doors ajar.

I walked into one of these and knelt on the floor beside a window, where the light from a street lamp outside fell yellow and bright enough to illuminate a patch on the floor big enough for me to do what I needed. I dug the rolled-up sock out of my purse and removed its contents. Sprinkling a tiny dash of each powder into the concave mirror of my powder compact, I added a squirt of water from the plastic cup, using the syringe as an eyedropper. I mixed the brown puddle with the needle's tip, sucked it into the syringe, and carefully emptied it into my arm. Then I filled the syringe with water and emptied it a few more times—a ritual—watching the thread of liquid arc through the shadowy emptiness as the high crept up the back of my skull. Just as I had tucked the sock back into my purse, I heard footsteps approaching in the hallway. The light didn't reach to the door, so all I could see was her silhouette for a few seconds as Rebecca hesitated in the doorway.

"Hey!" I called to her, knowing the huskiness in my voice was a giveaway. I rose to my feet, brushing the sawdust off my knees.

"Hey." She walked over and squinted into my eyes. When she reached for my arm, I felt twin surges of panic and nausea rise in my belly. Before she could see anything, I yanked my arm back and hoisted the window open, thrusting my head out to vomit onto the street five stories below.

# 9

THE DUNGEON'S OWNER and namesake, Mistress X, had once been an employee. In glossy full color she was shown to me in a book of Eric Kroll's photographs that decorated the Cross-Dressing Room's coffee table. A slender Latina in vintage lingerie, her doe eyes widened over a ball gag, she was pictured tied to a chair, or poised with a riding crop over another bound woman. Women who had been at the dungeon the longest had stories of her bursting in on sessions of theirs and jerking off their clients in order to vacate the room for the next waiting patron. Anna had once costarred in a minor fetish porno with Mistress X and reported that despite the staunch moral limits regarding sexual conduct adopted by some old-timers, "Mistress X would do most anything. She wanted them in, and out, whatever it took. She was always a businesswoman." In Lena's words, this was "a slut." Allegedly, I had been hired just after the birth of Mistress X's first child and some of her last appearances at the dungeon. While I heard once or twice of her making cameos in my absence, I was never to meet her. The only authority I ever negotiated with was Remy.

Originally from Argentina, Remy was a middle-aged man with a face nearly handsome, who spoke a broken English that took me months to accurately interpret. For a long time I would just nod at his wavering tenor and later seek translation from a witness more fluent in Remy's harried Spanglish. We all loved to rant and rail against him (as I am sure goes on today), but we could have had much worse to answer to. I never once heard of Remy making any kind of sexual advance on anyone, and though he could be unreasonable, he was predictable. By adopting a method of placation, I never suffered any major conflict with him; if anything, I received especially lenient treatment. In the end, all Remy gave a damn about was the money. If you expected to be treated with respect based on humane or ethical grounds, you would be disappointed. To get along with the boss man, you simply had to make him money, know when to ignore him, and avoid drama.

A late sleeper, he rarely showed up before 5:00 P.M. Unannounced, he would creep in via a back entrance, through a supply closet whose key he possessed the only copy of. Emanating waves of anxiety, he would pace around the dungeon, blotting his perpetually sweating forehead with a white handkerchief. He had the kind of face—forever squinting when he addressed you, his brow crumpled in distress as though he were speaking into a heavy wind—that begged for mimicry. Tacked to the walls of the kitchen, dressing rooms, and office we would find notes in his wake like the one I had seen during my interview. For the most part, we ignored these. If the esoteric message was repeated in subsequent notes, with increasing emphasis, eventually he would throw a tantrum—such as the time he burst into the kitchen with a knife, spitting and sputtering in Spanish, and sawed the cord to the television in half before exiting nearly in tears. When his frustration reached this level, we would lazily acquiesce.

Remy shopped impulsively, and the dungeon was full of his impractical purchases. One morning, we arrived to find in the walk-in supply closet a "Skybox" fridge that dispensed tiny bottled waters and cans of beer for our clients (he stopped ordering Diet Coke when he figured out that only we drank it). It was painfully tacky and so large that the door to the closet could no longer be opened wide enough for our full-figured mistresses to retrieve their supplies. We were convinced that he had found it on sale at Costco and couldn't resist. The supply closet also had an entire corner devoted to the storage of handcrafted Argentinean equestrian equipment, including spurs that fit no one, bits, saddles, and riding crops too stiff for our use. His fetish for electronic gadgetry explained all the cameras—they were rumored to be installed behind the mirrors of all the dungeon and medical rooms, as well as the magnetic doors. They also facilitated an intricate system of recording if, how, and by whom the rooms were cleaned properly, which would be as complicated and tedious to explain here as it was to perform. Rumors circulated periodically that he had once been Mistress X's personal slave, with a particular taste for brown showers. I also heard it said that he was gay, or a pornographer who sold illicit videos of our sessions in Europe, among many other theories. Although he did have a decidedly submissive personality—hence the walking-into-a-stiff-wind face at the prospect of even the most minor confrontation—I doubt many of the rumors held any water. I believe to this day that Remy was a shrewd businessman, an immigrant with a strong work ethic who, without harboring any deep animosity, felt generally harassed by us.

And so it would go, for two shifts out of my weekly four, I would arrive after my daytime classes around 5:30 P.M. to contend with this particular cast of characters. Jordan, the night manager, would already be manning her desk when I arrived. In her uniform black jeans, a black T-shirt, and her specter-pale complexion, she would inform me of my appointments, the half pound of sliced roast beef she ate every night sitting beside the appointment book, the evening's sound track of the Pet Shop Boys or The Cure already piping through every room of the dungeon. Although the majority of the night-shift sessions came in the form of meets, for which we all had to get tarted up and parade in one-by-one, it was on the night shift that I acquired my first regular. Vinny.

A burly Italian American with a potbelly and boyish features, Vinny was the type of client (like many) who slowly made his way through a string of mistresses. Reliable as an old dog, he would show up every night that his currently favored mistress was working until the point at which she could no longer stand him or whatever it was about her that had struck his fancy ceased to do so. The content of his sessions evolved similarly.

The scene went roughly like this: having reserved Med 1 (the smallest and hottest of the medical rooms) ahead of time, Vinny would park himself in the examination chair and select a porn tape to play on the wall-mounted television. Vinny had been pouring money into the dungeon for so many years and his porn collection was so extensive that he enjoyed the rare privilege of having it stored at the dungeon for him. Given that it required two massive wheeling suitcases—both large enough to hold any one of us—to accommodate his collection, it was also a kind of insurance policy on his sustained faithfulness to Mistress X's. Who could imagine him lugging those anywhere else? It wouldn't have been physically possible; it often required two of us to lug just one of those suitcases out of the hall closet. While widely varying, his taste in video ran along the lines of showers (he especially liked the foreign scat videos, in which the women always had natural breasts and spat foreign curse words while smearing feces on each other), corporal punishment (perpetrated on either sex), and enemas. Sometimes he kept a magazine (older women and hairy ones most often featured) open on the table beside him to glance at as well. For tips ($20 to $40 each) he would bring three or four other mistresses into the session. These visitors, along with his primary mistress, would be arranged as such: one very slowly inserting a catheter into his urethra; one perched on a stool beside him, torturing his nipples with her fingernails or clamps (they were deformed from years of this treatment); one squatting over a bedpan pretending to defecate; and one standing beside him threatening to pee into his outstretched hand, and eventually doing so. At least one of these roles would be altered slightly each session. Sometimes someone would be holding Vinny's arms behind his back, holding a butt plug in place, or whispering threats in his ear. It was imperative to him that everyone in the room remain expressionless, with immaculate poker faces. There were so many factors that had to be gotten just right: the perfect combination of intensity, timing, and company, only to be intuited in the moment, that Vinny occasionally failed to reach climax. Due to the strain of finding this ideal combination, the length of his sessions could vary anywhere between fifteen minutes and sixty. During my stint as his favorite, I saw him find many perfect elements: a particular new video, mistress, phrase, or outfit I would wear that had the power to immediately create his ideal. Once it was Cuban-heel stockings and a rubber dress with a nurse hat, once a fantasy we would discuss (in expressionless voices) about the perfect world: one in which we would all walk around naked, expressionless, holding hands, and releasing enemas anywhere we pleased—"true freedom," as he put it. Inevitably, the talisman would lose its power, and then it would be a week of taxing sessions that stretched on as his frustration grew, trying to re-create whatever feeling he was missing.

Vinny lived a kind of sexual samsara. To my surprise, the impetus of our relationship's end was not my own boredom and repulsion at his depravity but the empathic discomfort of having to not only bear witness but also be party to his pathetic chase. It was easier seen in his desperation than in the routine economical interactions of the day shift, our roles of not merely supply-and-demand but also pusher and addict.

This was another routine: I would sit with my back against the locked door of the Green Bathroom, the shower running, a Dixie cup of tap water on the floor before me, my spoon, works, and two tiny Baggies of white powder laid out on a purple washcloth from the towel rack across the room. I would mix a dash from each bag in the spoon with a few drops of water, stirring as they dissolved with the tip of my syringe. After I shot the speedball, I would lean against the door and let the hiss of water against the shower's wall ring in my ears until I knew I could stand without vomiting. Then, I would pack up my kit, smear a dab of makeup in the hinge of my arm, light a cigarette, and go kick ass.

# 10

ON WEEKENDS I sometimes worked nights. Saturdays were known for being slow; our clients took their girlfriends and wives out on weekends, spent time with their kids. Due to the low volume of clients, these shifts only required a few mistresses. I found the quiet of Saturdays cozy. The dungeon—emptied of voices, the click-clack of heels and bare feet thumping down hallways, the open and shut of doors, the shouts of *"Walking,"* and laughter— reminded me of a museum after-hours. It felt more mine. Also, Lena worked Saturdays. *Her* clients showed up every night of the week.

One such Saturday, I sat sprawled on the dressing room sofa, half watching television, half studying. I had a paper due on Tuesday and insisted on pretending, as usual, that I was going to start writing it before Monday night. I frequently lugged schoolbooks to and from the dungeon without ever opening them. The weight would remind me to read, I told myself while packing them, as if the problem were in forgetting. I'd been sitting there for an hour, partly enjoying my lethargy, partly trying to wish away the anxiety of work yet done. I often wished I'd simply fail for once, get an F instead of getting away with the least possible amount of work. Always getting away with doing so little stressed me out. I had just resolved to focus on my book when Lena walked in.

"Phew!" she sighed, grinning at me and kicking off her stilettos. Reaching behind her back, she deftly loosened her corset and then unhooked the front eyelets, revealing her torso, striped with pink creases where the seams had pressed against her for the past two hours. Tossing the corset into her open locker, she unhooked her leather bra and threw it in as well. I tried not to stare at her breasts. They were as big as mine—at least Cs or Ds—with pierced nipples and a snake tattooed between them. Breasts didn't usually make me shy. I didn't worry about staring at Autumn's. Autumn also had no interest in inciting my bashfulness. Lena held my gaze for a beat too long before pulling on a white wifebeater and collapsing onto the couch beside me. Wrapping her arm around my shoulders, she kicked my books onto the floor. I laughed at her brazenness, giving in to the warmth of her body next to me, and her attention. "What are you watching?" she asked.

"*Simpsons* reruns."

"Sweet."

I can't now recall what episode we watched, couldn't if my life depended on it. I remember that she laughed out loud a lot, turning her face toward me each time, so that the hot rush of her breath rustled against my neck. At one point, she idly wound a hank of my hair around her palm and let the weight of her hand gently tug on it. The excitement of being with her wasn't just a result of Lena excelling at seduction or touching, though she did, but of my trusting her in some unprecedented way, believing that she knew more than I about something. I didn't always know what she was thinking, and I loved that.

My flirtation with Lena remained within the dungeon walls for some time. Aside from a couple of frustrated, maudlin affairs with straight girls in my adolescence, I had only ever dated women who looked like boys. First I had gone from the dreamy, long-skirted, messy-haired girl to the ponytailed high school jock, and then the androgynous downtown college hipster, all the way to the androgynous downtown hipster transgender "boi" (female to male). I had been hoping to find, in their studded belts, narrow hips, and husky voices, some element of power that I could not find (and probably would not have accepted) in the men whom I loved. While I never quite admitted it, to myself or anyone, I expected to be dominated by these women. To my disappointment and eventual lack of surprise, I found that the more masculine they appeared, the more submissive the role they took in bed, and in every aspect of the relationship. Not that I was uncomfortable behind the wheel. I knew how make all the decisions, how to get myself (and them) to orgasm, how to fix things, break things, dance, fight, manipulate, get the drugs, drive the car, talk my way out of a ticket and into anybody's mother's heart. I knew how to be the girlier girl and the bigger man. All I had ever known was that safety, and that loneliness.

Lena didn't look like a boy. She didn't act like a girl, either. I wasn't sure how big of an act hers was, and didn't much care, as it was as good as or better than any of mine. It was nice to be convinced for once. Smelling of baby powder and musky perfume, she would walk up behind me and squeeze my waist with both of her hands, her breath on my neck, or reach across my chest to grasp my chin in her hand, turning my head to face her.

She would crawl under the blanket with me as I napped on the couch in Cross-Dressing, and we would faux-sleep, or half-sleep, in a sweaty knot of limbs, rising an hour later exhausted by the attention to every muscular twitch, every shifted hand or hip or breast, every consciously measured breath. Women do know better, that this is often the sweetest part, and how to make it last.

After an instruction session she had given to a group of new recruits, she finally invited me out for a drink. I had played teacher's pet while she listed safety measures (always ask if a client takes

Viagra before using Rush—the inhalant amyl nitrite, or "poppers"—as the combination causes seizure) and legal concerns (always make a new client insert the enema tube into himself). Choosing me as a model, she demonstrated bondage techniques and how to operate the rooms' various mechanisms (Catherine wheel, stocks, ceiling suspension, et cetera). The new hires giggled nervously when, following tips on anal play, including how to fasten an adjustable strap-on harness, what to wear (always a condom, no fancy corsets; keep a pair of rubber or plastic hot pants available for easy post-session cleaning), and how to carry forth based on the client's fantasy (lesbian sex-slave fantasy = easy does it; rape fantasy = not so easy), Lena announced that she was going to demonstrate on someone, say, Justine. After a long pause, she and I meeting eyes while the rest of the room tittered, she announced she was kidding, "kidding! Don't look so scared."

# 11

DECEMBER CAME FAST. When Fiona phoned about my first session with Elie, it was one of those afternoons whose cold is clean. Everything was fine and sharp, as if hewn by the hard sunlight—the trees, the tidy rowhouses, and the faces bobbing past me down the sidewalk. Between school, work, and everything else, my double life felt more like three or four, and I joked about needing a personal assistant. Fiona would often call if a favored client wanted to schedule an appointment on a day I wasn't in, or if she booked a session for which I'd need to prepare beforehand (by drinking extra liquids, or wearing the same socks for a few days). Though I had only just left a class whose final paper was due that coming weekend, I agreed to come in at 9:00 P.M. and stay for what promised to be at least a three-hour session.

"He asked for you specifically, Justine; have you seen him before?"

"No, I just went in for a tip on Lena's session the last time he was here."

"But you know what he's into? *Lots* of nipple work. His supplies are in the office closet with his name on the suitcase. It's a pretty corporal gig."

"That's what I'm counting on." And I was. But three and probably more like four or five hours was a long time to torture somebody. I would have to get some supplies of my own. After I hung up with Fiona, I paged a number from memory and took the West 4th subway stairs two at a time.

When I got off the train in Bed-Stuy, my little red phone was humming and blinking with a new voice mail. I dialed my code and a round, buttery baritone rolled out of the tiny speaker: "You page me? I be up round Eastern Parkway and Bedford in 'bout one hour. I got you covered, girl."

The flutter I felt in my chest, the sharpness of sound and light in that state of anticipation, I now recognize as a form of anxiety. The memory of that excitement is a bodily one, and when I recall it so do my hands, the small of my back, my chest and belly. It is the peak of the roller coaster, after the benign clatter uphill, but before the terrible fall.

Christmas was coming. The churches on my block had hung their wreaths and strung the trees outside with blinking lights. As the last sliver of sun was eclipsed by the rooftops, I huffed breath on my hands and squinted down Franklin Avenue for the bus. I had four twenties and a MetroCard tucked in my bra. As it groaned up to the curb, I hurried into the warmth of the #48 and sank into a seat by the window, my belly flipping like it did before a first kiss. It would only get worse until I didn't have to feel anything.

Eastern Parkway passes the northern tip of Prospect Park and heads east toward Brownsville and East New York. It is flanked on either side by a tree-lined promenade. Kevin wasn't hard to find, though as he walked up the sidewalk toward me I could easily have mistaken him for a man twice his size. Kevin carried enough merchandise on his body to open a kiosk: watches, jewelry, clothing, single-serving bags of nuts (cashews or almonds, roasted and un-salted), various herbal teas, bottled beverages, telephones, disposable cameras, cartons of Newport cigarettes, pipes, hair picks, and drugs.

It was night, but just barely, by the time Kevin and I finished our stroll down the promenade and he handed me a folded square of tinfoil. The sky was that royal blue that doesn't happen every night and, when it does, lasts only for a few minutes. The trees that lined the walkway reached over our heads, and with that luminous blue wrapped so tightly around me I felt that I could have reached my arm up and sunk a finger into it. To have something in your pocket is sometimes even better than having it in your blood.

I rode the train back into the city straight after meeting Kevin. It being a Friday, people crowded the subway on their way out for the evening, their faces fresh and hopeful. I knew I looked like them: students in trendy sneakers, slouchy jeans, and hooded sweatshirts. The disparity between how I looked and how I felt, indeed *who* I felt like, had long been a source of pleasure. Knowing the difference between where they were going and where I was going still had its sweetness, but the distance had grown further than ever. For a moment, as I was pressed against all those buzzing bodies who had nothing to hide, panic fluttered in my chest. The rush of wind outside the train crescendoed, the squeal of metal wheels on the track piercing. I had a fleeting vision of my body being sucked out of the train's car, swallowed into the black intestine of the tunnel. Cupping my hand over my mouth, I whispered my own name. I'd picked this habit up around the time I'd picked up hard drugs, in my late teens. "Melissa." In my name lay the memories of everything I'd ever been before this, before I'd ever carried drugs in my pockets, or gone to places where no one I knew could have found me, even if I'd wanted them to. It served as a password to an internal control group: a part of me that could not be cut loose. The other side of anchorlessness, and the perfect detachment of the high, and the secrecy, was a terror in isolation, a pure and senseless fear that could strike without warning, though it didn't often.

I took a few deep breaths. Stepping off the train at 34th Street, I told myself that it was natural to be nervous about the session. Walking up the subway stairs toward the street, I thought of the class I'd had that morning. We had discussed a Rita Dove poem about the goddess Demeter, her fury at her daughter Persephone's kidnapping. *The mystery is, you can eat fear . . . and become a queen whom nothing surprises.* As the meaning of Dove's lines emerged in our class discussion, I'd felt the same swell of excitement that I had as a kid, watching from the deck of a boat as the backs of whales crested above the ocean's surface. I'd left class light-footed, my thoughts fleet and electric, matching the crisp winter smells and the cheerful hurry of the sidewalk. Walking along the perimeter of Washington Square Park, I passed the windows of some dorms and saw students in the common rooms. They sat curled in over-stuffed couches with books, mugs, and earnest faces. Without warning, I had ached inside. A part of me belonged there, and sometimes I could feel how I was killing it; I could feel its deprivation in me like a great, sucking wind, an inverted scream. A part of me wanted to be *good*, to believe that I inherently was, and that everything would be okay, in warm places without secrets or the endless craving that drove me outside at night to fill a hole that was never full. But my craving was real, not only for drugs but also for things that could only exist in the limitless world outside those cozy windows. I knew I'd have to quiet some other inconsolable part of myself to live in that safe world and wasn't at all certain that I could, even if I'd wanted to.

Most of the time, my lifestyle felt like a choice I had made, because I was smarter, more complicated, terminally unique. But not always, and in these other moments when it felt like a bondage to something I didn't believe in I was choked with envy.

Corporal sessions are named for their distinguishing element: corporal punishment. These sessions may or may not include sensual

aspects, role-play, cross-dressing (i.e., feminization or forced feminization), and even switching—where the domme takes at turn at being submissive—but they always include a hearty dose of violence. In
retrospect, the word connotes beatings: flogging, whipping, slapping, spanking, kicking, paddling, and so on, although the term was
also used to describe sessions of a more precise violence, like Elie's. It
seems odd now, but I can't remember the word "torture" being used
very often, though that's what it was.

By the time I arrived in Midtown for my session, the office
grunts and tourists had already been replaced by clubgoers in their
leather, hair product, and sunglasses. Women with blown-out
highlights shivered outside the twenty-four-hour deli, smoking
and casting sidelong glances at their reflections in the windows. At
this early hour, the Garment District still showed life, but by the
time I left it would be a wasteland of locked storefront grates and
concrete broken only by steaming manholes and the whiz of cars.

Elie could easily have blended into the early-evening demographic, with his combed black hair and Mediterranean complexion. His jacket was leather, designer, his Gauloises ever present,
though as a Frenchman he would never do anything so crass as
wear sunglasses after dark. He was early that night, as I would
come to expect from him, and I hung back beside the newspaper
stand outside the deli while he rang the buzzer and was let in.
Shoulders hunched, he pinched his cigarette and sucked it down to
the filter before ringing the bell, shifting his gaze around the
street, behaving exactly the way I had trained myself not to while
buying drugs.

I waited a minute or two, then followed him inside.


Knowing the session would require dexterity, I decided to forgo
the elbow-length gloves that I usually wore on nights I was using.
In the bathroom, I waited until the angry red spot inside my elbow
stopped beading with blood to smear makeup over it. I had missed

the shot slightly, and my elbow went numb and tingly as the co-caine seeped through the tiny blood vessels under my skin.

The beautiful thing about heroin is that it eradicates fear. It's hard to know how much of it you suffer from until you experience total freedom from it. Most of the buzzing, the anxiety, the ticker tape that streamed ceaselessly through my mind, was motored by fear. *What's going to happen, how can I control it, what can go wrong, what has already gone wrong, how can I fix it, what if I can't fix it, what if I'm not good enough, what if nobody else is, what if there is no use in anything,* and so on, ad infinitum. Heroin pulls the plug on that. Imagine the quiet! The paradox of narcotics is that while they allow you to experience the present moment painlessly, the plug is still pulled, and so you are numb to it; nothing sinks in. The joy of the high never lasts longer than your drugs. It can make you feel as if everything is okay, but it can't make it true. While the bliss of a heroin high has a lot in common with the sense of well-being that years of meditation can give you, narcotic serenity is spiritually toxic. It's Sweet'n Low, fucking a prostitute, and cheating on any-thing (except maybe your taxes); it makes life less tolerable, not more.

So take the empty palate that heroin makes of your conscious-ness and splatter it with mania. Cocaine is drive. I've witnessed the mania of bipolar people, and the first thing that always strikes me is how identical it is to a cocaine high. It is grandiose, marveling, indiscriminate, tireless, and then suspicious, paranoid, angry, psy-chotic, debilitated. Heroin subtracts all the ugly parts. That's why I shot speedballs. The feeling of both well-being and ecstatic mania flooding your bloodstream is unparalleled. I become so agitated even writing about it, years after the last time I experienced it, that I have to make cup after cup of tea and start praying that the phone will ring. There is a retroactive fear that is slow to wane.

Though I had watched a number of Lena's and Autumn's corpo-ral sessions, which were heavy on verbal humiliation and torture, I had still been nervous to take them myself and found it difficult to imagine punishment coming as naturally to me as it seemed it did to them. But everything feels natural when you're high.

"He's in Med Three," Jordan told me as I walked into the office. "And he booked both you and Camille."

"Camille? Excellent. Is his stuff—"

"It's on your box."

I carried my box into the dressing room and dug through the black garbage bag on top of it until I found the aprons. Shiny and black, Elie's butcher aprons were straight out of a horror movie. They reached our shins, were adorned with wide pockets at the hips, and he couldn't session without them. He once ran out of the dungeon in a tantrum because they had been lost somewhere in the rubble of the office supply closet. I hung one around my neck and cinched it tight around the waist of my zippered white nurse dress. Walking up to my reflection, I reached into my locker and pulled out a tube of lipstick. Adding a coat, I smacked my lips together, leaned in to check out my eyes, and stepped back to make sure my arm didn't look like it had a botched fake tan. Assured, I grabbed another apron and headed into the smaller dressing room to see if Camille was ready.

Though Camille had only been hired a few months before me, it was difficult to imagine her doing anything else. With endless legs and a faint twang of Jersey in her gossamer voice, she collected vintage lingerie and already had one of the largest wardrobes in the house, full of genuine nurse, schoolmarm, and military uniforms. She had a dancer's body, not only in proportion but also in that mesmerizing agility that never becomes tiresome to look at. She smoked Benson & Hedges, cut her hamburgers with a fork and knife, and was the only domme I had met who was an admitted submissive, though never with her clients at the dungeon. Hers was the only affected girliness I've ever encountered that I didn't find insufferable. She lounged around the dungeon reading BDSM-themed books, from intellectual highbrow to pictoral how-to, and was always asking if she could practice some new bondage technique on you. "Ooohhhh! Isn't that beautiful!" she'd coo after you were trussed on the rug with your arms bent like wings behind you.

"Ready, Freddy?" I threw the apron at her.

She sighed and crinkled her smooth, white forehead. "He really is quite perverted, isn't he, Justine?"

"Oh, quite."

"I'm really looking forward to this." Camille had some connection to London, a parent who lived there or had lived there. It was enough to justify the accent that also sometimes crept into her speech, apparently—and something else that only on her person did I not find pathetic and irritating. She stared dreamily at her own reflection and made an imperceptible adjustment to the nurse cap alighted on her coiffed head. "It's from the sixties," she sighed. "I got it on eBay."


We made certain to walk heavily down the hallway, knowing how the click-clack of heels frightened the Frenchman, in a good way.

"Hello, darling," I greeted him. He stood in the largest of the three medical rooms, ashing his cigarette into the sink beside the steel cabinet that held most of our scopes, probes, pinchers, and other instruments that looked as cruel as they sounded. I saw that he had removed a pinwheel (like flatware with a tiny wheel at the end decorated with spikes) and some long-handled clamps and laid them on the stand beside the adjustable table.

"Oh! You are so beautiful, just as I remembered." His voice, thick with his native French, trembled slightly, as did his hands. He stepped forward and then back, sucking vigorously on the lit cigarette.

"Of course we are. Now come say hello," I demanded. He scurried forward and kissed both of my cheeks, then Camille's.

"Are you due for some punishment?" Camille asked him. While thorough and enthusiastic in her techniques, Camille didn't like to talk much in her sessions, and I could see that it made her nervous.

"I am." He looked so forlorn, and said it with such dismay, that were I not buffered by the drugs, I would have stumbled over my next words.

"Well then, it's time for you to put your apron on and let us worry about the next few hours; they are not your concern." It was with a kind of relief that he then stripped off his tailored suit and folded it neatly on the stool beside him.

I have always known what people want from me. This skill played a large part in my success as a dominatrix. That is essentially the job description: know what your client wants, and indulge or deny as prescribed. Of course, it's a more delicate operation than it sounds. And being high didn't hurt, as the quieter your own mind can be, the better to hear theirs. I could already see Elie's craving for maternal reassurance; he wanted to be told exactly what to do, albeit within specifications, not all spoken. A tall order, and a common one.

He let us tie his own black apron around his slender waist and guide him into the chair, which we reclined, and we firmly tied his feet to the stirrups, his hands behind the headrest.

It is too taxing to maintain strict character for the duration of a four-hour session. You end up slipping in and out of character ("out of character" not being yourself but rather a low-gear version of your domme persona), revving up at the client's cue, and giving him a rest when necessary. This improvisation requires a close attention to subtle tonal shifts in his responses and facial expressions. There is never anything so obvious as an "okay, let's get back to business, ladies." Many new dommes sour their business by being overzealous and not knowing how to discern when is enough. And so, after a slow crescendo that began with bondage (fishing line skillfully knotted around his nipples and strung to the great mobile lamp overhead) and ended with "fire-and-ice" (cigarettes and cubes from the kitchen freezer), we settled down into easy conversation and the slow process of emptying his bladder into a glass jar with a catheter.

"Now, here you're going to feel some pressure as it perforates the bladder." Elie moaned and squeezed his eyes shut. "There we go. Not so bad, was it?" I smiled down at him in perfect nursey condescension. He shook his head childishly. I left Camille holding the jar to go fix again in the bathroom.

On my return, a conversation ensued in which we learned of his deathly fear of water, due to an episode of maternal negligence at the shore during his childhood.

"Oh yes, I remember the fear of death vividly; even now I do. I have tried many times to swim, and every time it returns to me, just as it was that day when I was a boy. I cannot even take baths. It's very sad, I know."

Even at this early stage in my domme career I knew that nothing ever gets said carelessly in session. Camille knew the same. After she pierced his nipples while I held Saran Wrap over his face, we fed him a Dixie cup of water and stepped into the hallway.

"I have an idea," she whispered.

We found a large plastic tub in the closet where the cleaning supplies were kept. While she released him from the chair and blindfolded him, I filled it with cold water from the shower in the neighboring bathroom (the Green Bathroom—also where I had been fixing). Leaving it on the floor of the shower, I returned to Med 3. Elie was now standing, naked, still trembling slightly, though now it was probably less nerves and more adrenaline from the pain he'd just withstood. Hardened tears of wax and their paths down his chest clung to his goose-pimpled skin, his swollen nipples. He reached his arms out gently and Camille guided them behind his back to tie his wrists together.

"Where are you taking me?" he asked.

"That's not for you to worry about, now is it?" I said. "It wouldn't do any good anyway, would it?"

He shook his head.

We cautiously led him down the hallway and into the bathroom.

"It's cold in here, Mistress."

"You need to shut up now, darling. Nobody's wants to hear a whiner, do they?"

He shook his blindfolded head.

"Now you get down on your knees for us." Camille pressed on his shoulders from behind. In her heels, she was taller than him by two inches. He sank to the floor, trembling more violently now. I inched the tub closer to the edge of the shower, until it was just below him, waist high. He whimpered. Crouched on either side of him, Camille and I each placed a hand on the back of his shoulders, and his head. We silently counted together, *one, two, three,* and plunged his head into the bucket. The jolt that went through Elie's body was first one of sheer physical shock, as if he were being electrocuted. Then the terror shook him. A flash of something crossed Camille's face—the ripple of wind on a lake's surface—as he arched his back and bucked under our hands, but her expression resumed its placidity as her eyes met mine and said, *Now?* I nodded. We lightened our grip and his head popped up, mouth gasping fishlike, water streaming down his cheeks into it. After a few noisy mouthfuls of air, mine and Camille's eyes met again, *one, two, three,* and we pushed him back under the water. This time bubbles streamed up behind his ears and we could hear his submerged screams. His legs slid backward, bare knees slipping on the wet tile. We had planned to do three dunks but could tell we wouldn't be able to hold him down another round. We released him again, and after a few ragged gasps his body crumpled over and he let out a mournful moan. The three of us sat on the floor, damp and shivering. Camille and I rubbed slow circles on Elie's trembling back. Eventually we realized that he was weeping. Slow, wracking sobs, like fever chills, shook him for a long time. When they finally slowed, he pulled my hand under his body and pressed his mouth against it. At first he kissed my palm, wetting it with tears and mucus. Then I could feel his mouth moving, but it wasn't until he looked up that I could hear him saying, "Thank you, thank you, thank you."

. . .

Years later, during my first therapy session, I had to explain to my therapist what a dominatrix was.

"So, would you consider yourself a sadist?" she asked me, not a trace of judgment in her tone. I laughed. Of course I didn't; the suggestion was absurd. I could barely watch someone get beaten on television, let alone on the street; I hid my eyes and plugged my ears when rabid dogs were shot in movies.

But did I enjoy hurting people? Sometimes. But not simply for the sake of their physical pain. I couldn't fathom hurting someone who didn't want it, but how many people get to experience the moral loophole of hurting someone who wants to be hurt? I don't know what it means that I enjoyed it, or what percent of the population would, if given the opportunity. But for someone so bent on mastering her given conditions, on inventing herself and her world in opposition to convention, it was an act of supreme defiance. As I had crouched on that bathroom floor, held that man's head beneath the water, I experienced a kind of transcendence. It was that utter alienation from self, a loosening of the glue that made my reality whole. It felt both horrific and triumphant.

# Part Three

# 12

TEMPING?" my mother repeated. "But you've always hated office work." She stirred her tea and squinted up at me. "I thought you were catering?"

My brother stared at me over her head, waiting for my response. We stood in my mother's kitchen, my brother and I leaning against opposite counters with my mother sitting at the table between us. She had asked about my financial situation, which I assured her was secure. He knew the truth, as he always did before either of our parents. My father—easy to avoid, as he was often halfway across the globe—was usually last to know. My brother was a friend, a friend with an unparalleled capacity for giving me the benefit of the doubt. In my shortsighted arrogance, I couldn't foresee how I'd regret burdening him with my candor about so many things.

"I kind of have a new job," I said. "I've actually had it for a while." This wasn't the first time I'd broken unwelcome news to my mother, and while I knew how to keep an even tone, my stomach still fluttered. I wiped my palms on my jeans.

"What?" She recognized that evenness of tone. "What are you doing?"

"I'm a dominatrix."

She stared at me, her pretty face taut, practicing her own evenness.

"Do you know what that is?" I asked her.

"Kind of," she said slowly. God, I hoped she couldn't see through my calm as I could hers, and that what she saw beneath it didn't make her heart clench as mine did.

"I act out the role of a powerful, dominant woman. I tie men up, call them names, stuff like that. It's like a kind of therapy, really," I added, hoping to appeal to her therapist's sensibility, "reenacting childhood traumas."

She turned to my brother. "Did you know this?"

He nodded.

"I don't have sex with anyone, and I don't take off my clothes," I quickly added.

"Is it safe?"

"Of course!" I said. "Do you think I'd be doing it if it weren't safe?"

She just stared at me.

"Haven't I always taken care of myself?"

She nodded, though I couldn't read her face.

"Don't you trust me to make informed decisions? Hasn't it always worked out?"

"No, I do. I do trust you." She paused. "Not that I could stop you if I didn't." Was she accusing me? Reassuring herself? I couldn't tell.

"It's been great for me, Mom. It's given me so much confidence. I get *worshiped* for a living." Instinctively, I tried to appeal to my mother's feminist, therapist values. "The women I work with, they're amazing, strong, educated, creative women. It's not like I'm a prostitute or something. I'm in control of everything that happens. It's *empowering*."

She did trust me. At least, she wanted to. And I *had* always landed on my feet. So why didn't I feel relieved after telling her? Certainly, I hadn't always taken care of myself in the years since I'd moved out, but she didn't know that. I'd worked hard to conceal all the many unsafe conditions I'd sought out. I missed that sense of getting off the hook, of having the winning argument. I had a great argument; I really believed it, and kept on making it, but her face never relaxed. I told her about my alias, about medical sessions, about the money, about my nourished body image and my friendship with Autumn—what a kindred spirit I'd found in her. My mother kept nodding, but her eyes stayed worried.

My mother and I were inseparable for my first eleven years of life, and she spoke to me like a person before it was in vogue to be friends with one's children. In the long stretches of months that my father was away at sea, I was often her most available confidante. I don't remember grieving his departures much myself after the age of five or six, but when my father left, everything in our home would assume an aura of sorrow that lasted for weeks. Some things, certain times of day, were worse than others: the accumulation of shadows at dusk, beneath sills and chair legs; darkness slipping across the kitchen table like a drawn cloth; the faint fur of dust on the lip of a vase. After I reached a certain age, it no longer seemed as though this sadness originated in her, or me, but that it was organic to everything it afflicted. Our belongings emanated despair, as if they'd realized they were soulless.

By the time she became a practicing psychotherapist, I had already discovered men, and shut her out. When I slipped away from her, and began lying about where I spent my time, and with whom, she tried to rein me in with talk of rebuilding trust, with love and reason. This failed. Then she screamed and wheedled, and I grew to hate the stricken look in her eyes almost as much as I craved the illicit thrill of secrets and desire. She and my father sent me to a therapist of my own, who either bought my manipulations or gave up—I still don't know which. I settled down eventually, when

I scared myself enough. I don't think she ever stopped fearing losing me again. At least, she never pushed that hard again, never tried in earnest to stop me from doing what I'd set my mind to. Through my dropping out of high school and moving out at sixteen, she tried to mother me with support instead of judgment; she gave as much as I would accept and made a decision to trust me. We remained friends. Ultimately, we were similar in our self-sufficiency, though hers was the result of a childhood lived in poverty and neglect. She had had no alternative but to rely on her own resources, whereas I was simply determined to, for reasons mysterious to us both.

Not long after our first shift together, Autumn and I were talking on the phone daily. Our similar childhoods had eased us into fast friendship, and a slew of other likenesses cemented it. Together, we giggled and gossiped about the other dommes and delighted in our mutual appreciation for base humor and utter candor about all things sexual. The similarities seemed endless.

One night, while I was covering a shift for one of the usual nighttime dommes, Autumn poked her head into the kitchen as I was stuffing a load of laundry into the washing machine.

"Pssst! Justine!"

"What?" I peeled off my rubber gloves and pushed the "Start Cycle" button.

She beckoned conspiratorially and disappeared down the hallway. I sighed in mock exhaustion and followed her. Pulling me into the Green Bathroom, she locked its door and winked at me.

"What?"

"I'm bad," she said.

"Uh-oh."

"I've been a very naughty girl, Mistress Justine," she announced in a nasal, lisping tone.

"Well, perhaps Mommy Justine needs to give you a spanking," I growled.

Grinning, she reached into the cleavage created by her corset. Eyebrows raised in anticipation, she rooted around for a moment before withdrawing a folded square of paper and a twenty-dollar bill.

"Tsk, tsk!" I shook my head at her but then made grabbing motions as she set the white square on the back of the toilet and unfolded it.

"It's only a couple grams, but you have class in the morning anyway, right?"

I snorted. We both knew that as soon as she finished rolling up that twenty, having brain surgery scheduled the next morning couldn't have kept the cocaine out of my nose.

Sessioning on coke was unimaginable fun, so long as you didn't run out. The high raised you above the grim tedium of predictable sessions, the humiliation of sensual ones, and left you with the energy to get creative. Coke allowed everything whose sheen had dulled to shine again. A fair number of nighttime clients would bring their own stash to share with their domme, if she was interested. The dungeon traded in sexual compulsion, and with one compulsion you usually find others. Autumn and I were always interested. That night, we made a web out of a single endless twine of black rope and hoisted a 250-pound man seven feet off the ground. As he gently rocked from the ceiling-mounted chains, the soft flesh of his back bulging around the lattice of rope, we smoked and laughed, intermittently flicking his exposed buttocks from below with purple riding crops. We refused to let him masturbate to orgasm until he had drunk an entire pitcher of our combined urine from a plastic champagne glass. We heckled him, taking long swigs from a gallon jug of water, in order to keep replenishing the pitcher. At one point, Autumn laughed so hard that water streamed out of her nose onto the satin front of her corset.

"Well, that needed a good flushing out anyway," I said, and we cracked up all over again.

After closing the dungeon, we ended up at some signless bar on the Lower East Side, flirting with the lanky bartender and swiveling our hips to and from the bathroom every ten minutes to do lines. It being a weeknight, the bar was virtually empty by the time we licked that white square of paper clean and tried to suppress the instantaneous depression that follows every last line of coke. I silently concocted plans to get more, knowing them futile; it happened every time. Three o'clock in the morning was too late to call either of our dealers on a weeknight. Below my high lay the sheer drop of an excruciating comedown, compounded by the reality of a class that began in six hours and the fact that I'd spent more than I'd earned that night on shots. I kicked against the inevitable gravity of the crash, scrambling, determined this time to will my mind beyond the mental agony of withdrawal, the fever of worried despair and sleeplessness, that I could never seem to remember when I decided to inhale that first line.

Autumn and I had gotten loaded together a handful of times, nights that we began like this one: feeling beautiful and bulletproof, intoxicated with our power. By morning, I'd end up as I did after that night: at home in bed, alone, listening to the chatter of birds outside my window, with bleeding nostrils and suicidal fantasies, choking down gulps from a forty-ounce bottle of malt liquor from the bodega to soften the crash. The sound of car engines growling to life, apartment doors slamming as other tenants in the building left for work, and the squeal of city buses breaking to pick them up all sped my spiraling panic. Looking at normal lives from the ugly side of mine was a special hell. I silently prayed for sleep, and tucked tiny wads of tissue into my nostrils to stop the burning. Once, afraid to cross paths with Rebecca in such a state, I had urinated in an old coffee can in my closet.

Two days later, as Autumn and I crossed paths in the dressing room—she arriving for the night shift as I was leaving—I mentioned that feeling, made a joke of it, something about being glad I didn't own a gun, because I'd probably have killed myself that night just to escape another minute of it. She laughed with me, but the knowing I recognized in her eyes was as hopeless as my own.

A few days after that, I almost asked Rebecca to leave New York with me. Our final semester of college had begun, and having fulfilled all my credit requirements for graduation, I was enjoying a cushy schedule. Monthly, I met my thesis advisor at a coffee shop to hand her the next ten pages of my novel—already twice the required length of the thesis. My weekly classes consisted of photography, chorus, and a course on Romanticism that would have been more interesting if it weren't dumbed down for the design students it was intended for. Rebecca and I rode the C train into the city together for this class, which began at 9:30 A.M. The hardest part of my routine was getting there on time. Eight thirty cast a bad light on just about everything.

Leaning back against the scuffed train window, I watched Rebecca sleep, her long torso folded over her lap, cheek against her knee. She was a good friend, I thought, and looking at her softly mussed hair and flushed cheek, I appreciated how she managed to be both smart and innocent. As hard as I worked to annihilate my own innocence, I envied her sometimes. I hated keeping things from her, but how could I describe the misery of those sleepless mornings to her when I couldn't even broach the subject to Autumn without making light of it? I couldn't. I stretched my arms over my head, trying to shake off the dark feeling. The terror of nights like those usually slipped away after I finally slept, washed away in dreams and the particular amnesia of minds that, as Einstein famously defined insanity, "do the same thing over and over again, and expect different results." Only when alone, with a specific quiet of mind, did I find it creeping back in. I was often my most sober in the mornings, before the static of the day crashed over me, before I could smoke or swallow or shoot anything.

Watching her brow furrow in sleep, I almost shook Rebecca awake and suggested that we leave after graduation, go back to Boston and get a warm apartment, paint the kitchen yellow, and cook dinner in it every night. For a hopeful moment, I could imagine myself dropping everything in New York and leaving it there, living only as the version of myself whose name I whispered into my hand when I was afraid. What if I never had to see anyone's worried eyes again, not over me? And then, like a loose garment, that hope slipped off of me and slid to the floor. I nudged Rebecca awake with my knee.

"We're here," I said, and stood.

On my first and only date with Lena, we walked by that signless bar on our way to The Whiskey Ward, on the Lower East Side. After a few drinks, we moved on to some place on Eldridge Street. It was packed, dark, the kind of bar you want to be taken to by someone who knows the bartender, not to mention the pretty Latin boys selling coke by the ladies' room, so that you can get something better than the yellow mixture of baby laxative and gasoline they sell to the underdressed Jersey girls. I could tell she thought this was new to me, that I'd be impressed by her knowing Carlos's name, and flattered by the way she held my arm so that he'd know he could look, that she wanted him to, but that was all. I was flattered. But that was the only thing new to me. Cultural tourism had always been an obsession of mine.

The DJ played both of our favorite music for dancing, that is, any music not made by white people (hip-hop, reggae, Latin), and when Lena pushed a pill into my mouth I feigned hesitation. Happy to play the girl for once, I nestled my hips into hers but wished I had two pills, wondered if she had more. These are the scenes in movies when they employ tired camera effects to illustrate how fucked up everyone is: swooping shots that smear the faces in the crowd, paired with distorted audio to give everything a muddled, carnivalesque atmosphere. That was what I wanted, from the booze, the drugs, and the sexual charge between me and the people I chose. I wanted to lose control, to have things happen to me that I did not engineer or even anticipate. It never worked. No matter the number of pills or drinks or miles from my cultural landmarks, there always remained something that I could not disable. While I could occasionally disable myself physically, I still always knew what was going on and believed I had a hand in where it went. And so, though it became harder to walk in my heeled boots and my mouth stumbled against her ear when I whispered, I knew all along that we were going back to her place to fuck.

Sunset Park is in south Brooklyn, below Prospect Park and the baby stroller–studded yuppie haven of Park Slope. It is Chinese, Indian, Puerto Rican, Dominican, with wide avenues and squat commercial strips of bodegas, discount stores, and narrow ethnic groceries that double as social clubs. It was a warm night, for late January; it must have rained earlier. The trees shone, mostly bare, a few slippery leaves papering the sidewalk beneath our feet. The unfamiliar neighborhood at the end of a long cab ride (of which I only remember the mirror of the East River gleaming blackly beneath the Manhattan Bridge, and Lena's mouth on my neck) left me feeling stranded, which I liked. I clung to her arm and blinked at the streetlight in front of her building. Through my hazy high, the light was bloated, seeping into the dark like a billowing stain.

The light in her hallway was harsher and the dark of her apartment seamless after it. I followed the tug of her hand, rubbing with the pad of my thumb the uneven edge of one bluntly shorn fingernail as she opened one door, and then another, eventually guiding me up a wooden ladder.

Her lofted bed was flush with a window, and so I could nearly make out her face in the silvery light that crept through the branches outside. Spirals of hair stuck to her neck with sweat, she pulled off my boots and jeans and pushed my panties aside. She had mentioned keeping her nails short (unlike the talons of many of our colleagues) to avoid damaging the delicate tissues of her clients' vulnerable parts, and that night I was grateful for that consideration.

As a sometime lover of women, I have always scoffed at strap-ons. To me, the rubber penis was an impotent device in its sheer lack of reciprocity. While I liked being fucked, I suspected that in using one, or having one used on me, I would be convinced that my partner was simply waiting for me to finish so that she could have her turn. Did that say something about my view of relationships in terms of competing interests? I liked to be the best at everything I did, and the passivity of offering my lover an aerobic experience in exchange for my erotic one simply seemed bad form.

I could not see Lena's face with much clarity, especially once she had me on all fours with my face to the wall. However, when one has spent as much time as I had contemplating how and what it means to be desired, one knows what it feels like. I could hear her panting, and felt her fingers digging into my hips too spasmodically to be calculated. She was actually getting off by dominating me, regardless of deficient genital stimulation. I had always drawn a strict line between our clients and us, them being psychologically fixated in a way that interrupted "normal" sexual development and us just needing some good old-fashioned clitoral stimulation to get off. But never was the evidence more plain: Lena's desire was to dominate me, and knowing that made my stomach flutter, made my opinions about strap-ons melt away to leave only the bare physical sensation, the paradoxical pleasure of being objectified, which made me feel *more* real, not less. A total mind-fuck. While this experience did make the world of erotic possibility suddenly larger, it took me much longer to frankly apply the significance of that revelation to myself, in my private life as well as my work.

Usually, I negotiated the upper hand on dates, a dynamic further facilitated by my being a domme. On a date with a man I'd met online or at a party, I'd mention it early on, but after I'd established myself as not crazy. After the appetizer, and once assured that I'd captured their interest, I'd tell them. I enjoyed watching these men squirm, unsure of how to react. If they expressed too much interest, *personal* interest, the date was already over. I wanted admiration, to elicit desire prompted by my embodiment of both intelligence and sex, not by the prospect of exploiting my professional skill set. I never met with disapproval; without consciously doing so, I managed to never choose anyone who might judge me harshly. Whether for reasons I preferred or not, they were always impressed.

The only lasting romance I was able to sustain in the first year was with a woman I'd dated in college, and our reprise lasted only a few months, though not for lack of intensity. Gin was freckled, lovely, and lean, often mistaken for a boy by old ladies. "Why, thank you, young man," they'd coo when she held doors for them. Like everyone else, she was infatuated with this new facet of my persona. I was infatuated with how I looked to her eyes. She saw me as I wanted to be seen: wild, brilliant, sexy, and a little bit tragic, a force. But how could that possibly sustain us, when I knew it was at least partially an illusion? I could never trust others' perceptions of me—a terrible catch-22. Ultimately, my relationship with the job, and the drugs, didn't leave room for much else. It required a lot of energy to publicize only select aspects of each and to conceal the rest. I edited my experiences instinctively—there were rarely moments when I consciously decided to lie, willfully omit, or distort the truth—but it was still a sophisticated juggling act to ensure that I projected an image of seamless confidence and control. I found it uncharacteristically easy to stay out of long-term relationships in the early days at the dungeon; in many ways, it scratched the itch that my relationships always had. It was my *job* to be desired, rather than simply my most consuming pastime. Every "meet" was an opportunity to flex my seduction muscles, to prove once more that I had the power to compel, not with my own desire but with my will.

# 13

There isn't anywhere to hide in Tiffany's. The store is enormous, and jewelry is small. The twenty-five-foot ceilings don't accommodate much more than a few chandeliers and the fog of luxury that rises from those long glass display counters. On my first visit to Tiffany's, I breathed it in and smiled. The women behind the counters smiled back.

I had loved *Breakfast at Tiffany's* since adolescence, but I'd lived in New York for years without ever setting foot in the famous flagship store on the corner of Fifth Avenue and 57th Street. There were two reasons for this. One, I didn't believe in diamonds. That is, I knew that the racket of luxury goods and their value—invented merely to give those with too much money something to waste it on—was a disgusting hoax. My mother had always shaken her head at luxury cars and considered driving them tantamount to flipping all the poor people in the world the finger. To her, status resulted from humanism, not ostentation. I fancied myself too smart for Tiffany's.

Second, I didn't feel like I belonged there. Not that I grew up poor; in fact, I was shocked to find out as an adult how much we had during my childhood. But both my parents grew up poor, and poor children either turn into adults who worship money or firmly don't. My parents belonged to the latter group. So I never *felt* privileged. And while my disbelief in diamonds was tinged with pride, I still grew up in this culture, and no one is immune to the magic of luxury. Women who walked into Tiffany's did so swathed in a confidence I'd never had. A part of me knew that if I walked into Tiffany's, my raised-by-hippy shabbiness would emanate from me like a stench, draw glares, and the discomfort of not belonging would eventually drive me back out that revolving door, humiliated. I might have been a good many admirable things, but I was no Audrey Hepburn.

A year at the dungeon changed all that. I walked just about everywhere swathed in confidence now. And somehow, it didn't matter that I didn't *believe* in luxury goods, only that I now wanted them. I walked into Tiffany's in my red lipstick, heels, and fur-trimmed coat and felt completely at ease. I strolled along the carpeted floor, peering into the displays. I tried on a diamond bracelet, accepted the clerk's compliments with a smile, and finally settled on a silver locket, its chain a slender, shining thread, cool against my neck. As far as Tiffany's goes, a modest purchase, but spending many hundreds of dollars on something I absolutely did not need was, to me, a thrilling extravagance.

In the summer of 2003 I had money. Rolls of it nestled in between my paired socks and under my growing collection of slippery underthings—always more money for less fabric. There were fifty- and one-hundred-dollar bills tucked inside certain books: *Les Fleurs du mal*, a fat de Sade collection, a Bible with split binding. I found distressed twenties in jacket pockets, at the bottoms of purses, and in the Laundromat drier until I no longer did my own laundry.

When you work real jobs—jobs whose work consumes whole days ticked by on wall-mounted clocks—you know what you are spending when you hand money over a counter. A pair of shoes = five hours of washing tourists' dirty sheets and toilets. A taxi from Midtown Manhattan to Bed-Stuy at 2:00A.M. = four hours scrubbing chowder-encrusted pots and eating facefuls of noxious steam. A thirty-minute spree in Victoria's Secret = fifty hours of scraping paint off the bottom of a boat. But what are you spending when a man hands you hundred as you walk him out the door? Autumn once told me that there was no such thing as free money, but I didn't believe her yet.

For a time, I would do the calculations in my head, or on scraps of paper in the dungeon's kitchen while I smoked. Take Dave (one of many Daves), who came to see me once a week to arm wrestle for about twenty-five minutes. A good tipper to begin with, he would often cough up an extra $50 for each of us if I brought another mistress in for a tournament. He would occasionally win with the third party, but never me. A half-hour session cost him $100, $50 of which went to me, plus the $100 tip. If a second girl came in, the extra $50 then left me with $200 for about twenty-five minutes' work. That's $8 per minute. What's three minutes of arm wrestling in false eyelashes for a cab ride to Brooklyn that saves you an hour in travel time, not to mention the stench of the 34th Street subway platform and who knows what potential late-night dangers? Worth it from any angle I could see.

There were also slow nights: the preholiday slump when our clients' children were home for vacation, the clients' finances saved for gifts and trips abroad to allay the suspicion of neglected wives; nights of play-off games and Jewish holidays; inclement weather. If the clients didn't come, we made nothing. An average could have been calculated but wasn't, and so I never quite knew what a pair of shoes cost me in work. The $8-a-minute nights came to mind easier than the $0 ones when I was deciding between 300- and 1200-thread-count sheets at Bed Bath & Beyond.

Was it even work? Some sessions certainly were. Handling clients who didn't wipe properly was work. Cleaning up an enema spill from the medical room floor was work. Pretending to admire a 250-pound man in a ratty wig and pink muumuu with lipstick smeared on his teeth and pretending enough to play his lesbian seductress often required rigorous effort. When I had another mistress to share the burden, that effort was paid mostly to prevent hysterical laughter. Relentlessly spanking anyone for an hour is grueling. But I had never considered work something that shaped you; it was more like Styrofoam packing peanuts: stuff that took up a lot of space but was necessary for a certain degree of comfort. It certainly didn't define you. Being a dominatrix so quickly became a part of my identity. I watched it happen, watched myself turn into the women I'd seen on the day of my interview, felt myself absorb that confidence and sensuality. It bore such intangible results that I couldn't class it with any kind of work I'd ever done for money.

Law dictates that you cannot receive more than $10,000 per year as a gift without the IRS breathing down your neck. To be safe, we dommes rarely let banks hold our money, unless it was in safety-deposit boxes. The most successful (and pragmatic) dommes exploited the talents of their stockbroker clients, who were never in short supply. I never accumulated enough to stash or invest, and so I was simply cash rich: a dangerous status for someone who had never had much expendable income. I can tell you that to have a few thousand dollars in cash feels a lot richer than to see a number on an ATM receipt. It's also a whole lot easier to spend.

When I began working at the dungeon, the thought of taking cabs never occurred to me; it simply had never been an option. For all my years of city living, I had always walked wherever I could, biked from Brooklyn to Manhattan, and remained infatuated with the subway longer than anyone. But it took only a few weeks for impossibilities to become luxuries and for luxuries to become necessities. I took cabs *everywhere*. I ate in restaurants nightly and bought clothes without trying them on to kill time while waiting for a date. I could suddenly have bouquets delivered on Mother's Day and take the Acela train to Boston instead of Fung Wah, the gypsy bus that went from Chinatown to Chinatown for $10. Between my weekend drug binges, weekly mani-pedis, cab fares, and restaurant checks, I soon had a lifestyle whose financial demands eagerly rose to meet my income.

It wasn't only my economic status that had changed. My rise in popularity among the dungeon's regular clients coincided with the sudden privilege of a more flexible schedule and the disappearance of fines to my pay for arbitrary things like failing to follow room-cleaning protocol, leaving a shift early, or eating in the dressing room. I found myself one of the few mistresses whom Remy cracked bad jokes to and occasionally teased in his flushed, unintelligible way. It helps not to make enemies; I'd always known this.

Contention with phone girls would leave you undersold to clients, as every appointment had to come through Fiona, Jordan, or one of the other phone girls. While your income could plummet as a result of offending them, the reverse was possible if they liked you, so I made sure that they did. While there was a natural relay of clients between mistresses, overtly stealing someone else's regular slave before either party had reached the requisite state of ennui was bad form and could make your life hell in the dungeon. So I didn't. The same went for performing sexual favors in session that crossed a certain line. It was simple etiquette: if no one is giving blow jobs or getting naked, then the clients won't expect it and there will be a fair distribution of patronage. When it happened, it never stayed quiet for long. I witnessed many a rookie, not pretty or skilled enough to justify nabbing every walk-in who came through the door, finishing hour sessions in fifteen minutes. They never lasted. Physical confrontations were occasional but uncommon, though rare was the girl who could withstand more than a few weeks of our ostracization; the dungeon simply wasn't big enough. If social pressure failed, Remy could always be persuaded to fire them. The disgruntled consensus of his highest earners was powerful enough to end many careers. We used to kid about forming a union, demanding hourly minimums and health insurance, but so long as you were steadily earning for Remy, the threat of leaving for another dungeon was usually enough to get you what you wanted.

Still, there was jealousy, snotty asides from mistresses who had been there longer than me or whose look resembled mine (busty, petite, Betty Page haircut). There were also Autumn's former friends, who resented her neglect since my arrival. Recognizing my own naïveté humbled me early on, when it became obvious that the dungeon was no sanctuary from the atmosphere of competition between women that is fostered so avidly in this culture. I believed then (as I do today) that this is largely due to the conspiracy of a multibillion-dollar industry to convince women that we are not good enough and that good equals beautiful by its unattainable definition, so that we will buy more stuff. It was hopelessly naïve of me to think that the dungeon would be an exception. Sure, the sexual ideal of many of our clients contradicted that one paraded through SoHo on the thin, coltish legs of malnourished teenage models. Our clients often requested big butts, and bodies that smelled human; they fetishized body hair and physical strength. But these were still the characteristics that determined our value; it was still a sexual prescription. It was still a competition. I kept score, too. The ugly reality, like many, was easy to stomach while I appeared to be winning.

Though in my first year there I became more comfortable in my body than I had been since childhood, my confidence reflected a perceived sexual value. I had always thought I was smart, but I still changed my clothes inside my sleeping bag at summer camp. Despite my feminist 'zine making, unshaved legs, and proclaimed bisexuality as a young teen, I still silently behaved and thought like someone who hated her body. At the dungeon, I finally felt free of that, and the power of my sexual confidence and the money was intoxicating enough that I could choose not to examine it too closely.

This is not to say that the dungeon was the cesspool of cattiness, insecurity, and sabotage that I have heard strip clubs and escort agencies to be. It *was* exceptional in many ways. The women there spoke frankly about subjects that are aired much less often than they ought to be. Especially in my first year I admired them, when the mistresses were more experienced than me. They spoke about their insecurities and eating disorders (past and present). They discussed sexual abuse histories and unconventional sexual practices. Camille once told me, in a casual kitchen conversation, that she thought she'd been a submissive since childhood. As an adolescent, she used to scrub her vagina with a hairbrush in masturbation. Now as an adult she had a master in London who dressed in Nazi uniforms for sessions (his clients were mostly men). He and Camille were in love, she said, and would marry one day. He knew how to treat her tenderly, but he also carved designs into the back of her neck with a razor blade, locked her in the trunk of his car for hours, and flogged her back purple. She said that she knew it was a result of her history that she had desire so twisted up with hurt. "I accept that," she told me. In her way, she seemed more content with her lot than most of the women I knew. Who was I to judge her happiness?

I'd always had many more male than female friends, and it was an unexpected relief to spend so much time around women. I felt comfortable. We got our periods at the same time, bickered and made up like siblings. We laughed until it hurt. These women were the first people I ever felt comfortable being naked in front of. They tied my corsets for me, showed me how to be confident in my body and how to be a great dominatrix. But in the end, we were still lining up ten times a day like pageant contestants to compete for biggest turn-on.

After six or eight months, however, I had markedly less downtime in the dungeon with which to form alliances and rivalries; I was too busy. Like most new hires who were pretty enough and stuck out the first few weeks, I enjoyed an early boom in business chiefly owing to the same batch of dungeon regulars that every domme before and after me would know. We had nicknames for them, as we did for most of the clients we shuffled among ourselves. This first wave of undesirables included: Pilot Dave, Fish Bill, Pussy John, Hairless Billy, White Sneaker Fred, Fisting Jack, Dan Dan the Jerk-off Man, and Mental Dental Roy. Though they would occasionally reattach to a more experienced domme, they preyed mainly on new girls, who proved less adept at setting boundaries and more comfortable with sensual sessions. This motley cast made the rounds at every major Manhattan dungeon: Pandora's Box, Mistress Elizabeth's, The Ball and Chain, The Den of Iniquity, Rapture, Arena, and so on. On Internet forums shared by the citywide commercial S&M community, they were often mentioned, in jokes and warnings. I still saw some of them by the close of my first year, but my relationship with most had completed the life cycle from intimidating, to exhilarating, to more tedious than $75 could account for.

The easiest way to terminate with a client was to perform badly. While a fair number of clients paid to be ignored, insulted, and laughed at, the majority wanted nothing less than to see a dominatrix whom their fantasies bored. When yawning, monotones, and abruptly ended sessions failed, I would have to dump them, suggesting a recent hire whom I thought better suited to the job. Most of these scenes were relatively painless, with no more discomfort than my usual fear of others' disappointment and hurt feelings. In a few cases, they played the disconcerting role of jilted boyfriend, weeping, pleading, and calling repeatedly to beg for reconciliation. While it was part of my job to act as though I shared their fantasies, as if the money were a mere formality, the strength of their delusion in these cases was sad and disturbing. By the time summer rolled around, I had replaced them with regulars who were better tippers, more challenging in the good ways (creative sessions, intense roleplays), and less challenging in the bad ways (annoyance, attachment, hygiene, tedium, and sleaze factors).

And I had discovered something. I was good at my job. I greeted this discovery with genuine surprise, still believing that it was more chance than personality that had landed me in the dungeon. I lived in New York, had an open mind, and needed money, but I didn't want to strip or prostitute myself. It seemed obvious. I was surprised that I didn't know more women who had tried it.

# 14

THE LAST TIME I shot heroin was the day I moved upstairs from Autumn. I had left the Bed-Stuy apartment I'd lived in for almost three years with barely a glance back. Though if Rebecca had been home, I might have found that harder. She had helped me pack, though I wished she hadn't. I wanted to preserve my excitement about leaving, and her wistful presence agitated my doubts. I was moving forward—leaving behind the water bugs and mice, Kevin's wolf whistles, and the innocence with which I'd knocked on my neighbor's door that pivotal morning.

"Williamsburg isn't that far away," I said, though Rebecca and I both knew how little we'd see each other. As close as everything is geographically in New York, it's easy and comfortable to become cloistered in your own neighborhood. Factor in the lifestyle I was moving closer toward and how much it differed from hers, and the likelihood of our maintaining the same intimacy grew even less. But my desire for that lifestyle prompted my move: the shiny parts of being a domme. I wanted to move closer to the money, the invincibility of it, and how big it all made me feel: the shadowiness and the sex of it, the distance from any sense of insecurity or neediness. I wanted to feel that strong always. The old apartment, the decrepitude of Bed-Stuy, even my friends seemed like relics of an earlier, less knowing, more vulnerable version of me.

The tiny Williamsburg studio wasn't worth what I paid for it, but it was mine. My bedroom window looked out over our landlord's concrete patio. All day, the harpy matriarch would sit out on a plastic chair and scream at her husband and adult daughter in Italian, prompting the daughter to then scream at her own children in Brooklynese, leaving the children to torment the dog, an incessantly barking dachshund named Precious. "Go the fuck to sleep!" was their nightly refrain.

Autumn was out of town when I moved in, so I enlisted the help of an old boyfriend to carry my crates of books up the staircase. He brought with him five bags of South Boston dope and a syringe the size of a flashlight.

"What am I supposed to do with this monstrosity?" I said.

"I couldn't get to the needle exchange before I caught the bus," he said. "So I had to steal it from my doctor." Junky logic.

"You know that you can buy them at Duane Reade here?"

He rolled his eyes. "Oh, okay, sure. *You* ride the train into the city and go to the pharmacy. I will be here when you get back, enjoying these drugs."

So I stuck that javelin into my arm, and as soon as we could move, we moved.


It had been weeks since I'd gotten high—the longest I'd gone in years—so it was ironic that that was the night my problem became apparent to my coworkers. A few hours after moving, I was in session with Vinny and four other mistresses. As usual, we occupied Med 3, sweating beneath the mirrored ceilings and maintaining our stony faces. Bella was naked on a footstool, her blasé expression appropriate for once.

"Don't smile!" Vinny scolded the new girl, Sasha, as she tortured his nipples with a pair of long-handled clamps. Camille held his arms behind the upright examination table, her bored face resting against the side of his headrest, watching the wall-mounted television. On the screen, a potbellied man in riding pants whipped a woman tied to a wooden post. Hay lay scattered around their feet in an obviously haphazard attempt to create a barnlike atmosphere. Vinny preferred those videos that might have been taped in someone's actual basement or backyard. His favorites featured older women (*GrandMILFs Go Down*), unshaven women (*Hirsute Honeys XII*), and stars with cellulite, potbellies, and bad teeth. A part of me liked him for rejecting the usual choreographed, silicone-enhanced fare.

Miss K—a veteran with the duel honors of an Ivy League degree in architecture and the roundest ass ever seen on a woman of her stature and proportions—held a butt plug in place with one gloved hand. Situated between his stirruped feet, I teased his urethra with the tip of a catheter. The tube of rubber was as long as my arm and thin as a knitting needle.

"No, no, no," Vinny moaned, jerking against Camille's grasp. He spoke in his slave voice, which was higher pitched, and unheeded. He had a "safe word," as most sessions did: a code word to call out when "no, stop" could be mistaken for part of the scene. Vinny's safe word was "red," but he never used it, because we could always tell his real voice from his fantasy one. Vinny provided a classic case of topping from the bottom. He wasn't submissive but had a submissive fantasy. So we pretended to dominate him, under meticulous stage direction. He wasn't the worst case of this, but it added to the tedium of his fantasy.

Like any addict, Vinny had a high tolerance, and that night was not one of his easier ones. The hour felt interminable. Vinny wheezed and mewed, even his hairy shins slick with the effort. Sweat slid off my forearm and down the length of the orange catheter. Bella sighed, looking down to check her nails as she flicked her own nipples. Miss K wiggled the butt plug with one hand and reached up to rub her back with the other. Sasha increased the pressure of her clamps, Vinny's moaning building, building, building, and then waning. He did not look like a man indulging in lascivious pleasure. He looked like a man suffering from painful constipation. He was working harder than any of us, and his face began to take on a maniacal look of desperation. Then it looked as if it might happen. We all increased our effort, threw ourselves into as passionate an act of apathy as we could muster. Vinny announced, "I'm gonna, I'm gonna, I'm gonna—," and then my stomach turned. The catheter hit the floor with a little slap, like the tail of something. I lunged for the sink under the television and vomited into it.

It wasn't the first time Vinny had failed to climax by the end of his session, but it was the first time my coworkers had ever looked at me that way. "I'm sick," I offered as they filed out, pushing their damp hair off their foreheads. Vinny had booked the session with me, and so I stayed to clean up and walk him out. When he got out of the shower, I had already finished cleaning and sat on the disinfected examination table. Vinny smiled at me, removed the towel from his waist, and began buffing his shoulders and back with it.

"I used to have a coke problem, you know," he said.

"Oh yeah?" I stared at his genitals. They jiggled beneath his belly, purple and withered.

"You're on heroin, aren't you? I know what it looks like."

"I really just used to have a problem," I said. "I only do it every once in a while now."

His knowing look made me want to punch him in the face.

# 15

WALKING INTO an AA meeting didn't feel the same as walking into a party, but having Autumn beside me made it easier. I also felt buoyed by the social power I'd have as a domme; after all, I'd be in a room full of folk with an admitted taste for illicit activity. Autumn and I dressed to make an impression: jeans and knee-high leather boots, tight T-shirts, tattoos visible. Funny how bait and armor can be the same thing. We arrived a few minutes late, and the staccato of our heels echoed against the cathedral ceilings, interrupting the meeting leader, who read from a laminated paper to the seated crowd—close to a hundred, on folding metal chairs. Heads turned to look at us. I clenched my hands and relaxed my face, vacillating between wanting the attention and wanting to become invisible. We slid into a couple of empty chairs in the back.

The chair of the meeting finished his preamble, emphasizing that "we encourage the discussion of drugs as well as alcohol." Autumn nudged me, and I nodded.

The chair then introduced a speaker, a slender middle-aged

woman in a leather jacket who sat in front of the group, between two five-foot window shades on which were printed the Twelve Steps and Twelve Traditions. Though I instinctively rolled my eyes at the word "God," I didn't mind these so much. Their cultish tone irked me, but I had always been partial to lists and knew there was relief in clear instruction, though I'd gone far to defy it. I wanted stopping doing drugs to be simple; a step-by-step process sounded easy. At least, I'd always succeeded easily at that sort of task, when I tried.

The speaker had a good story, lots of heroin and 1980s Lower East Side debauchery. I loved the stories in meetings, like live renditions of my favorite books and movies. Alcoholics all sought extremity in some way, it seemed, all experienced an affliction of craving—even as children. There was a thrill in hearing a stranger describe my own private rituals, filthy habits, and obsessions. When the speaker described pissing in a bottle in her bedroom between lines of blow, and vomiting into her mother's kitchen sink, I laughed along with everyone else and marveled at the alchemy that could convert shame into humor. I admired her weathered, pretty face and gravelly voice and felt momentarily reassured that I could be both clean and cool. I didn't plan on becoming one of the bland, apple-cheeked women I saw in the rows in front of me, smiling down at their knitting and vigorously nodding whenever anyone uttered the word "miracle."

And Autumn had been right; there were *men* here. Sitting in a room full of men could be like having a pocketful of drugs—the *yet* of who and how I'd seduce comforted me; it was the longest distance from being alone. She and I were so full of desire—it wasn't sexual but something easily mistaken for it. We must have glowed, because the men all stared, and so we stayed. It only took me a few minutes to settle on a man across the aisle, a motorcycle helmet tucked under his chair, looking at me without looking at me.

.  .  .

At the time of the Vinny incident, it had been weeks since I'd last gotten high. I had already been to a few 12-step meetings, that humiliating last resort. It seemed I'd always known about them; my mother was a therapist, after all. The Twelve Steps were great, I'd always thought, for those who couldn't find their own footing. I had no doubt that meetings worked wonderfully for people who weren't strong enough to suffer their own craving, or smart enough to find a way around it.

My very first meeting I attended alone. One weekday afternoon, I slunk into a church basement in the East Village, hoping to go unnoticed. I mostly was, despite being virtually the only white person in the room and the only person of any kind under the age of forty. To my surprise, the people there seemed happy. They laughed and clapped and stomped their feet, and when the woman who sat at the front of the room told her story she talked about the misery of running back and forth between the bodega ATM, her drug dealer, and her apartment. I knew what she meant. I knew I was an addict; I just wasn't convinced that this was my solution. I was too young for AA anyway, I thought. I was only twenty-two.

Then, in the dungeon kitchen one evening, Autumn walked in for the night shift as I was folding towels, about to head home.

"God, it's wet out," she complained, tossing her umbrella into the corner and dropping her purse on the counter. She opened the fridge and pulled out a bottle of water. Unscrewing the cap, she hopped onto a stool and sighed. I joined her, reaching for her purse.

"Give me a cigarette," I said, rifling through the jumble myself. I spotted a gray booklet with newspaper-thin pages. *Alcoholics Anonymous*, it read on the cover. I pulled it out. "What's this?"

Autumn glanced up. "Oh, nothing. My boyfriend in California goes." She pulled her yellow pack of cigarettes out of the purse's side pocket and tucked one between her lips.

"Really?"

She paused for a long moment, looking at me.

"No, not really. I've been going myself."

"Yeah?"

"Yeah."

"Me, too."

We grinned at each other and laughed, sheepish and relieved.

"Where have you been going?"

"Well, not AA actually, NA."

"You should come with me to an AA meeting—they're better, less depressing. Cuter men."

"But I'm not an alcoholic."

"This is New York, Melissa. Half the alcoholics here are junkies anyway."

The motorcyclist was a painter, with tattooed arms and a vintage BMW bike. He was my mother's age, kind, and worshipful without passion. We attended that meeting weekly and others that he frequented in SoHo and all over the East Village. I loved swinging my leg over the back of his bike and pulling off the helmet, feigning nonchalance in front of the crowd smoking outside the church. He taught me to save my bathroom trip for when the boring people got called on, who the zealots were and the desperate women who would disapprove of him. "They're just bitter," he told me. "AA is full of bitter women." The painter brimmed with such nuggets of wisdom.

My job was a source of great amusement and novelty to him. The thought that the sexual nature of it could or even should be unacceptable to a lover never crossed my mind. I knew that were the tables turned, I could never accept such a situation. Money would not make it any less a betrayal. Do you see how I was able to decide where my reasoning stopped? Secrecy and careful selection of people was my armor. I had eliminated people from my life who challenged my drug use, and hid it from those who would have. I chose carefully the stories I told about my work, and lovers who would cosign it with their acceptance. There was never anyone who knew the whole truth. So it didn't exist. That is the magic of secrecy. It creates a vacuum. My secrets were like rooms where I could hide things and preserve the truth I designated for them.

His being twenty years my senior further facilitated this. I'd never gone for men that much older than me, but his age seemed to make him even safer. Part of the appeal of older men to young women is a way that they can never completely accurately see you; you are always a little bit of a marvel to them, an immigrant from another generation. To women who feel broken, or hidden in some way, it feels safe: they can hide behind the sheen of freshness that older men cannot help but see. Being with an older man makes you *feel* young.

The painter didn't ask questions; he doted on my precocity, my big breasts and hands, my little ears.

"Look at you!" he said once, after sex, lifting up his 300-thread-count sheet. "Every part of you is so smooth and perfect!" I blushed and scooted out of his bed, quietly loving it. His doting differed from that of my slaves; I got to play the child with him, and found that a surprising relief. After locating my panties and pulling on a T-shirt, I padded into the kitchen. I spent most of that summer like this: wandering around his central-air-conditioned house in my underwear—just a few blocks away from Autumn and my place in Williamsburg. I opened his fridge and stood in its pale light, surveying the contents. I grabbed a quart of organic yogurt, pulled a spoon from the drying rack in the sink, and headed back into the bedroom.

The painter reclined against his pillows holding a magazine, his reading glasses on. I curled up in a chair near the foot of the bed.

"What are you reading?" I said.

"Oh, just some stupid art magazine, did a profile on me." He folded his glasses on the bed stand and clasped his hands behind his head, looking at me appreciatively.

"So what about this whole sponsor thing?" I asked, with a careful

note of irony. "I keep hearing that I ought to pick one of those up."
I ate a spoonful of yogurt and raised my brows at him.

Smiling faintly, he shrugged. "It's a good idea, of course. But you
should be careful. You can't just take the first person who offers—
they're always the most desperate. There's a lot of people in the
rooms who get off on telling newcomers what to do, when it's outside
the jurisdiction of their own experience. Without sounding dramatic, it can be dangerous."

"Do you have one?"

"I have people who I call when I need to work something out.
That's what matters—that you know not to try and figure everything out yourself."

I put the yogurt on the floor and crawled up the length of the
bed until I was straddling him. "So, if I have you, does that count?"
I bent down, glancing up to see his smile broaden as I kissed his
chest.

"It counts for something," he said.

Most people in the program would have disagreed, of course,
but I was relieved. I wanted to hide out in his cool, dark house for
as long as possible. I didn't need the cool, dark escape of a high as
long as I had here to come to, it seemed. The painter had been sober for over a decade, and as much as he may have omitted in the
interest of keeping me around, I learned a lot about sobriety from
him, in his cool, nonchalant way. People in meetings could render
everything so life-or-death. His was probably the only way I could
have heard a lot of it.

When I arrived on his door one night with pupils pinned and a
husky heroin voice, he let me in and believed my lie about codeine
pills. However selfish his motives may have been, that nonplussed
acceptance made it easier for me to stick around, keep going to
meetings.

I think the only way I stayed as clean as I did was on the back of
the painter's motorcycle. At my request, we would speed up and
down the FDR Drive at night, flying along the East River, past the

Pepsi-Cola sign, and the park where I shot up with street kids during my first summer in the city. Back and forth from Brooklyn to Manhattan. New York at night, from its bridges, is a miracle. When I first came to the city, it took all my fantasies and set them on fire, turned them into flickering constellations of light. Then it did the same with my history. As a dark speck of energy hurtling over the water toward that galaxy, I felt myself disappear. Relative to that image of infinity I was nothing, a clump of quantum matter skidding through the ether. It was as good as any drug.

# 16

Is there anyone new to the meeting?" asked the meeting secretary, who made announcements and handed out coins after the
speaker finished their "qualification." The crowd clapped and gave
a, "Welcome!" in shaky unison after each person new to the meeting and each person visiting from out of town announced their
name and status: addict, alcoholic, addict/alcoholic, grateful recovering alcoholic.

"Is there anyone counting days?" Autumn, beside me, raised her
hand. The secretary smiled in her direction.

"Autumn, alcoholic, and I've got seventy-nine days," she said,
and everyone clapped, with a few hoots mixed in. As newcomers,
she and I were the darlings of our now regular Wednesday meeting, at least until we reached ninety days.

"Anyone else counting days?" asked the secretary, and Autumn
kicked my foot. I raised my hand halfway.

"Melissa?"

I shot a dirty look toward Autumn.

"I've got sixty days today," I said. More clapping and hooting. I felt my face flush and couldn't help grinning.

The secretary beckoned. "We have a coin for that, you know. C'mon up here!"

I rose from my folding chair and headed up the aisle as the clapping continued. When I reached her, the secretary handed me a plastic coin with a gold *60* embossed on one side. On the other side, in tiny print, read: *To Thine Own Self Be True*. As she hugged me, I felt a tiny crumpling in my chest. I hurried back to my seat. Autumn blew me a kiss, and I rolled my eyes.

"You should be proud!" she whispered.

I was proud. I couldn't remember the last time I'd been this clean. The program was, as they liked to say, *doing for me what I could not do for myself*. The thing was, I still couldn't stop getting high. The difference *was* radical: instead of getting high every day or every four days, I slipped every few weeks. To a junky, a difference of weeks might as well be eternity. Over the past couple years, I had been trying to stay clean for a consecutive week and failing. Leaving the country hadn't even kept me clean. This drastic difference, I told myself, was nearly the same as being sober. Hadn't I wished countless times for the ability to use just once a month or so? To be a recreational drug user again? I'd never planned on being completely abstinent. But that's what AA called for. I loved meetings, and my life had quickly come to revolve around them, around the host of new friends I'd found there. The people in East Village and Williamsburg meetings were people I would have gotten high with. I loved the stories, as I had always loved those kinds of stories. I loved having my four minutes to talk. It was all a perfect forum for me to practice looking and sounding the way I thought I ought to, which was its own kind of power. I did want help. I just didn't know any other way.

I counted the days I didn't use, and I believed most of what they said. I had never had a problem believing one thing and doing another. For a while, it continued to work. The meetings made me feel better. My dread subsided to a manageable size. But every three weeks or so, I would get obliterated. Lying in meetings bothered me some—especially during moments like that one—but telling the truth about my slips was unfathomable, unnecessary. Lies like this one had never eroded my self-esteem, as I had come to believe bigger lies did. Who was I hurting? Everyone took pleasure in being proud of my accomplishment, so what if it itched at me occasionally? Lying to Autumn bothered me more, but not unmanageably. I viewed other people's sobriety skeptically, too, finding it hard to believe that every single person who claimed that they had five, ten, twenty years without a drink or a drug had really *never* taken a sip, or a drag, or a snort, or a pill.

A few days after I accepted my sixty-day chip, my dad called to say that he and my grandmother were going to be in the city the next morning and would I like to have breakfast with them? I agreed. Autumn was out of town that weekend and had enlisted me to dog-sit her two pit bulls, Reddog and Little Girl. When Kevin called that night, I couldn't not answer. I walked those dogs halfway to Bed-Stuy and walked home with four sessions' worth of heroin and cocaine. With a syringe I'd saved in an envelope wrapped in a sock, wrapped in a sock in the back of my bureau, I shot up all of it that night. The way those dogs stared at me didn't make me start to hate myself until I ran out of heroin. Animals know things, and you can see yourself in anything that depends on you. Shame was unrecognizable to me then, but I felt its oily weight all through me, despite the drugs.

A speedball hits you like a huge, warm wave. The back of your neck throbs, your ears ring, and everything inside of you muffles while everything outside of you sharpens. The initial rush of it doesn't last long, a minute, maybe two. Then it's a downward slide into a normal high. Only the first one can be perfect. After that, you need more of everything. That night, toward dawn, after I had run out of heroin and was shooting straight cocaine—which shouldn't have had much effect at all, I'd done so much by that point—that minute or two stretched into eight. Instead of sinking, the rush rose and rose. I would have cried if I weren't too terrified of my heart beating any faster than it was. Breathing tiny sips of air, I focused on the grain of the wood floor between my feet. I recited multiplication tables, the names of my fifth-grade class-mates, anything that I thought would steady me. It was over an hour before I felt safe to move again. Staring at the floor that night, I had teetered on the edge of some infinity. I'd felt the way I occa-sionally had staring at high tide. Horrifically small. Right sized.

I had instructed my father and grandmother to meet me at a vegetarian café in Alphabet City. Sleepless and still high, I gingerly made my way into the city, trying not to vomit on the subway. You'd think I'd have been more anxious than I was. Partly, my anxiety about heading to brunch still high, with needle-bruised arms and a gray complexion, was quelled by the drugs. A heroin hangover has little in common with an alcohol hangover. Nausea is always miser-able, but much less so with opiates in your system. I actually enjoyed the vacuous, papery feeling that followed a speedball binge. I might have had the eyes of a zombie and track marks up my sleeves when I greeted my father and grandmother outside the café, but they couldn't see them.

"Hi!" I shouted when I saw my father and grandmother ap-proaching, determined to distract them from my cadaverous ap-pearance with enthusiasm. Squeezing them both in vigorous hugs, I hoped my hair didn't reek of cigarette smoke. I'd managed to hide even my smoking from my family for the last six years.

"Oh," exclaimed my tiny grandmother, "you're so *thin*!" I waved off the comment, leading them inside, to a booth far away from the window. I had plenty else to talk about. Amusing anecdotes about my landlords, the dogs, and my "catering" job filled the two hours, and neither seemed to notice that I didn't touch my food.

"Try some tofu scramble!" I urged them, and kept careful watch for the sort of worried eyes I had become used to getting from people. To my relief, my father and grandmother both appeared delighted by my energy and tales of my colorful city life. By the time our check arrived, I trembled with the effort it had taken to pull off. We hugged good-bye outside the restaurant. For a moment, as my dad gave me an extra squeeze, the familiar smell of his coat pressed against my cheek, I felt a surge of grief in my chest, and the corners of my mouth quivered downward. I squeezed him back, then pushed him away and smiled: "I'll hail you two a cab." I watched them wave through the car's rear window, and waited until it turned the corner before staggering into Tompkins Square Park to gather my breath. I sat on a bench and took a few deep breaths, watching the park's playground through a row of bushes. Nannies and mothers stood in clusters on the sidelines as their children ran and climbed, screaming with glee as they flung their tiny bodies around. I had survived. A familiar pride rippled through me. Things weren't as bad as I thought. I functioned under the assumption that when it got bad enough, I wouldn't be able to hide it any longer. If it ever got bad enough, my family would find out and I would check into a rehab somewhere. Junkies didn't graduate from college with a 4.0 GPA. They didn't manage brunch with Grandma. Relieved and wasted, I enjoyed a few minutes of happy exhaustion before the nausea returned and a sudden surge sent me running to a nearby trash can. I retched a few times, wiped my mouth with a napkin, and headed home, careful to avoid looking back at the playground to see if the people there had heard me.

When I first starting getting high, the world seemed to square itself. It was enormous; my thoughts were enormous; everything glowed with possibility. That magical defamiliarization had ended years ago, and since then the world had been shrinking. What I now called partying was hiding alone in the middle of the night and taking drugs until I made myself sick. I even had a special position I would lie in when I became too nauseous to move. Most of my time being high was spent waiting to stop feeling sick so that I could do more. Secrecy had whittled my life down to a single locked room with a glass of water, a bag of puke, and a coffee can full of pee in the closet, because I was too afraid of the floorboards creaking on my way to the bathroom. I couldn't leave the rug. I might have been a goddess all week long at work, but here I was a slave.

Pulling off the brunch with such success made me cocky. When I met up with Kevin again that night and he only had coke, I bought some, ignoring the fact that coke without heroin usually ended in miserable hell for me.

Autumn was home, and instinctively I lied, claiming that I was coming down with something and needed to hit the sack early. Her studio being directly below mine, I was petrified to walk on the creaky wood floor, for fear that she'd hear me and come up-stairs to see what I was up to. I made myself stay on the rug that covered a small area around my bed, sniffing lines off of a compact mirror. I spent that night organizing my sock drawer for six hours. There wasn't much else to do on the rug, and my obsessive drive had low standards for what occupied it. By the time I'd finished, my nostrils were stuffed with rolled-up toilet paper to quell the throbbing that ensued whenever I wasn't inhaling more coke. That was the fun part.

When I still had an hour's supply left, the scary part began. The insanity of how much was left and how to get more—as impossible and logically undesirable as it was at near morning—began in ear-nest. When I had lived in Bed-Stuy, it was possible to creep out of my apartment at dawn and roam the streets in search of more drugs. I had intentionally made this task harder. Crack dealers were not loitering in the alleys of Williamsburg at five in the morning. When daylight crept through the curtains and engines began rumbling in neighboring driveways, I felt skinless, as if some crucial outer layer had been ripped off of me. My cocaine crashes always shared this symptom with heroin withdrawal: painful sensory amplification. I'm not talking about a psychedelic, gaga sensory experience here; I am talking about what it must feel like to pop out of the womb. A menacing attack on the senses. Everyday noises felt like physical blows. Every smell was repulsive, gag inducing; every light, a blinding interrogation. The challenge was no longer how to get more drugs but how to quiet my anxiety. I had tried it all before: hot showers, aromatic candles, soothing music. Nothing worked. My body shuddered with nakedness; candles brought visions of house fire; soothing music was as useful as those $3 street-hawked umbrellas in a hurricane. Each only emphasized my powerlessness over the juggernaut of that feeling.

As I lay in my bed, every muscle clenched in the effort to relax, I prayed for relief. I didn't feel better for a long time, but one thing did become clear. I was waiting in vain to be found out and rescued.

# 17

H OW ARE YOU?" Rebecca asked me over lunch one afternoon.
I smiled at my steaming plate of kale and tofu. "I'm great!"
I didn't look up to see if she believed me. I had been great the last
few times I'd seen her, thrilled and overconfident in my success in
AA. Only in her relief at my sobriety had I first seen the extent of
her worry. When I told her I was clean, she described to me the
dread she used to feel when she'd come home to find me scrubbing the kitchen—an idiosyncratic habit of mine when high. While
I had felt uncomfortable acknowledging the addiction I'd worked
so hard to hide from her, I felt our friendship surge forward with
new intimacy. I told myself now that the usual ease between us was
missing only as a result of seeing each other less, though distance
had never much affected us. I saw her less frequently than ever
lately. My life had divided into such distinct parts: the dungeon and
meetings. The difficulty of maintaining friendships outside of these
only increased. I couldn't tell anyone the whole truth about either,
which burdened even my friendships *within* those spheres; it had
begun to feel like too much work to deal with outsiders.

"Good! Meetings are good? Any new clients at work?" She grinned, going for what had always been an easy topic.

"Not really." I beckoned to our waiter and asked for some brown rice. "I'm actually kind of bored at work."

*"Bored?"*

"I know, it sounds unlikely, right? But every day it's the same things; they all want the same depressing things. I'm sick of it."

She shrugged. "Well, maybe it's being sober. I mean, maybe you're too conscious, or something. I mean, it's always been bizarrely easy for you to *not* be affected by what you do there. Maybe you should take a break or something."

I nodded. This made sense, of course, but it's hard to accept advice when you never give all the facts.

Work had become miserable. I'd begun to dread my sessions weeks ago, but after that binge the scales tipped. I spent my shifts on the dressing room couch, swaddled in a blanket, praying that the clients wouldn't pick me. When they did, I staggered through the sessions, wondering how it had ever seemed easy. The closeness of their bodies was excruciating. It was another kind of feeling skinned. Previously, I felt protected from the depressing reality of my clients. They were powerless, craving animals, and I was a professional. My participation was elective, and thus I felt immune to their mucky baggage. This changed. If their powerlessness and shame were a bog that I had previously traversed untouched, stepping from stone to stone, I was now slipping. I could smell it—the brackish stink under me—on my hands and feet, in my hair when I woke up in the morning.

Conversation was near impossible, with them or anyone. The sad truth of things was so loud that I could barely speak and didn't see why to bother. I was waiting now to see whether my next step would be to move back home to my mother's basement or to check myself into a psych ward. Nothing *worked* anymore. Meetings seemed cultish and false. I stopped answering the painter's calls, and eventually they petered out. I was too anxious to even get high. The prospect of going to the old neighborhood, of shooting up, was terrifying. Things that had made me feel powerful now made me cower. The city was filthy, people weaving through the subways, sick and broken. Everything was either too sad or too hideous to behold. At parties I swiveled between grandiosities, feeling either taxingly omniscient or like a disgusting man with shit smeared on his coat. Misery and fear rose off of me in fumes. I hid in our apartment watching awful television, not eating.

"*Newlyweds* again?" Autumn would ask, walking into her apartment after work to see me camped out on the couch with Reddog, as usual. She had cable, and hated being alone, so I spent more time downstairs in her studio than in mine. "How are you not bored with this yet? You hate reality TV." She laughed, but I could feel her gaze on me, searching for an explanation of my radically changed behavior. We both had bad days in early recovery, but not like this, not for weeks at a stretch.

"What's wrong with you?" she'd ask.

"I don't know," I'd say.

I couldn't articulate what was wrong. It was in me, and it was in everything around me. Either I was going insane or the world had finally revealed itself as a miracle of suffering and ugliness.

Only in my very early days in AA was I green enough to think I could walk myself through Twelve Steps. I'd sponsored my own way this far without the help of a designated guide, I thought at first. *And look where that got you,* answered AA. My counter-argument had quickly run out of steam, the painter's studied nonchalance on the subject notwithstanding. I might have known a lot, about a lot of things, but I didn't know how to stop getting high. My search for the perfect sponsor commenced a couple months before the depression hit. The cardinal rule for selecting a sponsor, everyone told me, was to find someone who "has what you want." Many newly recovering souls had been sufficiently demoralized by the wreckage of their using to see sobriety as enough to fulfill that criterion; they just wanted the help of someone living significantly further from the cusp of death than themselves. They wanted someone who seemed happy some of the time. I envied these people for the gift of desperation, wishing I could also overlook the neuroticism and vanity in every eligible woman who spoke up in a meeting, who offered me her phone number. Most character flaws, or "defects"—as the parlance of AA went—I could accept in friends, people I admired and even accepted advice from, but not a mentor. I could not feel superior to a mentor; I knew that much. My search went on. At one point, I thought I had finally located her: a woman who was both cool and smart and sexy and tough and funny and warm and an artist, who made pulling it all off look effortless. Apparently, I was not the first person to think so. She kindly apologized for being unavailable for sponsorship right then. My search resumed. When the chairs of meetings asked if all the women in the meeting available for sponsorship could please raise their hands, I scoured every face and, finding a flicker of desperation, of *neediness*, in each, discarded them. I really did want to find the right one, I told Autumn, and everyone else who kept gently hounding me, but I couldn't afford to be wrong. I had enough trouble breaking up with lovers.

Then one rainy afternoon, as we concluded the Serenity Prayer and dropped one another's hands, a friend turned to me.

"Have you found a sponsor yet, Melissa?"

I rolled my eyes and turned to face her.

"No, Jen, I—"

"Because Greta here would be a really good fit for you, I think." She grinned and leaned back to reveal the woman seated on her other side. No older than thirty, the woman wore a bright yellow rain slicker and had lank blond hair that fell around her delicate face. She leaned forward and offered me her hand.

"Hi. I'm Greta," she said in a gravelly voice, and followed it with a gentle whinnying laugh, turning the awkwardness of the introduction into a joke between us. I took her hand, with its blunt fingernails—her grip surprisingly hard for such a pretty woman—and was a goner.

Greta and I strolled a few blocks from the meeting and sat on a bench outside St. Mark's Church.

"So, what's your story?" she asked me, half-smiling. Her gaze was direct, but I could tell she was nervous, too. It didn't matter; I had already decided on her.

"What's *your* story?" I asked her, more sheepishly than I normally would have returned a question I didn't want to answer. She shrugged and then told it. I related to a lot, beyond the drug hijinks, especially her affection for the feeling that one could *live on fumes*, as she put it, deprived of most human sustenance, but not caring. I knew the comfort of emptiness, the safety of knowing you could just drift through anything like a mote suspended in a shaft of sunlight or whirling on the breath of an opened door—it didn't matter, was all the same. I craved that feeling even as I sat on the bench beside her, mesmerized by the sound of her voice.

I trusted Greta, insofar as I trusted anyone. But I cared too much what she thought of me to ever be completely honest with her. I wanted what she had: effortless beauty, a one-bedroom, an unself-conscious indifference to people she didn't care about, a dog. The only one I ever admitted to was the dog. Greta talked me out of it. I believed she could help me, but was more interested in seducing her than taking her suggestions. I knew better than to try my usual tricks but didn't know of an alternative. So I just admired her, and felt awkward a lot of the time, caught between wanting to be her, wanting to sleep with her, and wanting to let her help me. The program was a system of vicarious reference: I had to trust in what she had done to stay sober enough to do it myself. I also had to tell the truth, AA doctrine said. But if I knew nothing else, I knew that neediness was not seductive. I couldn't bear the thought of being seen that way. So, I spent a few afternoons a week a few blocks south of Union Square Park, curled on her couch with the warm weight of her doe-eyed pit bull in my lap, as we passed AA's core text back and forth, reading a page aloud at a time. I gleaned what comfort I could from her—not an insignificant amount—without ever revealing the whole story, about my job, my desires, or my fear that I was one of those who could never stay clean, whom the AA literature referred to as "those unfortunates who are constitutionally incapable of being honest with themselves."

When my psychic state began spiraling, I didn't see what Greta could offer me, my problem not really being one of addiction. It seemed comically far-fetched that my problem had anything to do with accepting a false ninety-days-clean coin. I was an astute liar, a *gifted* liar. It worked for me, and I had been lying half of my life with an unwavering moral compass. The truth only *needed* to be spoken between me and God, I told myself, and whispered pleas before bed as if I believed in one. No, my problem had to do with the dismal state of the world, and possibly some irreparable psychic flaw of my own.

# 18

No, MISTRESS, the other paddle, the *sorority* paddle." Jack's plump hand strained against the rope that tied his ankles and wrists together, gesturing toward the pile of spanking implements. Glaring at his massive rear, I tottered over to the pile and selected the wooden oar with holes in it. "Yes, yes, that one." He wheezed. I walked back behind him and rested a gloved hand on his lower back. Like the rest of his body, it was waxy and white, like sweating cheese, with wiry hairs sprouting from its surface. My glove slipped as I groped for a firmer purchase.

"So the other sisters and I have noticed what a fabulous slut you've been lately, Margaret," I said. As Jack shifted his bulk, I tried to remember the details specified in the crumpled list he had handed me during our consultation. "And we have reached a consensus."

"Oh?" The breathy falsetto was three octaves higher than his paddle request had been.

"Yes. Whorish behavior demoralizes the reputation of the entire house, and we cannot tolerate it. You need to be punished, Margaret, and I have been elected to do it. I have de—"

"The purse, Mistress, *the purse!*" he whispered.

"Oh yes. First, I need to search your purse for, uh, evidence of your slatternly exploits." I balanced the paddle on his back and picked up the grandma-style clutch from the floor. "Don't let that paddle fall, Margaret," I warned him. Tipping the purse upside down, I shook loose a dozen condoms, a pack of tissues, a porn magazine with the cover ripped off, a pair of giant panties, and a huge mushroom-shaped butt plug. Jack whimpered. "Well, well, well. What do we have here, Margie, you little pig? Is this what you like to keep hidden in your panties? Maybe we should pop this into that fat ass of yours right now."

Jack cleared his throat.

"What's that?" I asked.

"My *pussy*," he whispered. "Call it my *pussy*."

Hasids often topped from the bottom. When I first started working and heard that Orthodox Jews were among our most frequent clients, I felt a pang of satisfaction. Of course they were! Repressive societies *had* to be the most perverse. It was exactly the kind of anthropological curiosity I had hoped to discover working here. The novelty quickly waned. The first time one showed up, his bespectacled face framed by two long curls and the sort of black wool hat that is ubiquitous in certain parts of Williamsburg, I was nervously intrigued. And then it was just me and another naked man alone in a room for an hour. A very bossy naked man. Jack fit the stereotype. He appraised me when I walked into the room but never met my eyes. I was appraised every time I walked into a consultation, but this was different. He was picky and already knew exactly what he wanted. My intelligence mattered even less than usual. The scan of his eyes over my body was mechanical, assessing, unselfconscious. I might have been a cow. He lacked the romanticism of many of my clients: I didn't hold a mystique that his wife lacked, and I wasn't the girl whom he could never have. I was ineligible for anything other than a sexual device and so was unconsidered. His gaze assumed that I already knew this.

Jack came with a typed list of instructions, but most didn't. I knew by now to ask every client what words were important, what stockings, music, and makeup. Clients who topped from the bottom specified little before the session began. They pretended to be a different kind of client. "Schoolmistress," they'd say, as if trusting that I would know all it entailed, which I did, just not down to the ordering of every last detail and inflection. I knew what "schoolmistress" meant and what kind of makeup and stockings and pain they required. But still I would spend an hour having every movement of my tyrannical role dictated to me. It was maddening, like being asked to run sprints in a straitjacket. I knew what to do, I was *good* at knowing what to do, but they still whispered the answers to me. I walked out of these sessions flushed with furious humiliation. I had signed up to be in control, I thought, to feel powerful. But still I saw these men. We all did. It was rare for anyone to turn down a session. They engaged a part of me that enjoyed persevering, which took pride in sticking out the painful ones. It was reminiscent of the state I entered while getting tattooed or waiting out a drug-induced sickness, or any kind of pure hell. It was an odd complacency, like when I was eleven and slept on a broken bed for a year, just because it seemed easier than requesting a new one. Either way, I was good at this, too; I could withstand.

As I became increasingly depressed, I increasingly avoided Greta. After that final weekend binge, I slipped even further from my daily phone-calling schedule than usual. I didn't have the will to assume any false cheer and grew tired of hearing the same suggestions: go to a meeting, pray, help a newcomer with less clean time than me (the last would have been harder than Greta knew). Her and Autumn's concern only seemed to drive me deeper in. The thought periodically occurred to me to confess my relapses, but I quickly dismissed it. Yes, I cringed at every reference to my clean time, but then I'd always known that secrecy could be lonely. I knew it wasn't the source of my misery and the humiliation of confessing, in addition to that of counting days all over again, would surely be worse. More concerning was my waning ability to work, the evaporation of my interest in anything but the fleeting escape of television.

Only when I had reached such a nadir that my only future options seemed to be checking into Bellevue or returning to Cape Cod to live out the rest of my days a recluse in my mother's basement did my resolve against telling Greta and Autumn the truth weaken. What did I have to lose? My life in New York couldn't go on much longer. I finally called Greta and made a plan to meet at her apartment, with the intention of telling her about my using. Perhaps, I thought, her disgust in me would make giving up the life I had here easier. I must have had some fragment of hope left, to have made the decision to confess, but it didn't feel that way.

I kept my eyes lowered on the L-train ride into the city; I hated the wild envy I felt when I looked at normal people, young and pretty and with a capacity for excitement about what might happen. What had changed in me?

"Hi," Greta greeted me at the door to her building, one eyebrow cocked. "Good to see you again." She pulled me against her in a hug, and I felt the strength of her muscular little body, her hands pressed against my back as if she hoped to imbue me with something. I plodded behind her up the stairs to her apartment.

"You want some tea? I have that soy milk you like."

"Sure." I sat on her couch, hunched over to examine some invisible message on my phone. After she had carried two mugs over and placed them on the coffee table, Greta pulled the phone out of my hands and placed it beside them.

"What's up?" She sought my gaze and held it stubbornly. She let the silence stretch on until I couldn't bear it anymore.

"I didn't really get ninety days," I said, my gaze skittering away from hers, settling on a knot in the wood floor. "I relapsed. A couple times." I swore I saw her frame relax slightly.

"Twice?"

"A few times. I'm not sure how many." I waited for her eyes to harden and quickly wished for a lecture instead of straight-out dismissal. I hoped our relationship could end on a decent note, with her giving me the opportunity to apologize and explain myself, though I had no idea what such an explanation might entail. I told her about the night of speedballs, the brunch with my dad, and the wretched sock-drawer organization that followed. "There were a couple others before that weekend, too," I glumly added, still inspecting the knot in the floor. "I figured I might as well tell you the truth, since I'm probably leaving town anyway. I know you can't fix this. I don't even know what's wrong with me." I looked up when I heard the familiar whinny of her laughter.

"Of course I can't fix this!" She chuckled again. "But I can tell you what's wrong with you." She smiled. "You're a fucking *drug addict*, Melissa. And congratulations; you've lost the ability to tell lies comfortably."

I kept listening, my eyes on her now.

"Of course you feel this way," she said. "Of course you relapsed and lied about it; you're a junky! But you don't have to do that anymore. And you don't have to feel like this anymore." She took my hand and stood, leading me to a clearing on her bedroom floor.

"What are you doing?" I asked skeptically, but I could feel a kernel of hope in me, swelling with every word she spoke that didn't tell me to leave. Standing before her bedroom window, Greta sank to her knees, pulled me down beside her, and in her husky voice she asked her God to help me. She prayed that my "god-shaped hole" be filled, and when she spoke that phrase, "god-shaped hole," something cracked open in me and that hope spilled out, threading through my body like some happy poison.

When I walked out of Greta's apartment that night, a veil had lifted, and the city shone for me as it had since I was a little girl—emanating its own sooty hopefulness, its promise that even if I stopped moving, got caught in some human inertia, it never would. Whatever dismal lens had slipped over my eyes lifted. I knew as soon as I'd heard Greta say that I had lost the ability to tell lies comfortably that it was true. At least about my sobriety. Something in the past months had magnetized my moral compass.

A lot of things changed after that night. Greta's laughter, her relentless acceptance, had tenderized something in me, softened me enough to let help in, to admit that I could be wrong. The evidence was hard to ignore, this time. It remained mysterious to me what about her prayer had cracked me open, but I was starting to figure out that some things could remain mysterious, that you could not understand them and believe in them at the same time. This relieved me, though I also still bucked against it. So much of my life had been lived with an opposite dogma: to believe only in what I knew and live accordingly. The moment I allowed myself to doubt that way of living, I stopped drinking and drugging and stayed stopped. I stopped lying. I stopped feeling smarter than everyone at meetings. I stopped stealing, even the duffel bags of books from Barnes & Noble that had been a monthly routine of mine. B&N might have been the corporate devil, but clearly I wasn't the best candidate to be making moral judgment calls. I wasn't Robin Hood; I stole because I didn't want to pay, and because I liked getting over, not because of any principle. Rationalizations fell away like scales, crisp and translucent. It suddenly wasn't enough to know, as I always had, that deep down at my core I was a good person, or to simply *feel* compassion for other creatures; I wanted to *be* good. Not *good*, but good. It was a huge relief. I had had no idea how burdensome it was to be a liar and a thief. The weight of my justifications wasn't felt until it lifted.

# 19

I COULDN'T COMPREHEND how domming fit into this new paradigm of living. You don't hear about a lot of bodhisattva dominatrices. But it must have fit, because I didn't stop doing it. When people asked me how the work affected me, my line was: "I don't know yet; ask me in ten years." When I thought about how long I would do it for, I assumed that there would come a day when I simply couldn't anymore, when everything about it had become banal and sad and I was done. While I wasn't completely oblivious to the failure of this kind of thinking where my addiction had been concerned, I couldn't imagine myself as a thirty-year-old dominatrix. There were plenty of women who made a career of it, but their interest was genuine, not born of curiosity and social touristing. Occasionally they would pass through the dungeon, working a few weeks as "guest dommes." Despite their obvious enthusiasm for it, and lack of shame, they scared me. Those women were cynical, and saggier than me. They had the rough voices of long-time smokers, and despite their profound expertise and wisdom on our trade, I sensed some essential immaturity about them and knew inchoately that the romance of this life was finite, only for the very young.

When an end came to so many other aspects of my life, I suspected that the end to this might come as well. I figured that the sessions would become harder without the drugs, without the haze of self-delusion that had accompanied them.

Some things did become more difficult. When my depression lifted, the world held light again. Some sights returned, and some were revealed anew. I was no longer amazed at my coworkers' ability to conduct sessions. What I found amazing was the contradiction of their lives, the hypocrisy. The women whom I'd idolized, who had taught me everything about entitlement and power, and in whom I had believed turned out to be shams.

The week of my rise from the walking dead turned out also to be a dramatic one at the dungeon. On one of my first normal shifts back, after an appointment with a new client, I carried my supply box into the dressing room, high only on post-session exhilaration, which so far hadn't waned as I'd thought it might. Camille sat curled on the love seat, clutching a silk kimono around her body, her eyes swollen and despondent.

"Hey," I said. "What's wrong with you?"

She answered without looking up. "It was all lies, Justine, all lies." Her chin trembled.

I dropped my box on the sofa and crouched down to face her. "Oh, sweetheart, what happened to you?"

"I can't believe I thought he was going to *marry* me." Her voice turned venomous on the final words, as she raised her eyes to mine. Camille's London master, the professed love of her life, turned out to have a whole stable of soul mates, whom he lovingly tortured and fucked on a rotating schedule. "We ate *scones* and read *The Times* together," she sobbed as I held her. The whole dungeon had watched love transform Camille. At her master's command, she had quit smoking, sent away for graduate school applications, and begun to exude a new air of self-preservation. The scars seemed more than a fair trade, in my eyes, and she claimed to enjoy them anyway. She had been *happy*. All that ended with him.

A few days later, I sat in the dressing room, organizing my locker. It had been a slow day, despite Bella having called in sick. Lena knelt farther down the mirrored wall, neatly packing some of her personal equipment into a leather suitcase. She wasn't working, had only stopped by the dungeon to pick up some things. I watched her wind wires around a "TENS unit," "TENS" being an acronym for "Transcutaneous Electrical Nerve Stimulation." A TENS unit is a small, battery-operated device used to send electrical impulses to select parts of the body. The electrical currents it produces, when mild, can prevent pain messages from being transmitted to the brain and are thought to raise endorphin levels in medical patients. At the end of the wires Lena wound around the palm-sized box—which had knobs designating settings like "pulse" and "ripple"—disposable electrodes could be attached and then adhered to body parts. Conventionally, that would be shoulders, neck, and joints. In our case, it meant nipples, scrotums, and penises.

"What plans do you have for this weekend that include that?" I asked her, smiling. After our one night together, Lena and I had settled into a flirtatious, comfortable friendship. It turned out she had a habit of sleeping with new blood.

"I've got a session planned for Sunday," she said. "I can't wait." I nodded, about to ask with whom when Fiona appeared in the doorway.

"How'd you like to take a sub session with a regular of Bella's? He comes every week, and I can vouch for his not being a psycho."

I glanced at Lena and then shook my head. "You know I don't do sub."

"Okay." Fiona shrugged. "But it's easy money."

I had never had second thoughts about submissive sessions but for some reason felt hesitant this time. I had been underearning for weeks, I thought, and had some catching up to do, now that I was able. But there was no chance I was going to agree in front of Lena. Maybe after she left I'd agree to consult with the client and see how that went.

"Well, he's going to call back in an hour to see if anyone is available, so let me know by then," Fiona said, and headed back to the office.

"You should take the session," Lena said, without looking up. "Bella is an automaton. The client could be yours after today."

"Yeah, but he's *a top.*"

"So, it's nothing that intense; I've seen him before."

"*You've* seen him before?"

"Yeah."

"I thought you didn't do sub?"

"No, I just don't take sub sessions that walk in here off the street. My session on Sunday is a sub session."

"It is?" I stared at the TENS unit.

"Yup."

"How much do you charge for that?"

"Nothing. I mean, not this weekend. Sunday isn't work; it's on my own time. He's *hot.*"

I didn't know how to react to this. I felt pissed off, as if I'd been cheated somehow. They'd sold me one thing, an image of one thing, and I'd gotten another. Was I the only one playing by the rules?

Even Autumn, my best friend, was at Western Union every week, sending money to her deadbeat boyfriend in California. This had been true since I'd known her, but I hadn't really *seen* it before, examined it in the context of who I thought she was: stronger than me. They had all not turned out to be the enlightened women I'd thought but suddenly seemed damaged little girls, compulsively subjugating themselves to men. My disappointment and disgust at this revelation burned away the glow I'd seen for my first year in the dungeon, the hope and invigoration that came from having proof that the world could have pockets of things I'd never imagined. This was a sight I'd seen before: women relying on men who let them down, *choosing* those men, men who were an expression of their own low self-regard. Even here.

We were all topping from the bottom, it seemed. Both my clients and my coworkers were designing their own humiliation. Freud said that there is no sadism without masochism. I can vouch for that truth in my dungeon. If any of us were sadists, we were the masochistic kind. And if there ever was a sadistic masochist in New York City, he undoubtedly crossed the doorway of Mistress X's. Jack was one. Those clients who preyed on new hires were looking for victims, not masters. I met many men whose real pleasure seemed found in demanding torture methods more humiliating for their domme than for them. It was their fantasy, after all. Is it worse to be fisted as you fantasize or to shove your arm up a strange man's ass for money? To have your yarmulke shat in or to have to shit in a yarmulke while a stranger watches?

"Mistress!"

"Yes, Margie?"

"Don't you think I deserve a harder punishment than that for what I've done?"

"Sure, Margie. Sure I do."

I unfastened the rope that tied his wrists and ankles together and then untied both his hands and feet.

"Up against the cross, Margie." Formally called a Saint Andrew's cross, the seven-foot wooden structure was secured to the wall, equipped with cleats like those used to tie boats to docks.

"But Mistress, I—"

"Please shut up. I know what I'm doing."

Jack staggered over to the cross in his giant stilettos and pressed his belly against its center. "No, facing me," I corrected him. After tying his wrists and ankles to the cleats on each leg of the cross, I gagged him, ignoring his protests. His body now mimicked the shape of the cross, only with a sagging belly in the center. The bikini he had brought with him also sagged, the weakened elastic of its strings hanging dutifully around his hips. He was pathetic. Looking at him, I felt like a dominatrix, like I meant it. I also felt free for the first time in our forty-five minutes together. I selected a whip from those hanging on the wall. Stepping back a few yards, I took aim and flicked the whip toward him. It snaked through the air with a sigh, only its very tip grazing the bulge of his testicles. He gasped around the gag and flattened himself against the cross. It was the first sincere expression he'd made.

Whips are the most elegant of a dominatrix's tools, mechanisms that rely on skill and accuracy rather than strength. Their strength is in simple physics. All the energy of that long tail's undulation collects in the narrow tip, and when it touches you it is a finger of fire. With that strength under my control, I did feel powerful. I took pleasure in his pain. The humiliation of the first forty-five minutes had cultivated that sadism in me. I had always thought of sadism as a predisposition, a condition you couldn't easily catch or shake. I had not thought it so fluid, something that could be engendered by an hour's resentment.

After a couple more well-aimed licks, I put down the whip and walked forward to face him. His breath smelled like rubber. The gag was wet, and saliva dripped from the corners of his open mouth. Though his eyes skittered across my face, their dark centers were level. Jack also knew how to withstand. Who was this man? What did we have in common to have both ended up in this room? I teetered over his face, peering into it for a dizzy moment. In what direction had this man come from, and where was he going? It was a feeling too objective to be compassion, but I suddenly felt on equal footing with him. For a moment, we formed two halves of a perfectly balanced scale.

And then I looked down at his erection and realized that the feeling was probably not mutual. The dungeon suddenly felt filthy, the film of dust and lubricant that covered it becoming a coating of hypocrisy, of lies and rationalization. No one was ever truthful about their motives for being here. There was a superficial layer of honesty, a line often given about consenting adults, people who were robustly unashamed of their desires. It was bullshit, and I knew I had a part in it. This place was so soaked in shame that I could hardly breathe sometimes. What were my lies, and what were they hiding? When I tried to figure out my part, it eluded me. My thoughts suddenly seemed abstract and arbitrary, like a lost memory or a dream, a tarp's loose corner flapping in the wind.

I could taste his rubbery breath, I was so close. I could smell the sweat of his scalp, the stink of long-congested sinuses. He flinched when I finally reached out my hand and lightly brushed it against the cup of his bikini top.

"You think these are tits?" I whispered. He panted around the gag, eyes down. "These aren't tits." I reached behind my back and unhooked my bra. His gaze rose slightly, moving from his body to mine. Sliding the straps down my shoulders, I let the bra slip to the floor. My breasts hung over the top of my corset now, nipples hardened into beads. I leaned close enough that they nearly brushed his chest, exhaling a few breaths on him before I spoke. "These are tits," I whispered. "You pathetic fuck."

# 20

SOME DOMMES HATED corporal, some sensual. Some hated talking in sessions, while others couldn't bear silence. Our tastes in role-play spanned a broad spectrum and usually changed over time and often from client to client. The fluidity of our preferences matched our moods, our experience, and the generosity of our clients. Limits were different. Hard lines were most often drawn short of switch, or submissive sessions, and those involving bodily fluids other than urine. If a girl wasn't comfortable with golden showers, she was wasting her time at the dungeon, where at least half of all sessions required them. It was an insurmountable handicap, equal to a phobia of dildos or high heels. But many refused sessions involving "bloodplay," which included piercing, cutting, severe corporal, and "ruby showers" (with menstrual blood). There wasn't much demand for "roman showers," so it didn't matter much if you were opposed to vomiting on someone. "Brown showers," however, were regularly requested. A small minority took these sessions, usually dommes who specialized in corporal and had a few years of experience. Lena did brown, Miss K, and Autumn, too.

A fair number of us would take switch sessions, which were often more role-play than anything. A primarily submissive client who claimed he wanted to give his domme "a taste of her own medicine," when asked to demonstrate in consultation, would often pat instead of spank, while inquiring obsessively about his victim's comfort. The dommes who took real submissive sessions were a small minority. In my 12-step meetings people liked to say that "some were sicker than others," and that was how I thought of those girls. To be pitied— albeit more generously than my clients—for their low self-regard and obvious trauma history.

From very early on, I drew my lines: no brown, no submissive sessions. I considered everything else worth experiencing, so long as I had my box of rubber gloves and bottle of rubbing alcohol. By my third year at the dungeon, I had established a reputation for corporal expertise. My list of preferences included electrical torture, piercing, verbal humiliation, spitting, face slapping, most forms of corporal punishment (whipping, caning, and flogging especially), and very nasty role-plays.

I enjoyed it, not only with the martyred pleasure of withstanding, or vengeance, but also more wholly. Even without the drugs, it could induce an altered state. I was good at it, and as in all things I've done well and with practice, there was a rhythm to be captured. A beat emerges, silent but sure, as if you can detect its vibrations in the air, in your blood, through the floor. In it, your movements string together with sound and consciousness to form one long, sinewy stroke. In the dark of the Red Room, with the right tools and my hands' intuition, everything else could just fall away, and I would be pure motion, pure drive. Maybe "love" isn't the word for how I felt about it, but one just as strong. I couldn't pinpoint what frightened me about this; it was only a small flutter, without any sound.

That kind of experience required a client who trusted me, like

Elie, and whose list of preferences matched mine. It required the right mood. The consistency of these variables could not be relied on. I might have a session like that three nights in a row; I might not have one for a month. In between was everything else, and everything else kept getting harder.

A more common session required constant redirection of tone, narrative, and the client's hands. I spent many hours wishing they just would shut up, that time would pass more quickly, that they would need an enema so I could smoke alone in the room for a few paid minutes. The dread I'd felt before every session during my depression had passed, but only as far as true corporal sessions were concerned. My limbs turned leaden when Fiona announced many of my regulars' names: White Sneaker Fred, with the roving hands and featherlight voice, who always left a box of Tic Tacs as a tip; Airplane Fred, the ticklish pilot with boggy breath who cooed and giggled and expected me to as well; even Enema David, who tipped heartily and spent most of his time in the bathroom, made me cringe with his need for affection, his demand to be petted like a child while the giant rubber udder emptied into him. There always seemed to be fewer Elies and more Tonys.

Tony was almost seven feet tall and bearded, with a voice like murmuring thunder. This towering Thor often came to see me multiple times a week. Stretched out on the bondage table, he was like a felled tree, and something in his size made me even sorrier to play his mommy.

There were mommy roles I enjoyed playing, the kind where I got to receive a phone call from an imaginary teacher and then chase my son around the room shouting threats, followed by an earnest spanking. If I was going to play mommy, I wanted to pull ears and break a sweat; I wanted to go all out and become a roaring hurricane of bitch. Tony's mommy was not a bitch. She was a creep.

The session would begin with Tony sitting upright on the bondage table. Facing him, I fought to maintain the distance between our bodies. The pressure between us was a constant contradiction of our roles. I was ceaselessly pushing him away and he drawing me closer. His hands grabbed at my hips, waist, and chest, trying to pull me into him, wrapping his legs around mine. This part was supposed to be the seduction. He wanted all the things that I hated doing, all those expressions of affection that repulsed me more than any spilled enema could. He wanted face stroking, tickling, caressing, and was always begging for kisses and hugs. "Don't you want to be a good boy for Mommy?" I'd ask, the negotiating molester. His voice in session was breathy and moist, octaves higher. "Ma-ma!" he would stutter. "Good boy for Ma-ma!"

In his baby voice he would ask me to undress, to "smother" him with my various body parts, to bring my pretty friends in to show him off to. There are only so many ways of saying no so that it doesn't sound like no. I invented new ones, reasons that used the logic of his fantasy. The charade of our role-play so thinly scaffolded our real negotiation that there was never a moment lost in the fantasy, not a moment that didn't require complete effort.

The second part of the session was easier because molesting him didn't require that I be so close to his face, or his hands. Sliding the slender vibrator in and out of his anus was mindless work compared to his groping, his breath on my face. Our idiotic talk would continue as he rubbed his penis against his stomach and spastically jerked his hips. "Who's Mommy's very best boy? Are you Mommy's bestest boy?" I'd intone. He would groan in his normal, deep voice and then speak in the baby voice: Mmmmmmm . . . Ma-ma, Ma-ma's best boy!"

Most of my sessions were this far from transcendent. Maintaining my physical boundaries was a tedious, earthbound task. It was repetitive and simple, like most of the physical work I'd done: washing dishes, painting houses, sanding boats. Maintaining the mental boundary was another thing. Domming was sex work. Sure, it was psychological, it was acting, it was physical, but above all else, it was sexual. After an hour-long session, my clients would head back to work, refreshed, or home to their families, lunch, a nap. After my hour-long sessions, there was always another man with a hard-on waiting. I had to match the pressure of their desire somehow, but to engage my own sexuality would have been a kind of suicide. I had to keep it separate. I wouldn't have lasted a week if I weren't able to do that. Most of the women who came through the door with their fantasies of being powerful and desired didn't make it to their second week. It required something beyond beauty, or seduction, or a craving for power and attention from men. These were useful, necessary even, but if you could not dissociate from their desire, no money would be enough for what you'd pay. Imagine reenacting the most painful traumas of people's lives all day, becoming, one hour at a time, the embodiment of their obsessions, their sexual fixations; it would suck the life out of you. Being raised by a Buddhist mother had instilled in me a reverence for the value of being "present" for life, and the 12-step program's belief in a spiritual path—however stumblingly one followed it—reinforced my trust in the practice of living mindfully, emotionally present. My efforts to do this did not transfer into the dungeon. I never made a decision to go emotionally numb in my sessions; I did it by default. Of course, I did *feel* things in sessions, though they all qualified as forms of excitement, that is, of anxiety, which was itself a kind of numbness, a lifting up out of myself. I didn't need drugs to do that, it turned out.

Getting high, and everything I did in its service, had required a similar level of dissociation. To stay clean, I had had to retrieve my conscience, to reconnect emotionally with my actions. Once that was done, I could no longer get high. The lies I had told myself in order to rationalize my using were so unconvincing that once I chose to see them, they shriveled like balloons, the illusion irreparably ruined. Once you know the sleight of hand that gives a magic trick its magic, that's all you ever see, as much as you may want to believe again. I could never again tell myself that I didn't have a problem, that I used drugs because life was too boring without them, that getting high didn't interfere with the rest of my life.

With this refurbished consciousness, I lost the ability to tell myself a lot of other lies, too. Once you get into the habit of second-guessing your own rationales, it becomes easier to see their basis in convenience rather than truth. I couldn't steal anymore. I couldn't lie to other people with the same facility I always had. I couldn't even enjoy sex with someone I didn't love. I would still push as far as I could go, but boundaries emerged where there had been none before. I was surprised and relieved to find that I was not, as I had thought, capable of anything. The truth would just pop out of my mouth, as instinctively as distortions of it used to. While home one weekend, I hurried through dinner and then asked to borrow my mother's car. Though I wasn't going to cop drugs, as I had after so many family dinners in the past, I didn't intend to tell her the truth when she asked.

"I'm going to an AA meeting," I said, my eyes widening with shock at my own words. My new instinct for honesty scared me, though it simplified things. The conversation that followed was not an easy one. I watched my mother's face as all the ill-shaped pieces finally slid into place.

"So, that time you disappeared to Seattle for two days?" she asked, and I nodded. "And all the mornings you'd come home and sleep for the next twenty-four hours?" I just kept nodding.

This phenomenon permeated every facet of my life, except at the dungeon. The rules were different there. Perhaps because it was my job, and because it felt increasingly isolated from the rest of my life, I was able to keep it separate. Whatever the reason, and whatever else I had finished with, I wasn't finished there.

I acquired a steady boyfriend around this time, Dylan. Tall and brooding and dryly hilarious, he thought my job exotic, funny to tell people about, easy money. He relayed my funniest stories to his friends—and saw the job's value to him, publicly at least.

I remember preparing for one of my first sessions booked out-side of the dungeon. Another domme had asked me to meet her at the Waldorf Astoria in street clothes—*nice* street clothes—for a double session with a high-rolling private client of hers. The client would pay for the room, she said, and I'd get $200 of the $500 he paid her. Ninety minutes before our meeting time, I leaned against my bathroom sink wearing stilettos, black stockings, garters, and a red bustier. Widening my eyes at the mirror to apply mascara, I listened to Dylan clanging dishes in the kitchen. A piece of silverware clattered against the floor and he cursed under his breath. As I penciled in lip liner, he appeared in my periphery, one long arm resting atop the bathroom doorway.

"So, are you going to eat something before you go, or am I fending for myself?"

Hearing the acid in his tone, I looked over, raising an eyebrow. I did enjoy his possessiveness, just a bit. "I'm fine. I'll eat something when I get home."

"When's that going to be?"

"When the session ends."

He glowered at me in the mirror, then hunched his broad shoulders to cough down the neck of his T-shirt. Dylan suffered from chronic chest infections. Privately, I suspected his sickliness was a somatic manifestation of repressed emotion. Having a therapist for a mother had long endowed me with a know-it-all-ism on the psychology of others. Besides, it seemed obvious. Dylan practically vibrated with anger so long ignored that it had settled into an oily reduction that coated all of him; it was part of what attracted me. It was charismatic, and maddening, and made for great sex. He sure could put on a mean sulk, though.

Dylan stayed in the doorway, watching me apply red lipstick. I felt his gaze harden further as I bent to adjust my stockings.

"What?" I challenged him, straightening my posture. Defiance can be difficult when you're nearly naked, but I had a lot of practice.

"Nothing. Just nothing."

"He's not going to lay a hand on me," I lied.

"I know," Dylan said, still fuming. For a brief, thrilling moment I imagined how he'd react to the truth.

. . .

The rest of my life was so divorced from my work that I would sometimes forget that they were both me. There were times, at a raucous dinner after a meeting, or just in conversation, that someone related an anecdote about a perverted friend of a friend, or an article they'd read about sex clubs, cross-dressing, or some obscure fetishism. I would react with the same gasps and "ews" as everyone else, blocking out that I had done that very thing the night before, had done it hundreds of times.

I didn't know where I'd acquired the skill and wasn't even quite aware of it. When friends reacted with shock and amazement at what I was capable of, I felt proud but couldn't really answer their questions about how I did it. What did they mean, *how*? I made a good argument for my adventurous nature, my open-mindedness, my compassion, the money. I still thought that it wasn't necessarily something specific to *me* that made me able, which kept me there. It was just social mores that kept other pretty, intelligent, open-minded women with thin wallets from doing what I did, wasn't it?

# 21

ONLY AFTER I STOPPED crossing certain lines in the rest of my life did I start crossing them in the dungeon. The first was brown showers.

Maybe I found it the easiest because it was so far outside of convention. You weren't going to feel like a slut for shitting on someone; there wasn't even a word for what that made you. Also, the extremity. To my anthropologist, interested in observing firsthand the scope of human experience, this was gold, the apogee of what most people would never know. Acts of extremity were my trophies. Like that moment before I first shot up, before I took this job, before I got my first tattoo, I felt that invisible wall whose authority I'd never thought to question, its force field of resistance. Then I stepped through it. Once I made the decision, it just disappeared.

It was the ultimate act of will. I might not have been able to will myself not to do drugs—I might have needed a higher power for that—but I could will myself to defy not only social law but also biological law. Humans are not meant to shit on each other; I am certain of that. The body doesn't want to do it. Why would it?

Ironically, it is also *such* a human act. Only in self-consciousness could an animal exact such will. I am certain of something else. They put water in toilets for a good reason: the smell.

Gerald was a regular. Though raised in Manhattan, he worked abroad, flitting from country to country to conduct his business—something to do with the buying and selling of companies. Though he only traveled to the U.S. twice a year or so, Gerald always managed a visit to the dungeon. Everyone said he was a sweetheart, nice to the managers, profusely grateful to his mistresses.

"Good! Go for it," Lena said when I booked the appointment. "He's easy, sweet, a good one for your first brown. You'll do fine. Just save your morning coffee and cigarette—they'll get things moving when the time comes." She showed me in which closet the industrial roll of plastic tarp was kept and advised that I secure the corners. "He wriggles around a bit," she added, wrinkling her nose. Although she and Autumn had described the details of his session to me many times—everyone in the dungeon knew about Gerald—nothing could have prepared me for it.

I prepped as well as I could: big dinner the night before, no coffee or cigarettes until he arrived. I was often nervous before sessions, just for a few seconds standing outside the door. In a way, every session felt like my first; I frequently experienced a moment of shock at what I was about to do, of fear that I would find myself incapable. Justine would slip away like a dropped robe, and I would think, *He wants me to do what?* Then I'd walk through the door and begin, after which point nothing was more familiar. That trepidation hadn't lasted more than those few seconds in years.

The whites of Gerald's eyes were pale yellow, his smile brilliant and frequent. He helped me stretch the plastic tarp over the rug of the Blue Room, securing its corners with his shoes and a couple heavy coils of rope. He then took off all of his clothes and stretched his lithe body out on the crinkling tarp. Blinking up at me expectantly, he announced, "I am ready now."

I picked my coffee up from the floor and chugged it. After

lighting a cigarette, I stepped onto the tarp myself. Standing over him, I didn't have to squat down to figure out that this was not going to happen without a toilet of some kind. Maybe in the woods I'd be able to shit without a seat, my thigh muscles tensed over rustling leaves, but not here. Not with someone breathing under me. I excused myself and retrieved one of the plastic-chair-style potties from the mop closet in the hallway. With cheap, metal legs and arms, it was like the folding chairs my family had kept in our basement for when more than a certain number came for dinner, only this one had a toilet seat where there wouldn't normally be a hole.

And then I did it. I sat on that plastic seat and I pooped through the hole, onto his chest. Thankfully, I'm a vegetarian and it only took a few seconds. I don't know if I could have withstood the humiliation of sitting there pushing. Afterward, I stood up, walked into the bathroom, wiped, flushed the paper, and took a deep breath. Then I smelled it. I think it's safe to say that most people don't mind the smell of their own shit as much as someone else's. Most people also don't experience that smell without it being tempered by water and quick disposal. Standing in the bathroom doorway, I told myself that the worst was over. I had done it. Another triumph over instinct. Another thing that could never be guessed by looking at me. I might not be capable of anything, but I was capable of a lot that most people weren't. There was satisfaction in that, even at that moment.

I could see Gerald writhing on the floor, his grunts audible over the crinkling of the tarp. I knew what to expect but was still incredulous. What was I supposed to do next? Breathing through my mouth, I walked toward him. Back then I had a masterful control over my facial expression but still could barely suppress my disgust and dismay at the sight of him. His eyes half-closed, trancelike, he methodically smeared my waste over his body. His fingertips together, he rubbed it like a paste across his chest, his navel, his genitals, touching his body gently, and with reverence, as if he were cleaning a baby. Streaks of it decorated his shoulders and arms.

Oblivious to me, he dabbed his thumbs in the concave of his chest and swiped them across his cheeks, down the bridge of his nose, and over his brow. He covered his face in a mask of it. Like clay, it quickly dried and cracked. As I stood there in the smell, looking down at him, my stomach lurched. I didn't vomit, but that lurching motion continued, spreading through my body, jolting my vision with ripples. Then I could feel my feet against the floor but nothing between them and my head. My heels felt like two pinpricks of light in a room gone dark. My mind floated, a balloon, over this scene, his caked body receding below me. Where my chest would be was only a faint streak of horror, a curling vapor that something burnt leaves behind.

The second line was harder to define. I never did aloud. I guess it started in that session with Jack. Before that, I never did sessions topless. Before that, I never heeded an impulse in session because it was exciting to *me*. Exciting the clients was satisfying, though never physically, and I wasn't willing to cross my boundaries in its service. Hundreds, perhaps thousands of times I had been asked to take off my top. After drawing the line in my first week, I never considered it. There was nothing unique about Jack. I had seen Hasids before, been topped from the bottom, felt hateful toward my clients; the session was perfectly run-of-the-mill. He hadn't even asked me to do it. It just felt good.

A couple of weeks after my session with Gerald, I was in Cross-Dressing with Mike, a firefighter from Queens. Mike just liked to talk. We made up stories together. It reminded me of babysitting as a preteen, when I would tell long improvised bedtime stories to my neighbor's children, adding new chapters to them week after week, of adventurous princesses who escaped from endless series of perils, that sort of thing. Mike's stories were the same, only instead of featuring princesses and talking animals, they were about Sally, the dirty slut. Sally didn't always escape in the end. Who knows where Sally came from or what she did to poor Mike, but we spent many hours exacting vengeance on her. Mike and I had our routine down so pat that we didn't bother with cordialities anymore; I'd walk in, and we'd get right into it. He would always start.

"So she's on her way home, and decides to stop for gas."

"On her way home from the salon, after getting her bikini wax," I added.

"A Brazilian wax!"

"She's still a little sore and swollen down there while she's driving, and it's distracting her, but in a good way."

"She kinda likes how it hurts a little bit, the slut." Mike started to fidget at this point, although he wouldn't start touching himself until we got toward the end of the story. He started throwing in cusswords when he got excited. "The string of her thong is pressing hard on her pussy and she's thinking about, uh . . . dicks." While Mike's narratives were deeply felt, he was no wordsmith. "Biiig dicks." He nodded appreciatively.

"What's playing on the radio?" I asked.

"Judas Priest." He answered without hesitation. "Judas Priest is playing when she pulls into the Shell station. 'Breaking the Law.'"

"She waits for the song to finish before she gets out of the car."

"Yeah, and when she gets out, her miniskirt is all rode up on her hips, and her ass is almost hanging out the back."

"She doesn't bother to straighten it, just struts over to the pump and slides her credit card in real slow."

"Slut!"

I laughed then, and he looked at me, startled out of Sally-world for a moment.

"Then she lifts that big, heavy nozzle and slides it into the hole," I continued. He nodded and turned away, like a child falling back asleep. "Every man at that gas station is watching her, staring at that shadowy little place between her legs, imagining what's just above the hem of her skirt."

"Her pussy." Mike sighed peacefully.

"She fills her tank, and slips the dripping nozzle back into the pump, feeling all of those eyes on her, like invisible hands, sliding up the inside of her thighs."

"She wants some gum."

"What?"

"She goes into the store to get some gum."

"Right."

"She buys some bubble gum, and puts a piece in her mouth. She blows a big, pink bubble and pops it with her fingernail. Then she asks for the key to the bathroom. She walks real slow across the store, to the door of the bathroom, and smiles at the dude behind the counter." A smile flitted across Mike's face.

"She winks over her shoulder at him."

"Yeah, and as soon as she closes that bathroom door, he locks the store door and puts up the sign that says: *closed*. Then he calls all the guys from the garage in through the back door."

"They're all sweaty and covered in grease, wearing coveralls with the sleeves rolled up."

"They're waiting for her when she comes out. She opens the door all confident, ready to tease them all on her way back to her car, but instead they're there, waiting. She looks nervous and tries to walk around them. They don't let her. 'You're a very naughty girl,' the one from behind the counter says. 'I think you need punishment.' Then he spanks her."

"Wait, how hard does he spank her?" I asked.

Mike looks at me in surprise. "Uh, hard?"

I got up off the couch and turned to face him. "So she walks out of the bathroom, and looks nervous." I raised my brows innocently. "Then what? Does he just grab her, or do the mechanics hold her while he spanks?"

"Uh, he grabs her."

"Show me."

# 22

IN MAY OF 2003, I graduated from college. My family came to watch me walk across the stage in my gown and to take me out to lunch. I was early to meet them at the French café on the corner of Sixth Avenue and 11th Street where I had spent many afternoons smoking at the bar over conversation and books of poetry or physics, acting and sometimes feeling like a normal college student, infatuated with my own green intellectualism. I had also gotten high in that café's restroom after classes more than a few times, along with the one at the student center, every Starbucks within a six-block radius, and even the piss-splattered McDonald's on a few desperate occasions. It had been months since the last time I'd used in that neighborhood, but when I locked the café's restroom door behind me I felt a rustle of dread in my chest, like water quickening, and wished I'd suggested somewhere else to meet.

It was a habit, throwing the pieces of my disparate lives together, as if in the spirit of a mischievous hostess with a seating chart. Still, I knew my motives were not so fatuous and assumed it was a form of self-punishment. Maybe if I wanted to enjoy the exhilarations of a life lived in multiplicity, I had to endure the rare, excruciating juxtaposition.

Spooked by the restroom's associations and without a book to distract me, I fidgeted at the bar, checking my cell phone repeatedly. I knew it would help to be in motion, and so I maneuvered through the busy blond waitresses to step back out in the springtime. Wandering around the block of my school, I thought how quickly my first three years in New York had passed. My eyes had changed since I'd seen these buildings for the first time on the day of my admission interview. Still a teenager then, I had taken an early-morning bus alone from Boston. I hadn't been to New York since a day trip at age nine or ten with my grandmother. The subway was stifling in the unseasonable heat. I saw my own desperation on every person's face and felt that stone of dread sinking in me, whose descent whistled that nothing, not even this drastic attempt to regain control of my life, would have an effect. And then I nailed it. Sweat and fear evaporated into the air-conditioned admissions office. I was an expert in discerning what people wanted from me, in who I was supposed to be. It didn't feel like pretending; I *was* that person, when I decided to be. I returned to Boston victorious. My determination was both that of a childhood dream (New York City!) and an addict's hope that a change in geography could induce one in self. I was so different now, I thought on the day of my graduation.

For the ceremony I was wearing a strapless black dress that I knew suited me. Without question, I dressed better than in those early days. I had more money, friends, and confidence. I no longer needed to wander the streets every few days, looking for a high junky to cop for me when I couldn't reach my regular dealers. I no longer lived in that tiny SRO (single-room occupancy) boarding-house, immobilized with loneliness and bad heroin, comforted by a pack of razor blades that I kept under my mattress like a trapdoor I could use if things got bad enough. I was finishing with a 3.9 GPA. I had a glamorous, lucrative, secret life.

So long as that list was longer than the number of ways I was hurting myself, I was winning. I counted its items as a way of lulling myself when anxious. It proved that I was okay. I had believed for a long time that I needed to get through college, not just survive it, but *win* at it. It would prove something, I thought, and then I could finally relax. But even with the end in sight, I tallied that list with increasing frequency. It was fundamental to the system of checks and balances that I used to allay the dread, a way of accounting for the damage I did. In its equation, straight A's offset crack smoking. Being publicly esteemed made up for all of my antisocial behaviors: the stealing, vomiting on the subway, and promiscuity. I don't know where I learned it, but I could not remember a time after puberty when I did not believe that to the degree I succeeded by public standards, I could covertly defy them. I could only be as *bad* as I was *good*. Each carried a separate worth, and mine was based on what wealth I could have in both.

That morning was beautiful, the spring air creased by the laughter of brunchers at sidewalk tables. Something ragged in me made it lonely, though, some fear emerging like a jetty from an ebbing tide—far from the excitement and pride I'd been anticipating feeling. The rationalization equation contradicted the way I felt. I had spent so much time lamenting the amount of time and energy that school consumed and calculating how much more money I could be making if I didn't have papers to write and classes to attend that I had taken for granted what it gave me.

School had been my cover, from sixth grade on. A's came easily to me and were a free ticket to get away with whatever badness it was that I wanted—or needed—to be doing. When I was drinking and lying about my age to high school boys at twelve years old, it was my cover. When I was tripping on acid, sniffing coke, and skipping every afternoon in high school, it covered me. When I was smoking crystal meth, popping ecstasy pills like aspirin, and robbing the cafés and tattoo shops that employed me, I was also getting A's at Harvard's night school, and no one asked questions. Lying came easily to me and I never asked for money, so how would anyone looking at me from the outside have known?

On the inside cover of more than one journal during my college years I had printed F. Scott Fitzgerald's assertion that "the test of a first-rate intelligence is the ability to hold two opposing ideas in mind at the same time and still retain the ability to function." If this was true, then I embodied first-rate intelligence, of a certain kind anyway. Success in the environment of small, discussion-based classes came easily to me. I knew how to talk better than I did anything else. I could feign expertise with only a shred of knowledge and never wrote a paper sooner than the night before its due date. I'd always cruised through school this way and figured that in college my hand would be called, but it wasn't. In a few classes, I did sweat over the work, but I never could have said with confidence that I'd done my best—being an academic con woman meant I avoided that, even when I did care.

Some of the ploys I pulled to get out of having not done the work make me cringe to think of now—what performances! I faked sicknesses, deaths, once even a pregnancy and subsequent abortion to avoid getting anything less than an A. Not doing the work was more work than doing it, sometimes. The steadiness of my hand when it came to crossing certain moral lines didn't concern me then. I took pride in my ability to work systems and people; I was simply getting from Point A to Point B, I thought—besides, if I didn't work the system it would surely work me. With this kind of survivalist mentality, you'd think I'd had a hardscrabble childhood, known poverty or hardship in a way I never had.

The thing was, I loved college. I had always loved school. Not only because I was good at it and because I wanted to be *good*, but also because nothing compared to the explosion that happened in my mind when I understood the concepts of physics or unlocked the meaning of a poem. I craved the pop and spark of ideas, of new pathways searing through my consciousness. The excitement I felt in classes and in writing felt pure.

There had been moments as a teenager, reading alone, when the prismatic, interconnected meaning of things exploded into my consciousness and I would feel as though I had stumbled up to the lip of a canyon, paralyzed, but vibrating with inspiration. And in college, there were teachers who really *knew* things, who had learned out of love, and the experience of learning from them felt like a kind of love itself.

But my desire for that feeling had always been trumped by my desire for escape, and the quickest escapes, I quickly learned, were found in the illicit. Even as a kid. In fifth grade I was at the right age at the right time to participate in the D.A.R.E. program—a short-lived and impotent crusade in George Bush Senior's War on Drugs. As the final presentation given by a rotund lady cop my class was presented with what we would take to calling the drug box. It was a metal briefcase that opened into a kind of medicine cabinet, with Plexiglas panes covering about fifty cellular compartments. In these compartments were an assortment of colorful pills, roach clips, joints, bags of white powder, and even a blackened teaspoon with a mottled crust in its concave. I had counted the days leading up to this event. The anticipation that mounted in me was marked by the same piercing thrill as secrets and, imminently, boys. As we crowded around the display I thought, with a matter-of-fact sort of clarity, I would do any of it. Maybe it was a subconscious desire to rebel against the prescription to just say no, or the pragmatic ideologies of my parents—a psychotherapist and the son of an alcoholic—but it didn't feel defiant. It was a conviction that drifted up through me like a leaf in water to rest on the surface, as much an unconditional truth as the sky's being blue, or the fact of my own name. It was with this same tranquil assurance that I knew I would become a dominatrix.

As a result of my tendency to fall down stairs and walk into walls, my family nickname as a child had been Crash, so it was a characteristically miraculous feat of clumsiness that I managed to give myself a paper cut on my eyeball minutes before the graduation ceremony. Seated in the front row of the auditorium, I couldn't open my eye without tears streaming from it. I dabbed mascara from my face through all the speeches and fielded curious looks from everyone who crossed the stage. By the time my family and I made it outside, my eye was horror red and I had to hold it shut. My parents chuckled sympathetically, in familiar wonder at my knack for calamity.

We made our way northwest, toward Chelsea, where I had made reservations at a Thai restaurant. We were a sizeable group for Manhattan sidewalks and fell into single file by twos. There was my mother's sister, my father's tiny Puerto Rican mother, my maternal grandmother, and my three immediate family members.

As we walked together, my brother handed me an envelope.

"Open it!" he said. Tearing the seal, I pulled out a handmade card. On the front was a colored pencil drawing of me, in graduation cap and gown. From under my hem poked out a pair of stilettos, and my hand held a whip that wound its way around the card. The drawing was good, and I laughed.

"Let me see!" demanded our father from behind us.

My brother and I exchanged a look. I felt my mother's look as well, though I didn't turn to see it. Sometimes I regretted having told her. Like the moment when she spotted the leather strap-on hanging from the back of my closet door and simply looked at me and said, "I know what they make you do with that." For as much as she didn't say, she saw a lot. I didn't know if I wanted her to see less or say more. We both feigned comfort with the knowledge of what I did between us, but every time it was mentioned the look on her face sandpapered my insides.

So I handed my father the card. The silence while he examined it shimmered between my brother, mother, and me, disrupted only by the scrape of our shoes against the sidewalk and the murmur of my aunt's telephone conversation ahead. My grandmothers lagged a few yards behind in silence, having accepted the failure of Grammy's hearing aid.

My father looked up at my mother and brother and me, and I didn't need to turn my head to recognize the furrow of his forehead, to feel a pang of anxiety and faint revulsion at its innocence.

"I don't get it," he said.

"I guess I have to tell you something, Dad."

"What?"

"I'm a dominatrix."

My dad has an assortment of laughs. His loudest is reserved for moments not necessarily of great hilarity but of surprise. The three of us, my mother especially, had spent many moments blushing with embarrassment in the darkness of movie theaters as my father bellowed with laughter at dinosaurs tearing human bodies apart with their teeth or scenes of bloody murder. When other people gasped, my father shook with uncontrollable laughter, his hand clamped over his mouth. I knew it was a nervous instinct; I had experienced the occasional spasmodic smile while being reprimanded as a child or in reaction to a piece of shocking information. But other people didn't know that, and to them there was simply a sadist in the middle row.

This was the laugh that greeted my news. While it lasted, I chose to look at my brother but not my mother. What had shimmered between us in my father's silence continued for his laughter. When he stopped and wiped the tears from his eyes, his first question was, "For how long?"

"A few months."

He laughed briefly again.

"Wait, so you guys both knew?" His eyes shifted between my mother and brother.

They nodded.

He looked back at me. "I can't believe I was the last to know!" he shouted. "*I'm* the cool parent!"

As it turned out, a young coworker of his at the Berkshire retreat center where he had worked between voyages had also worked as a domme. I gathered that she had censored her anecdotes as I would have, saving me the assurances of my safety and dignity. He was delighted.

Something relaxed in me that afternoon, but not the part that held my dread. A future was sprawled out before me, one in which I was free to continue on the path I had taken. No one was going to protest; I had made sure of that.

# 23

Toward the end of my second year at the dungeon, I had started cruising the craigslist job listings outside of "Erotic Services." It was a response to the gnawing feeling that my eligibility for other kinds of work was slipping away.

As a young teenager, I would ride my bike to the ocean at dusk. When the sun landed on the horizon, the beach would be empty except for a few people with their dogs, and couples in parked cars watching the sunset spill red across the water. The lifeguards were off-duty, and I would swim out until my shoulders throbbed. Right at the point where I tired there was a buoy moored. It was an old nicked thing, white with a red stripe around its potbelly. I would cling to its neck and catch my breath, watching the dogs on the beach glide like gnats in wide figure eights. Without the buoy I probably couldn't have made it back. I had been foolish enough to try the distance once, and then it became my routine. Sometimes, bobbing there with the waves softly slapping my back and no human sound except for my breath, I would hallucinate the shore receding, the tiny figures of people becoming tinier. Panic crashing through me, I'd be certain that the buoy had lost its mooring, that I was drifting out to sea.

I had moments like that at the dungeon. When I heard news of an acquaintance's success at a normal job, acceptance to graduate school, or engagement, panic would again crash through me. I was drifting too far away; by the time I turned back the swim would be too long, the water too cold, the fear too great.

It was a slow but insidious transformation of my thinking. "You are what you do, not what you say," they told me in meetings, and it was true. What I did dictated who I felt like, and in direct proportion. When I was getting A's in college and shooting up every day, I felt like a smart junky. When I ran twenty miles per week, I felt like a runner. By my third year of being a dominatrix, I felt like a sober sex worker. I spent all of my time concentrating on not getting high, and becoming men's sexual fantasies. Being in recovery was the first time I felt like an honest person, and not that deep-down-inside-God-knows-I'm-good feeling, but like someone who actually tells the truth. You can't get as honest as I did about my drug use and still do it. You also can't spend every day banking on your sex appeal and not start feeling like it's the most valuable part of you.

When I sent my résumé out in response to the editorial assistant position, it didn't feel like anything. I had no plan to leave the dungeon; I just wanted to know if I could still get a real job, if I could still pass so easily for normal. I just pressed a few buttons on my computer and a list of my accomplishments up until college graduation zipped through the Internet ether. I didn't tell anyone, so I wouldn't have to tell them that I had been ignored, or rejected. My whole life I had expected to win things. School readathons, friends, spelling bees, lovers, internships, attention, permission—I just always had. I didn't think twice about dropping out of high school, I was so sure that it was an obstacle to my success. It was childish grandiosity and my intelligence helped, but hunger is what made it so powerful.

The office was in the Brooklyn Navy Yard, an industrial park that looked across the East River at lower Manhattan. I wore the same outfit that I had to my interview at the dungeon. All my business clothes purchased in the last few years had been for sessions, not actual offices, and I knew better than to show up at an interview dressed like a pending sexual harassment suit.

I took the bus through Williamsburg, watching the skinny hipsters with asymmetrical haircuts change into Hasids with all their black wool, beards, and kerchiefed women ushering broods of children across the streets. I glided by men in suits, clutching briefcases and barking into cell phones. One in particular—a thick, jowly man with a clipboard, leaning against a sedan—struck me as familiar. Whenever I vaguely recognized a man on the street, I felt a pang of anxiety, my mind flooding with all the things I might have done to him, the ways he might have seen me. Occasionally, I did see clients out in the world. How many did I not recognize? How many of the men I passed in the street had been to Mistress X's? What did they think when they stared at me deboarding the bus? I knew that all of them weren't perverts and that it was wrong of me to think that way. Still, I couldn't help feeling as if they recognized me, too, as if in the meet of our eyes all pretenses fell away and we were simply dominatrix and client, meeting in the street. I couldn't help feeling that we knew each other's secrets, as if in passing each other our clothes fell off. It felt both humiliating and privileged. I had lost my anonymity, in a sense. If I could not see these men without imagining them groaning in a puddle of urine under me, how did they see me? I did not even share their obsession. How did any of my clients see women as anything else?

The press's office was in a large, open space on the fifth floor of a warehouse. The editorial, payroll, and copyright departments were separated only by tall, metal shelves full of collections like that of their annual volume of Dickens criticism, from the last fifty years. I was interviewed by a woman my own age. The first minutes were awful. It felt like the first date after a divorce. To be questioned by this stranger, to even be sitting so close to her, felt oddly intimate. I was so used to being immediately privy to the needs and shame of strangers that I almost felt I knew hers already. I could see it when she tucked her hair behind her ear and in the bulge of her belly when she sat and plucked at her blouse, in the shift of her gaze. It took me a while to turn that off. I didn't have to find her shame to get this job, as I did at the dungeon, but I looked for it habitually. I took control of the interview the way I did pre-session consultations. I began asking the questions, squinting and nodding at her answers as if in careful consideration. She had to want *my* approval. I left feeling that I'd won. Two days later she called to offer me the job. Impulsively I accepted. It felt so good to be wanted.

The job paid $12 an hour and required a minimum of twenty-five hours per week. I hadn't worked more than twenty-five hours per week in years. There was no way I could maintain my lifestyle on $12 an hour, but I had wads of cash hidden all over my bedroom and wasn't thinking longitudinally. I didn't want to quit; I just wanted to know that I could. I considered it an experiment, a way of assuring my easy assimilation back into the real world, whenever the time for that arrived. Keeping the wheels greased. Remy agreed to give me a few months off to take some imaginary classes. Autumn was skeptical.

"You're going to work in an office? Eight hours a day? You're going to hate it."

"How do you know?"

"Because I know *you*, stupid. You are going to be bored out of your mind. Have you ever worked in an office?" I hadn't really. "Why don't you just swallow your pride and get a job waiting tables?"

She had quit for good a few months before, under more dramatic circumstances. Remy had used spyware to break into her e-mail, and when she found out Autumn had raged through the dungeon, cursing at him while packing her things. A blowout like that was something to be grateful for, she said; it made it impossible for her to go back.

"You could always go somewhere else," I had told her.

"Yeah, but I won't. I'm done."

I both pitied and envied her. While I was expecting to feel as she did, what I was doing felt less like putting something down than running away from it. I was afraid of drowning, not sick of swimming.

Having cobbled my concept of office life together from movies, I was surprised to find that I did not spend my days clicking around the office in heels, answering phones, and flirting with handsome coworkers. Nor was I actually editing, or wrangling with difficult though genius writers over the phone. My days were an endless spool of quiet, miserable boredom, punctured only by the scrape of metal from the construction site outside my window. My coworkers were all women. The one with whom I had the most contact was Ilse, the office manager. Ilse had been with the press for thirty years and was easily in her seventies. She must have once been beautiful, with an angular face that years of scorn had sharpened into a shingle. Shrewd and efficient, with no use for social niceties, she would have made a great domme fifty years ago, I thought. I had joked many times about wishing I had a domme of my own in college or at the gym, someone to make me get my life in order. I always knew I could do more to please someone else than myself. Ilse was not this person, although she acted like it.

"Melissa!" she would bark my name across the office. When I made it over to her desk, she would glower at me, her eyes pointedly resting on the tattoo peeking out of my sleeve. "What are you doing?"

"Uh, I am proofing the Dickens annual."

"Stop that. File these." She would point to one of the decrepit towers of paper on the wall of shelves behind her desk, which held all the company's records before 1980.

I didn't have a computer, only endless yellow pads of Post-its.

Ilse was in at six every morning and left at three in the afternoon. After the click of her heels faded down the hallway toward the freight elevator, I would read novels and sometimes the *MLA Style Manual*, picking choice citations from it, or the payroll secretary's personal calls, to write on the yellow squares.

After a month at the new job I went on a fast. "The Master Cleanse" limited my diet to laxative tea and a mixture of water, lemon juice, maple syrup, and cayenne pepper. Maybe I missed the extremity of the dungeon, or maybe I just wanted to quit. Boredom was something to withstand, but it wasn't what I was used to; there were no sharp corners of boredom, no distance to fall. Monotony has blunt edges, unchanging landscape. It was an Oklahoma highway of time, my month there.

I started my diet on a weekend. The first day of no food was invigorating; I was hungry, but what was hunger to me? I had survived a disease of craving. The second day I was exhausted. The third day I went to work. At nine in the morning, on my way to work, I stood outside of pizza shops, the scent of melting cheese bringing tears to my eyes. This hunger resembled only pain in its power to subsume all other desires. I had always marveled at the way a splinter or stubbed toe could suddenly put things into perspective. Other ambitions are the luxury of those whose bodily comforts can be taken for granted.

I read the same cumbersome sentence all day at my desk, little red pencil poised between my fingers. My dysfunction felt like being stoned, minus the fun. I could not complete anything or focus for more than a few seconds. All I could do was space out into vague anxiety, watching the construction site out the window, the crane bending its great skeletal arm to scrape through the dirt.

"Melissa!"

"Yes, Ilse?"

"Come here."

(Long shuffle across the office.)

"Yes, Ilse?"

"What are you doing?"

"Proofreading."

She suspiciously squinted into my eyes.

"Sort these files."

The fourth day, when I walked into the office with my jar of spicy lemonade there was a bag of muffins on the table by the refrigerator. They were blueberry Hostess Mini Muffins, mushed in a sealed bag into an exquisite clump of sugar and preservatives. My taste buds spasmed, flooding my mouth with saliva. I shuffled to my desk in agony and, sitting, nestled my face into my folded arms.

"Melissa?"

I could not move. I could not answer her without those muffins.

"Melissa?"

"Yes?"

"Come here."

"Yes?"

"What are you doing?"

"Nothing, Ilse."

"Finish these promotional packets."

For the new annuals, we sent out publicity materials made with colorful paper, glue sticks, and Ilse's typewriter. Ilse was usually too fetishistic about straight corners to permit me this task.

At noon, I put down my scissors and glue stick to retrieve my "lunch" from the refrigerator. The muffins were still on the table. The payroll secretary stared into the microwave, watching the carousel of her own lunch, which was always the same: diet meals in plastic cups that she had mailed to her by the caseload. They made the whole office smell like canned dog food and SpaghettiO's. Sipping from my jar of lemonade, I stared at the muffins.

"Better not!" The payroll secretary smiled, stirring her cup of orange stew. "I think those are Ilse's. You know how she is." She smiled conspiratorially and wrinkled her nose. "I think she'd notice." I wrinkled my nose back at her and returned to my desk.

Three hours and two glue sticks later, I heard Ilse push back her chair. She clicked her way over to my desk and surveyed the mess of sticky paper cuttings.

"What's this?"

"This is what you asked me to work on."

"This is a mess. Where are the finished materials?"

I handed her a card on which I had typed all the publishing information before gluing it onto a red background. She examined it, scraping at a minuscule clump of glue with her fingernail. "Look here." She ran her fingernail along the edge of the card. "It is crooked." She dropped the card onto my desk. "Do it over." She clicked back to her desk and I heard her chair's legs scrape the floor once more, the tap of her typewriter resuming. Beyond the window, the crane shuddered in mid-air, clumps of dirt falling from its blunt bucket hand. Rage made every sound louder: rips torn in the quiet. Ilse slammed a desk drawer, and the payroll secretary whispered into her phone. I couldn't do it. Whatever had prompted me to get and keep this job was dwarfed by my fury. As soon as I stood up and knew my intentions, it drained out of me and I was free. I tucked my chair under my desk and walked into the kitchen. The muffins squished inside their bag when I squeezed them into my pocket. I left my lemonade in the fridge and walked out.

# Part Four

# 24

The frayed edge of the rug was just discernable through the slit at the bottom of the blindfold, and I used it to navigate my way toward the bathroom, groping the air with my hands until they found a wall. Pulling the bathroom door open, I took tiny steps, wary of water on the floor in my stilettos. Feeling my way along the sink, I moved on to a marble shelf bearing a stack of Dixie cups, an industrial-size bottle of Scope, and a collection of disposable toothbrushes individually wrapped with their own tiny tubes of fluoride paste. After I navigated along the heated towel rack, my shin finally bumped into the rim of the toilet.

"Today, Justine . . ."

Larry was closer than I thought. If not in the doorway watching me, he was almost that near. His eyes on my back, I unfastened the top button of my white shirt.

"Are you going to make me come in there and do it myself? Are you *trying* to provoke me?" Hurrying, I removed the shirt, pausing with it bunched in my fist as goose bumps rose along my back and shoulders. "Turn around, Justine." I turned slowly, the cold lip of the toilet against the back of my calf as I faced him, conscious of my nipples, taut under the breath of the air-conditioning vent overhead. "That's it. Good girl." After he appraised me, his footsteps descended to the opposite side of the Blue Room. The door of the wardrobe against the far wall groaned as he opened it, and I heard the scrape of heavy chain across the wooden shelf where chains were kept. As the chains clinked against themselves in his hands, I could tell he spoke over his shoulder.

"Stop fucking around, Jus; I want it dripping. Do you hear me? Dripping. If it's not dripping, Jus, I'm gonna to stick your head in there; I'm gonna wash that toilet with your hair. Got it?"

"Yeah." My own voice sounded frail and ambivalent; gone was the husky assurance with which I denigrated my clients.

"Not 'yeah,' Jus', 'yes.'"

"Yes."

"Good girl, now hurry the fuck up."

Crouching over the toilet, one hand bracing myself in the treacherous heels, I dunked the fist holding my blouse in the toilet water. It was freezing. Squeezing the sopping fabric gently, I attempted to wring just enough liquid from it to still qualify as dripping.

"What did I say about dripping, Justine? I can hear what you're doing in there, and you'd better not squeeze another goddamn drop out of that shirt!" Standing up, I peeled the fabric apart and found an armhole. Streams of frigid toilet water slid down my breasts, back, and belly onto the bare skin underneath the waist of my pleated skirt as I buttoned the shirt.

I might have engineered this punishment in one of my own dominant sessions. It was the familiar choreography of verbal humiliation and psychological mind-fucking that impressed me. Larry knew what he was doing, and that's how I could let him. I actually stole a few of his tricks to use on my own submissives.

Larry was a big man at six-two, a little hefty, with warm eyes and a solicitous disposition. He bred Yellow Labs and in our first meeting reminded me of one. Before we even got to his to-do list, we bonded with the instantaneous goodwill and enthusiasm of two dog lovers. After we traded stories of canine food allergies and yeast-infected paws, the conversation rolled around to his erotic penchants, which included face spitting, forced gagging, and intense verbal humiliation. Larry's fantasy was a common one and a personal favorite of mine: the high school bitch. It should be surprising to no one that she made such frequent appearances here, where our business traded so often in the resurrection of childhood tormentors, both real and imagined. She was of the most requested bullies, along with mom, stepmom, teacher, babysitter, and nurse.

Larry wanted the tight jeans/braless T-shirt/high heels/ponytail combo, in which I was to strut around the Blue Room in cock-teasing antagonism, batting my eyes and coyly suggesting that he'd been staring at me an *awful lot* in algebra and how would he like to help me with my homework after school? This masterful plot would of course end in evil laughter, some humiliating remarks about the size of his penis, a swift kick to the balls, and a loogie in the eye.

"Just give me a safe word and do whatever you want," he said. There was nothing I appreciated hearing more, especially in a session whose fantasy I might enjoy. I heartily endorsed the idea with a handshake and promise to return in ten minutes.

Don't mistake my enthusiasm for identification; I was not this type of girl in high school. While commanding a certain amount of respect from my peers, I was an outsider, with no status to lord over lesser social castes. I had neither the motivation nor the capacity for this caliber of cruelty. The closest I came to antagonism as a teenager were a few instances of championing the more endangered passengers of my school bus. An empath by nature, I could barely stomach the gait of my neighbor's three-legged cat, let alone the humiliation of those with a surplus of social handicaps to begin with. High school was painful enough from a voyeuristic standpoint.

So how did I transform so comfortably into this sadistic persona? Perhaps I longed for a sort of freedom from conscience, or at least the ability to override it, that would sanction cruelty. The dungeon was the only forum in which I could enjoy the fancied freedom of cruelty, and there was a part of me greedy for it.

So I dressed with gusto: black stilettos, tight ponytail, and lipstick so sharp and bright it might have been a tear in the olive slope of my face. I slathered my hairless limbs in scented lotion, not unlike the fruity kinds popular with teenage girls; olfactory triggers can't be beat for evoking memories of sexual awakening and its subsequent traumas. Clicking down the dim hallway to the kitchen, I sucked down the remains of my morning coffee under the eye of the camera perched over the washer-dryer unit. The lazy swivel of the fan over the door forced me to waste one, two, three matches before my cigarette lit and I took a hungry drag before heading to the Blue Room.

"You're for sale, Justine. You're on the auction block. Show them what they'd be paying for." Larry trod a slow circle around me, prodding my ass with a riding crop. "Don't let those chains fall, Jus. You can't blame me for what happens if you do; you'll only have brought it on yourself."

My shoulders were on fire. Still blindfolded, I was balancing in the middle of the room on a small podium that usually bore an ornate wooden throne from which I would degrade my own slaves. Just that morning, one of them had been fellating the heel of my boot while I sat in it. Now I wore only the sopping white blouse and heels, whose punishing angle was cramping my arches so badly I feared collapsing. In each outstretched hand I held four feet of heavy chain.

"How many times have you done this to some poor fuck that was paying you to abuse him, Justine? How many times?" He rapped my tit with the tip of the riding crop, catching me off guard. It took me a few seconds to regain my balance before I could reply.

"A lot."

"You bet a lot. And much worse, huh, Justine? This is kiddy stuff, isn't it?"

I nodded.

"How many times have you humiliated some poor bastard with a choice like the one I'm giving you: hold up the goddamn chains or drop them and get punished? I know you can't hold 'em up forever, darlin'—that's the fun part."

As he spoke, I let my arms drop slightly, hoping he wouldn't notice their incremental sinking. All those hours at the gym would only get me so far. The burning in my shoulders was spreading, smoldering down my biceps and into my forearms. After Larry came to see me, I was always sore for days.

"How much, Justine? How much would you go for? How much would it cost to sell you on the block for an hour's time? How much for some stranger, some sick fuck, to fuck your brains out, kick your ass, do whatever he wants to you for sixty minutes? How much are you worth, darlin'?"


Explaining the bruises that dotted my arms and legs never posed much of a problem; I had always collected bruises as a by-product of my daydreaming. My hip never met a table corner it didn't like. I moved too quickly and haphazardly for someone so prone to spacing out. I did manage to hide my ass from Dylan for ten days once, until a particularly telltale purple stripe faded. But the only real worry any of the minor wounds inflicted by submissive sessions gave me came when Larry's sloppy bondage pinched a nerve in my wrist. See, I had never pinched a nerve. During my post-session shower, when my left hand began tingling, I first thought I might be having a heart attack. I crouched under the stream of hot water, bracing myself against the shower walls, pulse racing. The cold sweat of panic ceased when chest pains failed to follow. The tingling, however, continued to creep up my forearm. By the time I returned home after work, a solid stripe of numbness covered the distance from my elbow to my pinky finger. I hadn't lost mobility, only feeling.

"You okay?" Dylan asked me that evening as we watched a movie.

"Sure." I shrugged. "Just tired. Long day with the perverts." I flexed my hand and surreptitiously pinched the outside of my wrist, waiting for the movie to end and for him to leave so that I could scour WebMD.com, where everything always ended up being a symptom of cancer. There was so much I still hid; it must have often seemed to him that I'd pinched more than a nerve. I never lost my mobility, but I sure spent a lot of time gone numb.

Larry was too big to pick up and dunk in the toilet, as I would have liked, so I just made him crawl, kicking his ass, clad in a pair of huge pink panties, the whole way to the bathroom. This must have been our second or third session. When he was finally kneeling before the toilet, I stepped over him and hiked down my Levi's.

"Are you thirsty, Larry? Did all that studying make you thirsty? I hope so. I would make you close your eyes, you little sicko, but I want you to see this." Standing over the raised seat, I peed for a good long time, holding his gaze the whole while. Pulling up my jeans, I stepped over him again and planted myself behind him.

"Drink it." He hesitated. "Drink it, you little fuck!" He leaned forward, but that was all. I grabbed a fistful of his hair and dunked his face in the yellow water. "How. Dare. You. Even. Speak. To. Me. This is what you get, you pathetic piece of dog shit, for thinking for a second that I would even want to be seen speaking to you in public, let alone go on a *date* with you!" I pulled his face out of the toilet gasping, water streaming down his chest.

"*Eww!* You are getting piss-water on my shoe! What are you going to do about it, pig? Huh? What are you going to do about that?"

"I dun-nun-nun-no, Mistress." Larry's sub voice was unrecognizable from his normal speaking voice. Like most of my clients, the change in persona he underwent in session was so thorough that everything from his facial expression in repose to the tone and manner of his speaking was transformed.

"Well, I have a fucking idea, Little Lara; why don't you clean it off with your scummy little mouth?" He didn't resist.

With Larry blindfolded and kneeling execution-style in the middle of the room, I finished the session whispering in his ear.

"Show me how you touch yourself at home, Larry; show me what you do when you think about me alone in between your Superman sheets after you've finished your homework. Show me how you diddle yourself every night so that I can tell the whole cheerleading squad and the football team and we can all laugh and point at you in hallways and call you Little Larry. That's right, Lar, I'm gonna divulge to the whole goddamn student population precisely how small it actually is."

He came into his own hand.

"Eat up, Larry, down the hatch."


Afterward, I pulled my hair back in a bun, kicked off the heels, and donned a clean pair of latex gloves to wash the dildos in the sink while he showered.

"That was amazing!" he shouted through the steam.

"I'm glad," I answered, peeling a condom off a black trunk as thick as my arm. I was surprised he didn't split his lip trying to get his mouth around it.

"Do you ever switch?" he asked.

"Not often."

"Why not? I bet you like to."

I paused, deciding whether or not to let this pass. We weren't in session anymore and I liked Larry, so I decided not to correct his presumptuousness.

"Have you any idea the types that come through here? They have no clue what they're doing. I end up having to run the session myself, so why bother? I'd rather just top than top from the bottom."

"Can't blame you for that. So you don't have anybody good that you see regularly?"

"Nope."

"Shame."

"Why? Have you got designs on me, Lar?" I laughed.

"Yes."

Well. It was true that ever since my failed reentry into the straight job market, I had been experimenting increasingly often with submissive sessions, taking ones I never would have in my first years at the dungeon. This evolution had partly to do with ennui, sick as I was of seeing the same sorry twenty clients for almost three years, and partly the laziness that resulted of my boredom. Like my powerful, Armani-suited slaves, I had grown tired of my monopoly on executive power, which also meant doing all the work. Having sole responsibility for conducting my sessions, for injecting them with the imagination and enthusiasm that had made me so successful, had become burdensome. Passivity looked like vacation. But this was not enough to justify a dismissal of boundaries as stringent as mine had been. I had always had a lot of submissive fantasies, though not to the extremity of my clients; I dreamt more of being ravished than ravaged. But now, almost exclusively in my private fantasies, I had become the subjugated. On a few occasions, I had actually reversed scenes from my workdays and imagined myself in the position of my clients, though it was never they whom I envisioned dominating me, only a faceless male figure, a masculine phantom of myself. I would surmise that even the few sessions in which I had trusted the expertise of my dominant enough to let go and successfully submit, it had been essentially an autoerotic experience. The conditions of my switch sessions always included being blindfolded, and the men were prohibited from all but the most rudimentary verbal interaction. To hear my pathetic, panting partner's voice—the desire in it, let alone any trepidation or nervousness—was a certain mood killer. To experience pleasure in submission I had to be able to remain in my fantasy without the intrusion of their personality, without any reminder of the reality of our business arrangement. And I was not as disconcerted as you'd think, to witness in myself what I had judged my coworkers so harshly for. It seemed so separate, the way all things that I never spoke about did. It just *was*, not existing in the context of anything else.

"Well, what would you have us do in such a scene, Larry?"

"You mean what would I have you do? Or do to you?" He turned off the shower and pulled a fluffy white towel from where it hung over the shower stall door. Facing the vanity over the sink, I could see his silhouette as he dried himself, his hulking form obscured through the opaque glass behind me.

"I suppose that's what I mean."

"Well, I would say I'm best at doing what I enjoy having done to myself."

I laughed, slightly relieved at the obvious improbability of such a scene.

"Yeah, I don't think I'm going to be drinking anybody's pee in the near future. Sorry to disappoint."

"Well, not that necessarily," he replied, stepping out of the shower with the towel wrapped around his waist. "I know how to respect limits. What I meant was the general tone of my sessions. I like the psychological aspect to it. The physical, too, of course, but I'd like to get in your head."

Our eyes met in the mirror, and I couldn't help smiling.

"I don't know if I could let you in there, Lar, even if I wanted to."

"You'd be surprised, Jus; dommes usually make the best subs. Why do you think I'm so fun to abuse?"

"Oh, so now you're a dom?"

"Most of the time. This is just to balance it out."

"Uh-huh."

"Don't get me wrong, I'd hate to lose you as a domme; you're fantastic. But I get this sense about you. And I think we both know you can't do both with one person; there's no such thing as a real switch session; either you're on top or you're on the bottom."

I could taste the soap still on Larry's fingers when he shoved them down my throat. Saliva ran from the corners of my mouth as my throat lurched around his fingers, my whole body convulsing with the gag. As it sank toward his knee, Larry pushed my forehead up with his free hand, looking down at me like a hardheaded dog, his tone firm and patient.

"Look at me, Justine. Right here." He pointed toward his own eyes. "I want you to look me in the eyes while I do this to you." He tapped his fingers in the back of my mouth again, prodding my uvula and instigating another short round of gagging. "I know how easy it is to just go to another place, to leave your body while I humiliate it, but I'm not going to let you do that. I want you to feel every minute of it. I want you to think about this, my fingers in your mouth, when you are fucking your boyfriend. I want you to think about me when you are kicking the shit out of some guy later today."

An ugly sound came from my throat. As it echoed around the cavernous room, I heard how animal it sounded. The involuntary voices of our bodies are so strange to us, who are used to controlling them, calculating the way that others hear us. The guttural cries that came from me were painful in their betrayal of the facility with which I manipulated language and how expertly I enlisted its power to disguise this bestial truth. It was excruciating to be exposed in this way. And also freeing.

Though reflexive tears already wet my face, I felt the sudden urge to cry. It was not an urge of pure grief, and the grief in it was not that of my predicament there, with that man's hand in my mouth, but of other bondage, which abhorred the naked humanness in my submission, its discomposure. The pain I felt was mingled with gratitude. Maybe because I was incapable of freeing myself from the bindings of power, of self-control, without help.

To me, desirelessness had always meant power. The people I have been most instinctually attracted to are those who are unavailable to me; their power is irresistible. The arousal I felt as a dominant was not sexual but psychological: my submissives desired me, and without any desire myself, I enjoyed the freedom to refuse them. It was in this freedom that I entertained the possibility of a greater power, of mine as an agent in my own life, a person without need of faith in anything but myself.

When the session was over, we each showered and then sat on the leather bondage table to talk dogs. I felt more at ease and warmhearted toward Larry than any other client of mine. In fact, it was through my sessions with him that I began to develop an unprecedented empathy for my own submissives. After dominant sessions, I was often exhausted, peeved, and anxious to get them out and put my sweatpants back on; I resented their dewy gratitude and lingering, their chatty amicability. Preferable, most days, were the ones so consumed with shame, with the immediate emotional hangover, that they fled without showering or ever meeting my eyes.

After a session with Larry, the peace of our induced intimacy was a warm place to be, and I was not anxious to leave it. Having survived something, I felt lighter and strangely hopeful. In defying my own boundaries, I nurtured a hope for the illusory nature of other limits and in my own ability to set and break them.

# 25

"UGH." AUTUMN SLUMPED BACK against the sofa, the book sliding from her hands onto the floor. "I'm cooked. Stick in a fork in me, my love, because I'm done."

"Oh, stop," I said, looking up from my carton of Chinese food. "School is easy. *Life* is hard." I ceremoniously lifted a piece of broccoli with my chopsticks and stuffed it in my mouth.

Autumn snorted. "School is easy for *you*, smarty-pants, but thanks for dropping some knowledge on me—that was deep."

I rolled my eyes and put my bowl on the coffee table. "Give me the book."

"It's killing me, Melissa. It's like breathing sawdust."

"See, that's very creative—just use that in your paper!" I laughed and took the slim volume from her. "*The Metamorphosis*? This is a classic!"

She raised her eyebrows and mouthed, *Nerd*.

"You just have to get used to the language—it's old." I smiled at the book. "I've written papers of my own about this story."

"Great! Can I borrow them?"

"Let me see what you've got so far," I told her.

Autumn was midway to finishing her bachelor's at Long Island University and was considering switching focus from criminal psychology to nursing. I was of no use when it came to her science homework but regularly helped her out with English, which she hated. Working on her papers thrilled me, more so than working on my own ever had. I'd had to scale back my editing after she was gently accused of plagiarism by a professor.

I disappeared into the work—plucking at sentences, scanning the pages of familiar books—the way I sometimes disappeared into sessions, but without any hangover that followed, no shame or disgust, only a sated wearines. I missed the way I could disappear into that kind of work; I'd forgotten how easy it was, how fast time flew when I was engrossed. I still read a lot but found it increasingly difficult to focus on anything for long. Gone were the days when I could read for five, ten, eight hours at a stretch. Downtime in the dungeon I spent perusing the newspaper or magazines or wandering around online, killing hours in the vortex of Friendster—the soon-to-be-obsolete precursor to Facebook.

Autumn flipped through the television channels while I sat with her computer on my lap.

"What are you doing this weekend?" she asked absently.

"Black & Blue Ball is this weekend."

"You going?"

"Uh-huh. You want me to get you a ticket? I'm picking mine up from Purple Passion tomorrow." Purple Passion was our favorite supply store: a small, intimate boutique in Chelsea that sold high-quality corsets, leather goods—cuffs, crops, clothes—and even the medical supplies appropriated by our profession, like sounds, TENS units, and clamps.

"No, I have a test on Monday. That thing is too crowded for me, anyway. I want to leave as soon as I get there."

"Suit yourself."

The Black & Blue Ball is one of the biggest fetish events of the year in New York. At a different venue each spring, its spectacle draws an international audience of thousands. People go for the art, the music, the cameras, to schmooze and publicize themselves, to see and be seen. It was worth it just for the outfits.

That year, Camille, Miss K, Fiona, Georgina, and I met at the dungeon to get dressed before the ball. All of us crowded into the dressing room while the fresh-faced twenty-year-old night shift gawked from the couch. Miss K glued on two-inch magenta false eyelashes as Camille tucked peacock feathers into her headdress, and I baby-powdered the inside of my rubber minidress (latex is impossible to get on otherwise). Wanting to keep it simple, I smoothed some product on my black bob, put on red lipstick, and donned my most comfortable platform stilettos. One of our coworkers was performing. I loved to see the clothes, the local celebrity performers, the Amazonian trannies with their glitter and implants, and the dommes from other dungeons, but my reasons for going were also more pragmatic than any of that. There was business to be drummed up at the B&B.

When I left the dungeon for a "real" job, it had a lot to do with my limits and their disappearance. When I went back, that didn't change so much as my attitude about it. If I was going to go all out, I was going to get paid for it, I thought, and that made it seem more like a choice. I also couldn't get the rumors about Remy out of my mind. Supposedly, he had cameras rigged behind all the mirrors of the dungeon. To an onlooker, what I was doing in sessions may not have seemed much more intimate than before, but I knew it was. Whether or not Remy had cameras in the dungeons, it was paranoid of me; even if they existed, girls had been doing what I did, and much worse, for years before I got there. But it wasn't getting in trouble that I was afraid of; it was being seen. Where I had gone in my sessions felt like stepping off of that cliff, as I had my first day, but it felt wilder, steeper, darker below. It didn't feel completely within my control, and the way I controlled things was in secret.

Even as a kid, I'd found power in the ability to claim a hidden world. Selecting items from my household that would be wondered about but not missed, I would bury them in far corners of our rural backyard or off the banks of the pond our house sat at the edge of. I hid detailed maps inside a diary with a minuscule lock, whose key was hidden in a copy of *Anne of Green Gables* whose final chapter I had hollowed out with a pair of sewing scissors. It wasn't to prohibit others' use that I did this but to claim the knowledge of the items' whereabouts for my own, to stake out a metaphysical territory over which I had sole control. In my closet, I kept a Mason jar filled with the ashy remains of other expendable household materials. I would put bits of paper, fabric, plastic, hair, and food in the jar and burn them with long kitchen matches. Watching such vivacious transformation of the mundane mesmerized me.

I needed a more controlled space to observe the transformation of my sessions, like that jar in the bag in the back of my closet or a hole dug in the backyard. Some things I needed to bury to keep. That wildness promised destruction if not contained.

Skye, our colleague, was up on the balcony that overlooked the main floor of the club. They had oversold tickets worse than usual that year, and everyone you would have strutted by in years past you were now instead pressed up against. There was a glammed-up band playing, fire-breathers, and some sideshow sessions going on, but we couldn't see any of it over all the heads. At five-two I had enough trouble seeing over the heads of other women, let alone men in heels. I found some breathing room on the balcony.

I knew that Skye was into suspension but had never seen it before. We milled through the crowd for a while before finding her. I posed for cameras with a group of gay rubber fetishists, their perfectly sculpted bodies ensconced from head to toe.

"There she is!" Camille finally shouted, and pointed to the corner where a tighter crowd had formed. We found Skye at the center. She had sculpted her black hair a foot high, weaving razor wire and Kewpie dolls into it, among other things. She smiled down at us as we pushed our way to the front of her audience, and I could see that her eyes were glazed with something. She'd probably taken painkillers in preparation. Dangling off the ground by a few feet, she wore a spangled bra and hot pants. Strung from the ceiling by rope were two large, silver hooks. They pierced through the flesh of her back, and from these she hung, a head about the crowd.

As a teenager I had had needles stuck through my nose, lip, navel, and ears; I had stuck needles in my veins fairly recently, and I pierced slaves at the dungeon all the time. This was different. Session piercings were usually superficial; they only punctured the topmost layers of skin and never bled much. Regular piercings hurt like hell for about three seconds. This woman was hung by deep-sea fishing hooks, as thick as my thumb. They had to pierce through enough flesh to support her entire body weight, to avoid ripping through her. They pulled handfuls of her back into two symmetrical tents of flesh.

At that point I was hard to shock; in fact, I had been for a long time. As if I had a lost gag reflex, there wasn't much that made me gasp or cringe. I stared at the blood-encrusted holes in her back, her glassy eyes, and the shimmering light her spangles threw across all the upturned faces and I wasn't shocked or disgusted or scared, but there was something. Skye once said to me in the dressing room that she considered herself an artist and that she was her own work of art. I thought of this as I stared up at her. She was magnificent, in a way. The idea of doing it myself was frightening, unappealing, but I understood the impulse and her limp satisfaction, and maybe that is what disturbed me.

On my way down the stairs, I paused. Squeezing my eyes shut for a few seconds, I asked myself what if I could have seen this as a younger me, a glimpse of my future life. I had always wondered what I would be like at the age of eighteen, twenty-one, twenty-three. It was an impulse that reminded me of my childhood fantasy games, when I would lie in the woods, close my eyes, and open them as someone just born, someone from another planet, to see everything so new and strange. Now I opened them on a writhing ballroom, strobes from the cathedral ceiling bathing everything in purple light: half-naked men and women led on leashes by towering she-males and dommes with cinched waists and rubber catsuits; a fire-breathing, Hula-Hooping troupe clad only in body paint and piercings; slaves in masks crouched over and used as stools by women at the bar; and behind me a woman hung by hooks with razor wire in her hair. Someone down on the floor called my name: "Justine!" I blinked, reached into my cleavage for a stack of business cards, and descended the stairs.

# 26

~~

In the beginning, $75 had seemed like a lot of money. After a few years, it no longer did, not when I knew it could be more. For the small minority of dommes who stayed in the business longer than a year, mine was a common trajectory. After a time, you stopped focusing on the fact that you made $75 an hour and started thinking more about how you were getting $75 out of the $200 that your client was paying. Then you started talking to independent dommes who set their own rates, paid for their own space, booked their own appointments, built their own Web sites, and set up retirement funds. Then you figured out that that's what the most senior dommes at your own dungeon were segueing into; they didn't work fewer days only because they booked so many sessions but also because they were doing sessions elsewhere and harvesting new clients from the house. I wasn't interested in getting a lease in Manhattan and investing in all my own equipment; I couldn't afford it and believed that I might spontaneously quit any day now. But so long as I was still in it, more money and privacy were necessary. So I had my business cards made, and I started slipping them to clients who tipped well and whose sessions interested me. I could charge what I wanted in private sessions; it was a sliding scale based on what I thought a client would be willing to pay. Most sessions ended up at around $300 an hour, four times what I made at Mistress X's.

My first was with Tony. He constantly said things in sessions like, "Doesn't Mommy want to take Baby to the ATM and make him give her money?" As promising as that might have sounded, I never took him up on it. Primarily, I hesitated because it would have looked suspicious, me going downstairs in the elevator with him. I also figured he was bullshitting. The man didn't bother to tip in session. But while he wasn't a favorite, he was familiar and benign. I didn't know if he was bluffing about the ATM, but I did feel certain that he posed no physical threat to me, and that was my first criterion for taking sessions "outside," as we called it.

I hated the phone part of it. What the managers at Mistress X's spared me from I didn't know until I started booking my own sessions. It was so *awkward*. Not to them, I don't think; my affectation over the phone remained as seamless as in person, but to me it was harder. It discomfited me to hear those voices while wearing my street clothes, in the midst of my "regular" affairs, to talk into the same phone I spoke to my mother on. In effect, I was Melissa, not Justine, during those conversations. I missed the transitional elements: the dungeon, the clothes, and the darkness; without them it was jarring, and it took time for me to be able to slip in and out of character that quickly.

Autumn told me about a hotel in the Meatpacking District, right on the West Side Highway. It was cheap (for Manhattan), not too filthy, and rented rooms by the hour. Tony agreed when I suggested it but asked if we could meet at a bank ATM a few blocks away.

"Perfect," I told him.

We met just after dark on a Friday evening, a mistake I wouldn't make again. I was early and made my way west from the Eighth

Avenue subway station. West of Ninth Avenue the crowds thin and the shops, while still chic, are farther apart. The blocks go from quaint to industrial, all loading docks and the locked grates of galleries. I stepped carefully in my heels across the cobblestones and was glad, then, for the early clubgoers who straggled past me on otherwise deserted streets. Even with the glowing ATM and a nearby gas station, our meeting place was desolate. I smoked outside the glass doors and fiddled with my phone until he arrived. It was odd, waiting there with my suitcase of dildos and rope. I felt both vulnerable and excited by the nearness of my two lives. It seemed so brazen. His familiar stride and shining head bobbed toward me under the streetlights.

"Hello, Mommy."

I felt a wave of embarrassment, hearing that voice outside the muffled walls of the dungeon. Like sudden nausea, I suppressed it and smiled. "How is Mommy's baby?"

"I'm very good, Mommy. Does Mommy want to go into the ATM?"

"How did you know? You're so good at pleasing Mommy, aren't you?" At the dungeon I had become used to this kind of talk; I did it automatically, unselfconsciously. Here, though—hanging in the air over the cobblestones, the river of traffic behind us and the Hudson shining beyond that—the words rang false. In the open air they sounded phony, the way they had during my first session. It seemed the world was too honest for them, as if the river and the sky and the street were too real to suffer our falsity. We could only get away with it in an environment as contrived. I was struck with sudden fear: What if I saw someone I knew? What if my suitcase fell open on the sidewalk, dildos rolling into the street? What if Tony and I were arrested for some reason? What if I couldn't do it? What if this was the moment when it all stopped? Tony clearly did not notice or share my discomfort.

Unlocking the door with his card, he opened it. I followed him into the glass cubicle, turning to squint at the street behind us for signs of life as he settled himself in front of a machine. There were only a couple of cars at the gas station on the next block, too far away to see us in detail. Joining Tony, I saw that he still had his card out and was smiling at me expectantly. Before I could think of what to say, he reached for the zipper of his coat and pulled it down slowly. Watching this towering man sensuously lower his parka zipper, coy as a burlesque dancer, would have been funny if Autumn were there. Knowing this only made me more alone, made our scene in this fishbowl more lurid and sad. The jacket covered him to mid-thigh, and when he unzipped I saw that the zipper of his jeans was also down, though the waist buttoned. His semi-erect penis was threaded through the hole, clasped lightly in the teeth of the open zipper. He must have arranged this before even leaving his apartment, titillated by the concealed transgression as he walked here through the Friday crowds, perhaps even brushing against anonymous hips with his hidden member. He disgusted me, and his perversion acquired a kind of menace here, where I could not meet its enthusiasm. The disconcerting parallel was not lost on me: both of us with our secrets, precious and thrilling.

He smiled down at me and reached into his pants' hole, fishing around for a second before retrieving a knotted white string, about six inches long. He reached down for my hand and pressed the string into my palm. Closing his fist around mine, he jerked it toward me. His penis jiggled against the leg of his jeans, and I could see that the string was tied around its base.

"Is Mommy going to make me take money out of the money machine for her? Mommy knows how she controls the Baby."

Not meeting his eyes, I tugged stiffly on the string (something I had done hundreds of times in the dungeon). "Oooooooh, Mommy, look what you do to me!" I tugged more violently. "Lookwhatyoudotomelookwhatyoudotomelookwhatyoudotomelookwhatyoudotome!"

"Now put your little card into that little hole," I said.

"Yes, Mommy."

206 · Melissa Febos

After he punched his code I pushed his hand aside and selected "Withdrawal from checking." I withdrew $500 from his account and folded it into my coat pocket.

"Now let's go," I said, dropping the string so that he could tuck himself back into his pants, or at least zip his coat back up.

He did neither. Instead, he lifted the string toward me again and cooed, "But Baby doesn't know where Mommy is taking him. Doesn't Mommy want to lead the Baby there like a good little doggy?"

How could he not have known how little I wanted to do such a thing? My eyes said as much, I know. His eyes reminded me of the money in my pocket. We stared at each other for a long breath before I picked up the string and pushed the glass door open.

I was petrified the whole way that I would see someone I knew, that we would see anyone at all. I felt like a dog pulling on a leash, pretending that I didn't get my dinner from the other end of it. "Why so fast, Mommy?" he whined. At one point, a couple passed by us on the other side of the street. My heartbeat matched the hurried click of the woman's heels against the street as they neared. Wrenching on the string, I pulled him up beside me, between the building's façade and my body, hoping to hide him in shadow. They looked at us as Tony took advantage of the close range and reached for my face, prompting me to dodge him awkwardly. I doubt they saw anything lewd, but my whole body burned with humiliation anyway.

We made it to the block of the hotel without further incident. I stopped at the corner, from which we could see people smoking outside the lobby doors.

"Close it up," I said, and he did.

It being Friday, there was a wait for a room. This might have been the worst part. We sat silently together on cheaply uphol-stered chairs by the checkout desk, which was protected by a bul-letproof glass window, like those in taxis. After a drunk man with an overly made-up woman in a wig tossed his key through the opening in the desk window, I paid for an hour. The clerk avoided my eyes and only looked directly at me for a brief moment, but in that moment I knew he saw a prostitute. Maybe he noted that I was more sober or cleaner than most, but maybe he didn't see anything beyond an image of me having sex with the big bald man behind me for money. I wanted to protest that image but was helpless. I felt trespassed, the clerk's glance a subjugation much worse than any client's appraisal. I elected to be seen as a sex object at the dungeon; the clients *paid* to see me this way. I had an absurd urge to show the assuming concierge my college diploma, to use vocabulary that he wouldn't understand, to explain that I was *a dominatrix*, not a whore. He wouldn't have cared. He wasn't even smug; there was no spite in his assessment of me, only casual certainty and dismissal.

The room was hideous, with a mirrored ceiling and bony mattress. I turned the sound up on the television and did my best to avoid the mirrors. It was the usual exercise in withstanding. Afterward, I sent Tony away and took a shower in the yellowed stall, scrubbing my body with a tiny bar of soap. I sat on the closed toilet seat wrapped in a nubbly towel and waited to stop feeling like a whore, waited for the swell of accomplishment. It came, albeit slowly, and not quite until I emerged from those lobby doors, the shame seeping away like soft steam from the cracks in that room.

# 27

THERE WERE A FEW MORE sessions in that hotel and then never again. From then on I stuck to Miss K's place: a small loft on the line between SoHo and the West Village. She had a massive industrial loft out in Brooklyn and maintained this one just for work. There was a tiny kitchen and lofted bed, both of which she had outfitted with black curtains that could be pulled to hide them, leaving only the main area, about twenty square feet. Its theme was hot pink, with lots of black and Lucite accents, mostly made by her. Along the walls she had installed rows of silver hooks for paddles, floggers, crops, and every thickness of rope. The opposite wall shelved an impressive (and mostly pink) dildo collection. There were drawers of gloves, condoms, clamps, needles, cotton balls, alcohol wipes, and lube, whose use was included in her hourly rental rate of $75. She made me my own set of keys, and I started sessioning there weekly with a select group of regulars.

There was Tony, whom I hated but whose session was usually short and the money good. After his sessions, I would tell myself that it was the last time, and so it was, until I needed money or wanted to call in sick to Mistress X's. Then I'd give in and schedule him again. Thirty minutes of hell with him often seemed easier than a whole day in the windowless dungeon. Our ATM charade became a miserable routine.

There was Albert, the Englishman who lived in France and worked in fashion. Albert was a round, scruffy beaver of a man, with ruddy cheeks, a man purse, and a full-length fur coat. He had the body of a stodgy British businessman and the fashion sense of a Parisian fag. He liked switch sessions, and when I saw him he dommed me for an hour, then I him. We went out for dinners beforehand, and he always brought me a bottle of perfume.

There was Billy, the blue-eyed stockbroker, dubbed Hairless Billy at the dungeon, as he shaved everything but his legs and armpits with a razor. Occasionally shaving would be incorporated into his sessions. Once I got over the fear of accidentally slicing his balls open, it was something I looked forward to, a session consisting of mindless grooming and chitchat. But mostly he wanted his extraordinarily small penis tied up with string and pulled on while I laughed at him. At the dungeon a few times, we played jump rope this way. Being filthy rich and dumb as wood, Billy scheduled a lot of sessions and never tired of the same scene, the same lines. Sometimes I would blindfold him just so that I didn't have to make all the facial expressions. Once in a while, he would let me mummify him with latex ribbon or put him in a body bag, but he wasn't into sensory deprivation, so those parts never lasted long.

And then there was Jacob. Jacob was different. We sessioned once at a Holiday Inn in Queens and every time after that at his apartment. I had seen him for a couple of years at the dungeon, but he was Autumn's client first. We all passed clients between us, after we got sick of them or they got sick of us. Jacob was a kind of ideal client, at least to me. First, he was young. Usually sessions with younger men, men my own age, or even within ten years of my age, were uncomfortable. The likelihood of our social spheres overlapping was too great. I don't mean that we might have friends in common (though that did happen once), but that we might be able to put each other into a realistic context.

But it wasn't awkward with Jacob. It was *fun*. With other young men, they were too close but also too different and our sessions felt like trying to fit two slightly mismatched puzzle pieces together. I was always afraid of what they'd glimpse, how they would interpret me, what they would assume. With old men, I was a chess pawn and they were a checker; I just played their game and they never knew the difference. Jacob and I were alike enough to escape unease. We actually fit. His session didn't turn me on sexually, but it was wildly fun. Sometimes we used a specific fantasy; schoolyard bully was a favorite. I would taunt him, imitate the lisp that he actually had as a child, and there was always a lot of spitting and face slapping. I didn't know why those were my favorite things; I'm not sure he did, either. They were the pinnacle not of pain but of humiliation. Even now, I can think of few things more offensive than spitting in someone's face. You have to look into their eyes to do it.

Jacob was short, clean, cute in a blue-eyed bashful way, and funny. Sessions were always so dead serious; that was part of what made them exhausting; there was no room for the actual absurdity of what happened in them, only a manufactured mocking. That's why I loved doing sessions with other mistresses, Autumn especially. A witness lessened the pressure, allowed for the humor in the ridiculous. Jacob did this, too. I often laughed genuinely in his sessions. He could allow his own objectivity to slip in and consciously self-deprecate, acknowledging that he could see the humor as well. These were the least lonely sessions I ever had. In order to enjoy sessions, I had to enter the world of my client's fantasy. But, until Jacob, I always had to bear the truth alone, to carry the full weight of objectivity.

Jacob had a girlfriend and a studio apartment in Astoria, a sweet residential neighborhood in Queens. He would drive his Saab to Williamsburg to pick me up and take me back to his place to session. I loved getting into his car in jeans and a T-shirt, no lipstick. With him, the overlap of the "real" me and Justine didn't feel awkward or false; it felt like a kind of freedom. I knew that I was a fantasy to him beyond our sessions and that he was a little bit in love with me from the very beginning.

# 28

RICK WAS A REGULAR of mine. He was a nice, clean, single guy who made good money tutoring rich Westchester brats for the SAT and ran the marathon every year, and it took him years to work up the courage to walk through the door of Mistress X's. I was the first domme he had ever seen, and after his inaugural session he came back every second Thursday for a year straight. Occasionally we did a stock medical scene, but usually I impersonated his tutoring clients, donning my schoolgirl outfit and pigtails. I had begun wanting to apply to graduate school around this time and considered offering to trade sessions with him for GRE tutoring but never did. I had the books to make our sessions authentic, at least. It was a switch session that began with him making lecherous advances on me, his student, lifting my pleated skirt to spank me when I didn't finish my practice tests. This part I always tried to prolong.

"But Mr. MacDonnell! I didn't study my vocabulary, either! Are you going to have to punish me for that, too?"

"Of course I am, you naughty little girl! You are going to get a spanking for every word you didn't learn!" Then he would pause, rubbing my lower back as I waited, bent over the desk. "What's that I hear?" he'd ask, and I would sigh, resting my cheek against the open Kaplan book beneath me. "Could your mother be home early?" Then I would have to run out of the room and change into my Mean Mommy business suit.

I wasn't proud of the clichéd route my own fantasies sometimes took, but on some level I had accepted them. The fact that I was ideologically opposed to my own misogynistic, youth-fetishizing turn-ons actually made them more exciting. Succumbing to my submissive impulses reminded me of discovering drugs as an adolescent; a door had opened into something big, something that made me feel both empowered and captive to it. It was that feeling of something awakening in me that I didn't quite know and couldn't quite control.

I was so weary of Mean Mommy. Rick had a startlingly high-pitched and nasal submissive voice, and I loathed the second half of our session doubly for the fun that preceded it. But he paid well and his sessions were easy to hurry. I could depend on his $300 for thirty minutes of work every other week, and when I started moving clients out of the dungeon he was one of the first I took.

Most of my clients were lonely, and their sessions demanded a certain amount of pretending that you cared about them and their problems. After my first year at the dungeon I no longer took clients who wanted sessions that were half domination, half therapy; they were more work in most cases. Still, when Rick called me one Sunday in November and invited me to go to the New York Marathon Expo at the Javits Center in Midtown, I agreed. I had made a lot of money from him and figured it was a shrewd investment, something I wouldn't have to do more than once a year, like a company picnic. If he wanted to pretend for an hour that we were friends, I could stand it. I guessed there was a chance I could finagle a new pair of running sneakers out of it, too. My feelings about my job were complex, but sometimes I could be just that shrewd and shallow.

He made a surprisingly heartrending sight, waiting for me by the entrance in his matching hat and mittens.

"You came!" he said gratefully.

"I said I would, didn't I?" I gave him a lopsided smile and kissed the air near his cheek.

I followed him through the aisles of merchandise tables, carefully sifting through piles of ankle reflectors, water bottle belts, packets of carbohydrate gel, and sweatbands. After a half an hour of smiling encouragingly every time he looked back and proudly held up a find, like a kid doing tricks in the pool, I began tiring.

"How about a T-shirt?" I asked him, holding out a find of my own. He hesitated before adding it to his shopping basket. *Asshole,* I thought; he was ungrateful like a child, too. I suddenly wanted to go home, to get away from him and his cloying loneliness. He was a finicky, needy man; it was no wonder he was lonely. That was my job: a guard against loneliness so that he could enjoy his hobby for an hour. I imagined running a marathon with no one to cheer me on. The dense mixture of frustration and depression I felt at his vulnerability was familiar, an old burden. It was the feeling that had hung like a perpetual dusk over our home during my parents' breakup. The dark outside seemed to mimic it, the smell of imminent winter leaking in through the lobby's revolving doors.

Laden with plastic shopping bags, he found me staring out of the giant windows by the escalator.

"Time to go home?" he said. His acknowledgment of that single authentic feeling of mine prodded my own loneliness, and I felt a surge of gratitude.

"Yeah, I think so."

We glided down the escalator in silence. Out on the chilly sidewalk, he insisted on hailing me a cab.

"See you in two weeks?" he asked as I slid into the backseat.

"Sure," I said, and squeezed out a smile.

"Oh, wait!" He grabbed the taxi door with his mittened hand as I went to close it. Pulling off the mitten with his teeth, he reached into his back pocket and pulled out a wad of folded bills. "I almost forgot." He smiled again sheepishly as he tucked them into my hand and slammed the door, waving as we pulled away. As my cab sped down the highway, I counted the bills. It was $300 in twenties, the same as for a session.

And so this became our new routine. For formality's sake, we did have one more session after that, but when he called to invite me to dinner the following week we both knew there would be no spanking, no Mean Mommy. He took me to restaurants uptown that he had carefully researched to make sure they had vegetarian options. I learned all about his students, his aging mother, his psoriasis and obsessive-compulsive streak. There was a mood we maintained that prevented it from ever feeling like a therapy session, a lightness that I know he kept calling me for, which he didn't feel in his immaculate Westchester condo. I talked about myself, too. I didn't lie about anything, but there was a way the truth was omitted, even from those facts. Maybe it was a natural result of my altered personality. He called me Melissa, knew where I was from, where I had gone to college, that my parents were divorced, even about my addiction history. But any evidence of grief had been bled out of my story; I might have been pulling figurines off of a shelf for him to examine, they had so little to do with my actual experiences. That was what he wanted, to borrow an aura of ease for a few hours. He believed that being me was light and fun and easy, and so with him I got to become that.

There were bad moments, a sucking black hole of loneliness that opened in me, when our conversation lulled, but mostly not. Mostly I felt safe, in a contained space. We stayed far enough outside of my usual stomping grounds that I didn't often fear bumping into anyone I knew. And oh, the getting over! I was making money to be taken out to dinner! Yes, something flinched in me when I realized that I was being paid to go on dates with him, that that was what we were simulating. But what else had I simulated? What was this by comparison? I knew it couldn't last forever, that I couldn't simulate what develops after so many dates, but I didn't know who would stop first.

# 29

"STOP!" Dylan shrugged me off as I tried to kiss his cheek. I had just arrived at his apartment, coming straight from a session at Jacob's place. Dylan frowned. "I need you to feel my forehead. I think I'm running a fever again."

I sighed.

"What? Do you think I like being sick?"

"Of course not." I wasn't so sure, though. I knew *I* didn't like his being sick and it was only getting worse. Dylan seemed to come down with something every other week. Last time it had been a bizarre infection in his elbow, an unlikely affliction prompted by nothing the doctor could think of.

"Then why are you looking at me like that?"

"I'm not looking at you like that; I'm feeling your forehead." I pressed my fingers below his hairline and looked at the floor. While he didn't act like someone enjoying himself, chronic sickness did give him a convenient reason to act like a miserable bastard, I thought. I sure spent a lot of time taking care of him for how contemptuous he could be. More and more frequently, his minor emergencies seemed to coincide with my private sessions. A guilty conscience could have been a factor in my noticing this; Dylan had called while I had been in the car with Jacob, laughing. I felt a pang of annoyance when I saw my boyfriend's name on the phone, followed by shame. The sound of his voice when I answered—forlorn and a little desperate—intensified both my annoyance and my shame. His neediness when sick disgusted me sometimes. How could a man who found it nearly impossible to tell me he loved me expect me to coddle him? I couldn't help tallying the affection owed me, and I was losing hope that he'd ever pay up.

"How was work?" he asked me.

"Fine," I said, ignoring his tone. I didn't really want to get into it with him, not when I was already feeling guilty. "You need some Advil to bring the fever down. I'll go to my place and get some."

"Thanks," he said, and rolled over to face the wall. I still had my coat on and was outside in seconds, tasting the freshness of the open air. By the time I got back he'd be asleep.


Jacob was the counterpoint to Rick. Jacob and I talked on the phone at least once a week, those hour-long, muffled-because-you're-lying-in-bed type of phone calls, the kind that only happen between girlfriends and new lovers. We also went out for meals, but their pleasure was wholly different from that of sharing a table with Rick or any of my other clients. I missed Jacob when he didn't call. Then I started calling him. We went Christmas shopping together, to the movies, The Home Depot, and the flea market. He bought me a vacuum cleaner for my birthday. We traded mix CDs and family stories. He paid for everything, and he paid me, though we always did a session. I made sure of that. Even when I knew his interest in them was waning. I wanted the money, I thought, but that wasn't what I missed when I missed him.

When we had been sessioning privately for a few months we would go out to eat afterward and he would drive me home to

Brooklyn. One night, as we parked outside of my building, he handed me some money and I put it in my pocket but didn't get out of the car. I could smell night through the cracked car windows and thought of how I'd feel walking into my apartment, slightly less alive.

"It feels like Sunday night." I said.

"I think it *is* Sunday night."

"Ha-ha. No, I mean it feels like Sunday night used to feel when I was a kid."

"School the next morning, homework not done."

"Yeah, but just that *sad*, too, like something is over. Like the night is just a symbol of something else that found you after all, something else you can't escape."

"I don't want to go home alone."

"Me, neither."

We looked at each other in the almost dark, and then he started the car again. We drove farther out into Brooklyn. "Right!" I would shout at a red stoplight, and he'd turn. "Left!" I'd shout at the next. It became night, and we drove through neighborhoods where trash cans rolled through the street; those where inside every lamppost outside of every brownstone a light blinked cheerily; those where the streets widened and buildings hulked gray and industrial, no soul in sight. I felt happy. In his car there crackled the known magic of desire, the comfort of his wanting me, but that wasn't all. There was something else, some other sweetness that I didn't want to let go of. I wasn't in love with or attracted to him, not in any regular sense. But I wanted that feeling with him more than I did any other then. It wasn't only in that dusk that I was reminded of my childhood. There was a safety with him that came from more than just his wanting me. I felt known by him in a way no one else made me feel. Autumn and I had an unspoken understanding about each other's sessions; I am fairly certain that ours took a similar path. Now, more than then, she and I can admit that there was more to it than money or rebellion, but then it was tacit at best. She and I did plenty of sessions together, but their pleasure was only ever of humor. She, like most of my friends, only knew the "real" me. Then there were clients, like Larry, in whose company I enjoyed things that would have shocked most of those who knew that "real" me. That pleasure was also real. Jacob was the only person with whom I felt known in both senses. I never privately practiced the things that aroused me with him, but I related to his pleasure freely. He was the only man I knew of who embodied both truths. Sure, there had been young, attractive clients before, photographers who wanted to trade photo shoots for sessions, a personal trainer at my gym once, but I always felt estranged in the company of these men from that "real" me; with them I still had to maintain an invulnerable persona, and it was often more lonely than the company of my usual clientele, who didn't presume to relate to me socially.

Of course, I never thought any of this at the time. My experience of it was instinctual. I wanted to be around Jacob, and sessions were the way to be around Jacob. Even when he stopped wanting them. I could tell, perhaps even before he could, that he was losing interest in that part of our relationship. For me they were as fun and invigorating as ever, but that wasn't why I kept initiating them. The intimacy of our friendship had surpassed the power of his fantasies, and they started to feel false. Both of us wanted to simply be around each other more than we wanted to act out those familiar scenarios. We would go out to eat, watch television on his couch, laugh. Before the evening could end, I would start something, and he wasn't able to say no. Partly, the impulse was still strong in him, and partly, he knew that I required it. I felt guilty but relieved every time we parked outside of my building and he handed me that money. Eventually we talked about it. He told me how his exasperated friends kept insisting that I was using him for the money, that he was a dupe for believing that we were actually friends. To myself, I thought that it was about the money, but also I knew that we were genuine friends, that the comfort and pleasure of being with him was separate from the comfort of the money. I told him it was because I had a boyfriend.

"It satisfies my conscience. It doesn't feel like an infidelity if it is still technically a business relationship."

"And just being friends would?"

"Friends who used to have this kind of business relationship, yeah."

"But if you already *know* that that's why you're doing it, how can it still work?"

I laughed then, because it was a good question and one I hadn't bothered asking myself about years of past rationalizations, because it *did* still work and I didn't need to know why. Also, because my excuse was a lie. It was so ironic; I knew my self-deceits well enough to create an incredibly realistic lie, and to him it sounded implausible. In truth, I hardly felt guilty at all on my boyfriend's behalf. But there was something about the money that did seem to legitimize mine and Jacob's relationship, and the prospect of not having it made me uncomfortable. So we went on that way until our comforts went threadbare and he started to resent me. I wasn't ever going to transcend the pageantry of our business relationship and become his girlfriend.

"I'm too short," he'd say.

"You're too nice," I'd reply, half-kidding.

A whiny, childish side of him emerged as his frustration grew, and our barbed joking increased. We bickered. I became crueler and condescending, angry at him for changing what we had, for needing more. Then he fell in love with someone else, and I was relieved, and scared. I felt splintered again, not sure how to go on as I was, and not sure if I could stop.

# 30

WHEN I LAID OUT all the applications on my bedroom floor, consulting lists of deadlines, addresses, and requirements, I counted five out of ten applications that were to out-of-state schools. Moving hadn't helped me to relinquish anything in the past, but I still hoped it might this time. Not that I was certain that I wanted to quit domming. My uncertainty was the problem. My hope was that a geographic change would eliminate the need for a decision. I doubted that I had it in me to start domming all over again, especially in some leafy New England town without proper dungeons and S&M weeklies. It was just that it was so *easy* in New York; here, the clients found me. To quit would mean gutting my life, and my identity. What would I be without it? Sober, yes. That was the only other thing I had going for me, the only thing that allowed me to consider quitting my job. But besides that? A drone at some publishing house making enough money to buy coffee and canned beans? I would end up some post-college cliché, worrying about her future, getting older, marriage; I would become *average*.

. . .

"I don't know," I said to Greta. "It's hard to imagine myself without it. What would I do for money?"

She smirked faintly. "You'd think of something." She pushed a lock of blond off her forehead, and I could see her searching for the right words, her blue eyes resting on something outside her apartment window. "Whenever I let go of something I'm that attached to, an idea of myself as bigger than I am, my recovery grows in a way I couldn't see I needed before. I have to jump before I can see the other side." She looked at me. "That's where faith comes in."

"You think I should quit," I said, though I had known that for a while now. "And I will, eventually. I just need to figure out what to replace it with."

"Sometimes," Greta said carefully, "when I think I'm afraid of something concrete, like money, I'm really afraid of not being good enough."

"Good enough for what?"

"To have a happy life, be a part of society. To be a worker among workers."

I cringed at this and made a face.

Greta laughed. "I know that's not how you want to think of yourself."

"Not exactly. 'Not good enough'? It sounds so fucking Oprah."

Greta laughed again. "Okay, fine. But there is a way that your addiction kept you from participating in life, and—"

"And now you think this is."

"Yeah, I do. I think that your playing outside the rules has more to do with hiding on the sidelines," she said. "And you're outgrowing it."

I knew it was more complicated than that, and also that she was right. But in getting clean, I had needed death as an alternative to prompt my decision. I had no such incentive here. I couldn't imagine willfully stopping and had no idea what was on the other side of it if I did. So I got on my knees and prayed every morning for an acceptance letter from one of those five schools.

All five rejected me.

"Congratulations!" Jeremiah, my new client, reached across the table and squeezed my hand, though we had only known each other for the length of the current meal. "Sarah Lawrence is a fabulous school! You'll do so well!" He returned to his salmon fillet with gusto. We sat around the corner from his Bond Street loft at a restaurant where the entrées ranged above $100 and the waiters looked like soap stars.

A sober friend had given me Jeremiah's e-mail after learning that he was looking for someone to dominate his girlfriend. Lean and gray, Jeremiah was a millionaire record executive with the overzealous spirit of a dad trying too hard to be cool for the kids. He was old enough to sound ridiculous using adjectives like "fierce" and powerful enough that no one ever told him so.

"I'm gonna order some more wine," he announced. "Is that okay with you? I know that you don't drink and everything. . . ." He trailed off, waving the waiter to our table as I nodded. The affectation, though embarrassing, made Jeremiah easy to talk with. I could see behind it traces of the weary, shrewd man he concealed.

"So," I said, wanting to get to the point before he started drinking and talking.

"So," he repeated, theatrically arching his eyebrows and then laughing. "I like that! A woman who gets to the point." I gave him a big smile, knowing that people with that much money know not to get hustled and that I needed to be canny in my delivery, to nail the right combination of getting-to-the-pointedness and solicitation. He tucked a hunk of fish into his mouth and smiled back at me around his chewing. I sipped my water and waited for him to swallow before speaking.

"So you have a girlfriend?" I asked. "She's lovely, I assume."

"More than lovely." He leaned in, resting his elbows on the table. "And very naughty." I flinched inside, my own weariness sinking in as my endive salad hit my stomach.

"Interesting . . ."

"But here's the thing." His voice cleared, and I knew we were going to talk business. "She can't know that this is a business arrangement."

"Sure, we'll sort that out beforehand."

"I'll slip an envelope into your purse when she's out of the room."

"Perfect."

"There's another thing." He smirked coyly at me, but his eyes were direct. "You're a lesbian."

"Okay."

"She's very jealous, and it wouldn't work any other way. So don't come in any professional-looking outfit, or bring too much equipment, all right?"

"Got it. I am your lesbian buddy who simply wants to come over and spank your girlfriend."

"Exactly." He smiled at me, leaned back in his chair, and lifted his glass.


Eva was a beauty. When I stepped out of the elevator into Jeremiah's living room she hung back, shyly clutching a wineglass. She was dark haired and curvy, and her body had the languidity of those who have borne children, still slender but with skin that moved, was draped more loosely over bones than that of the very young. They'd already had dinner and a bottle that cost more than my monthly rent. I smiled at her with what I hoped was the right combination of a girlish entreaty for friendship and assured desire. I knew how to seduce men and engender quick intimacy with women, but this was more complicated than either. Not only did I have to accomplish both with her, but I also had to seduce Jeremiah without appearing to.

My palms had gotten sweaty in the elevator, considering the complexity of this task. The cockiness I had felt picking my way through the cobblestones of Bond Street in my designer heels had quickly drained when I faced his door. Walking toward the posh address, I had felt excitement. It tugged, umbilical, on an old pleasure, a swaggering childish exhilaration, like that I'd felt reading in the corner of the bookstore as a kid. I was living that illicit fantasy; I was beautiful, calculated, and adept—a Chandler seductress. It felt simple, powerful. But its dimensions, borrowed from some childhood longing, were limited; there was no room for my fear, the context of my emotional past, my awareness of humanity beyond romance. When these elements entered, the fantasy began to collapse.

When I tried to lie outside of work, I now failed miserably. I had mostly stopped trying. My fear and hope was that this inability would eventually carry into my sessions, eliminating the need to choose whether I did it or not, eliminating my ability to do it at all. As much as I privately hoped this would happen, I didn't look forward to the session in which it first did. *Let it not be this one*, I prayed before every session, and doubly hard before this one with Jeremiah.

Once I began, though, the performance was usually intuitive, much easier in practice than projection. Like any skill, the idea of managing the individual parts was overwhelming, but the doing was habitual, depending more on motor memory than conscious thought. This session would be like that, too, I told myself. I'd always hoped for more female clients at the dungeon.

Working with Eva *was* different from working with my male clients, partly because of her femaleness and partly because she wasn't really a client. She made me nervous, similar to the way clients close to my own age did. I was afraid that she would see through me. Women were as easily duped as men in their desire; that I knew. But did she have desire? Other than that to please Jeremiah, I wasn't sure.

I kissed her. I had never kissed a client before. They asked, sure. But I never did. They always knew (even when they pretended not to) that it was a business relationship. If I were really her boyfriend's lesbian friend who wanted to spank her, it would seem, at the very least, odd if I didn't want to kiss her. Probably she would be offended. Ditto for the rubber gloves. I hadn't thought of this before I got there. After I led her to the bedroom and blindfolded her, took off both of our shirts, and began wondering what to say that wouldn't sound false, she leaned in and kissed me. She missed the mark somewhat because of the blindfold and left a sticky smear of lipstick half on my mouth, half on my cheek. By the time she leaned back in, I still hadn't thought of a believable reason not to, and so I kissed her back. I felt a fleeting flash of disgust but suppressed it, concentrating on what to do next. Under her jeans she wore black lace panties tied at the sides with pink ribbon, obviously expensive and new.

When I had my entire hand inside of her and Jeremiah was masturbating beside us on the bed, murmuring encouragement, I realized that I was working a lot harder than usual. *Look how elastic her cervix is*, I told myself, trying to summon the clinical anthropologist, to remember how exciting it was to be working with a woman— *a baby's head is actually bigger than your fist.* I did my perspective trick, pulling away from the present to look at it objectively, as a stranger would, or a younger version of myself. It wasn't working. Even from that distance it didn't seem wild or glamorous or shocking; it seemed grotesque. It was Jeremiah, I thought. If only he would shut up. But when I imagined him gone, the scene became even scarier. His presence provided a buffer between her and me, and whatever I feared there.

Here was the thing: I wasn't buying it. All her mewling and writhing wasn't convincing me; I thought she was faking it. Here was an intelligent, experienced, successful woman, and she was going to believe mine and Jeremiah's bogus story? Some mysterious lesbian shows up with a bag of rope, fists you, and goes happily on her way? It sounded ridiculous. I knew that experience skewed my perspective. None of the women I knew, lesbian or otherwise, would be interested in doing this for free. I told myself that probably she didn't know the kind of women I did and could imagine that such a lesbian was out there being friends with her millionaire boyfriend. Still, my intuition told me otherwise.

Sometimes, back when I was a pot smoker, this awful thing would happen. I would be in a social situation, a party, dinner, or just hanging out with friends, and suddenly all of the embedded social dynamics would be exposed to me, like a sheet stripped off of a stained mattress. All the unspoken desires, motives, resentments, and insecurities of everyone in the room would be revealed, on their faces, in their movements and words, emanating from them like body heat. I would tell myself that I was just paranoid, but I wasn't; I knew that what I was seeing was real and was always there, and it filled me with terrible sorrow. Everyone was so afraid, so needy. My session with Jeremiah and Eva had an element of that. I didn't know how Jeremiah felt at that moment, but the fact that he had gone to such lengths, felt the need to go to such lengths, to feel desire, well, it suggested desperation of some kind.

Eva and I were performing for Jeremiah. We also performed for each other. I was on to her, and I think what frightened me was the prospect that she might have been on to me. The truth hovered between us, as we moaned and whispered not of lust or pleasure but of what? Our desire for what? We did share something and could not avail ourselves of the comfort, could not even look into each other's eyes for fear of seeing ourselves. What did that make us? It made me feel like howling with sorrow.

After her yowling climax, Jeremiah gestured me to the side and climbed on top of Eva. I watched his bobbing behind, a buoy glowing in the dark of the bedroom, for the two minutes it took for him to orgasm. His, I believed, was genuine.

As Jeremiah lay stretched out on his bed, grinning, Eva put on an oversize T-shirt of his and sat cross-legged beside him, not meeting my eyes. I sat around with them, chatting about how great it had been for as long as seemed necessary, and then left. I had been there approximately one hour. After changing into my sneakers in the elevator, I felt around my purse for the envelope. Tucked between two books, it was slim, decorated with the bank's insignia. Inside was $1,500, in crisp hundred-dollar notes.

By now, Autumn had moved in with her boyfriend and I lived in a loft with two other sober girlfriends. When Jeremiah e-mailed me a month later, asking if I was free that weekend, I turned to them for advice. I was hoping, I think, for permission to say no. They knew all about Jeremiah already; I had briefed them in comic installments. This presented the problem; no one could give me accurate advice, because no one knew the whole truth. It had been the same with my addiction. The stories I told about the dungeon were carefully slanted. People loved them; they were *funny*. The reasons why I wanted someone to tell me to stop I kept hidden, and so no one did. In my telling, the job became alternately gross, hilarious, tedious, sexy, glamorous, and shocking. It depended if I was trying to befriend or seduce you. I had become an expert at discerning immediately what a person's response would be and how to play it up or down. No one heard about the real disgust, pleasure, or sexuality my job involved. I wouldn't have known how to describe those aspects if I wanted to.

And so when I went to my roommate and expressed my reluctance, she looked at me in disbelief.

"Yeah, he sounds really annoying. But fifteen hundred dollars? Come on. I would do it if I could." What she meant was if she had the opportunity. At this point, I was starting to know better. When I began using hard drugs, I thought that if everyone knew how good it felt, they would do the same. I figured it was only social stigma and cowardice that kept other people from going to the lengths that I did. But I could not imagine my roommate going through with what I knew that session entailed.

Fifteen hundred dollars. For an hour's work. It sounded amazing, when you didn't know what the work meant, or when you pretended not to.

# 31

I WAS ENROLLED in Sarah Lawrence's insurance plan. When I called Health Services and requested a referral for a therapist whose fee my insurance would cover, they said I would have to make an appointment with someone on staff first.

"I'd rather not, if possible," I told the friendly receptionist.

"I'm afraid it's required."

"I'm afraid that I need someone with more experience. Off campus."

"It's just the one appointment, miss, and our staff is *very* experienced." Most of the warmth had left her tone. "When would you like to come in?"

It was uncharacteristic of me to be so confrontational. My fear of conflict in everyday life (however ironic) extended even to phone conversations with strangers. I was much more the be-friendly-and-accommodating-now-and-fume-later type. In this case, though, I was filled with panic at the prospect of saying aloud what I planned to say, to some idealistic ignoramus in a room only yards away from my professors' offices. It wasn't what I had imagined.

Not that I had imagined ever telling anyone the exact details of my sessions. Spilling my secrets was a last resort. Still unsure if I wanted to quit completely, I had tried stopping, to see if I could. It was harder than I'd hoped.

Most of my private sessions were made by e-mail at this point. My clients would contact me to discuss a session, and then I would either book a private space or have them call the dungeon to make an official appointment on one of my two shifts there. All I had to do was not check that e-mail account. I called in sick to Mistress X's and committed to no sessions for one week. It would be easy, I thought, a vacation. All I would have to do was my homework. I knew how to *not* do things, after all, didn't I? But I couldn't stop checking that e-mail. I made it the first few days, but my head was crowded with earnest reasons why this was the wrong time to take a break. The holidays were looming; I was still building a private client base, trying to get rid of the Tonys; didn't I promise to get back to Albert about the following week? It wouldn't be cheating if I just wanted to reply to someone and let him know I was off this week; it would be professional courtesy. This logic was good enough, and I ended up doing one session that week and scheduling three for the next. I finished the session anxious, instead of exhilarated; I had failed to uphold my commitment. No, the timing had been bad, and I had *chosen* to reconsider my decision. Who was I letting down anyway? Satisfied with that explanation, I tried again two weeks later, with the same result. When abstaining, I obsessed, and when I gave in, I felt guilty and anxious. The money offered a fleeting comfort.

When I had first begun working with Greta and was only a few weeks off heroin, she made me look up the word "compulsion." I had been arguing with her over the idea of powerlessness. She said I wouldn't stay clean unless I could admit mine. I said that I had survived by my own agency. According to the dictionary, a compulsion was *an irresistible impulse to perform an act that is contrary to one's will.*

"Do you believe in truth?" she asked me.

"Of course."

"How about caring for yourself?"

"Sure."

"And you want to practice these things?"

"Yeah."

"But do you?"

I saw then that I could not even abide by my own beliefs. I had kept getting high long after it stopped being fun, after I began wanting to stop. In order to abide by my craving, I had acted contrary to my beliefs, to what I knew to be true. I had always suspected that I felt capable of anything because I was morally corrupt, or intellectually superior, or both. I discovered that my compulsions were simply stronger than my will. Never mind taking care of myself, I had tried everything within my power to stop shooting heroin and cocaine into my body. Telling the whole truth had been the only thing that worked.

"But why?" Dylan asked when I broke up with him. We fought more days than we didn't, but I had still known that it would catch him off guard.

"I just don't think we can change fast enough to love each other well."

He squinted at the pillow in his hands.

"We haven't been very good at it for a while," I said.

True as this was, I had other reasons. I wanted to take a clearer look at my job, and in order to do that I needed to disentangle from his vision of me—and all the omissions in his version of what I did. I wanted a clean palette. I had a list of other reasons for leaving him, including his chronic sickness—which I, ever the psychotherapist's daughter, considered a somatic manifestation of his anger at his parents. Also, his inability to express verbal affection. And then my general feeling of resentment and malaise in the relationship. I didn't actually count among them the confusion of my desire to get honest. I couldn't admit then that I resented his tolerance of my job. I didn't consider how my own behavior had damaged the integrity of our relationship, and underestimated the corrosive power of what I kept from him. I don't think we ever could have recovered. I had chosen him partly *because* he would cosign what I did, like the painter had, and my parents, and everyone else I told my half-truths to. In a way, Dylan and I were perfect for each other but also doomed: in our silence we simultaneously protected and betrayed each other.

The counselor at school was probably five years older than me. I had become nauseous a few hours prior to my appointment. I felt like a defiant child walking into the Health Services office. The counselor looked nice, her face studiously free of suggestion or judgment. It occurred to me, looking at her well-meaning face, that she would pity me for what I did. I wasn't used to telling anyone about my job who wouldn't be impressed by it, find it shocking in a *good* way. I felt angry then, at her, for that pity.

"I'm Megan." She smiled. "What's been going on?"

"I torture people for money and I can't stop," I said, wanting to punish her for my shame.

They referred me to a woman whose office was on Fifth Avenue, just west of Union Square. Dressed conservatively—as I was most days by this time—in jeans and a turtleneck sweater, I exchanged covert once-overs with the other woman in the waiting room and took that same old pleasure in her likely misconception. I probably looked as if I worked for a magazine, a publisher, a designer. She did. She probably assumed I was just like her: same cool job, boyfriend, sadness. When a man in a jacket opened the door and smiled at her, she followed him out into the hallway. I wondered if

I shouldn't have asked for a referral to see a male therapist. That would have been less intimidating. I would probably have been feeling excitement rather than dread at that moment. Which is why I knew that a male therapist would have been useless. I knew a lot about myself in fact, and when my own therapist led me into her cozy office overlooking 16th Street, I proceeded to inform her of it for the next thirty minutes. I needed her to know exactly how knowledgeable I was.

"You should know that I've been to a number of therapists in the past," I told her. "My mother is a therapist. I have all that vocabulary; I practically learned to read on *Codependence No More*, *Healing the Ties That Bind*, *The Road Less Traveled*, all that stuff." She only smiled at me, nodding encouragingly. "And I'm sober. I've been clean and sober in AA for two years now. So I've got all that information, too, about addiction, and spirituality. I'm a good person now. I sponsor people. I have a lot of self-knowledge. I pretty much know how to change; I mean, I *am* changing. There are just a few things I can't seem to stop doing. I mean, I *get* them; I just don't know how to stop. That relationship between knowing and changing, I mean, applying my knowledge to my actions, it's always been hard for me."

"Okay," she said.

I heard my own voice as I spoke, and it sounded false. I sounded desperate, defensive, like I was trying to prove something. I sounded like someone who was trying to sound like she was fine. But that was what I had always done. The difference was that I didn't want to hustle this woman; I actually wanted her help. So why couldn't I sound honest? I sounded like a *kid*, all trembling bravado. It was pathetic, but I couldn't stop. I kept trying to emphasize how ready I was to change, to accept help, to find a solution; I kept trying to get the tone right, to sound sincere and present. My effort only made it worse, only made me sound more desperate to convince her of something I feared wasn't true. Distressed, I finally shut up. We stared at each other.

"I sound like I'm trying to convince you of something," I said.

"Yes, you do."

"I don't know why. I'm really trying to be honest. I just think there is a lot you should know."

"Why don't you just tell me why you are here?"

"I want to stop being a dominatrix. I mean, I think I want to stop. I want to be *able* to stop."

"What is a dominatrix?"

I gaped at her. Of course, my perspective was also skewed by my own experience in this regard. I wouldn't have expected her to know what a roman shower was, although it was quotidian vocabulary to me, but I still found it hard to believe that there was a person in New York City who didn't know what a dominatrix was. There were beer commercials featuring dommes and entire fashion lines derived from our costumes; Madison Avenue featured a Diesel Jeans billboard advertising women with whips, for God's sake! But she didn't. So I had to describe it for her. This was so much harder and more humiliating than I ever would have imagined. I had always enjoyed shocking people, having the privileged information. She wasn't shocked, though, not visibly. She just listened. She listened to me describe a job that entailed acting out the sexual fantasies of men who want to be tortured by women and dressed in their clothes; who want to relive the trauma their mothers inflicted upon them with enemas, high-heeled shoes, paddles, and verbal abuse. I explained how we all had to file in to meet new clients and wait for them to choose whom they wanted to pinch their nipples or coo obscenities in their ear. It did not sound glamorous. It did not sound tough, or cool, or sexy. It sounded humiliating. She didn't react at all. All these judgments welled up in *me*, as I spoke. If I had been eavesdropping on our conversation, I would have judged my words the way I did other dommes': as the misguided rationalizations of someone in bondage to her sex issues, man issues, daddy issues, trauma history, whatever. "It's really just one of the few well-paid acting gigs in this city," I told her, having delivered that line hundreds of times. I gave her all the neat and clever explanations that I had in stock. They sounded as flimsy and transparent as the insults I had shouted in my first domme session.

In meetings I spoke a lot about perspective, about context. It was important to actively seek out things that shifted your perspective, I often said; *it's all about context*. Well, taken out of context, my job became a wholly different beast. My perspective shifted so violently, the bookshelf might have spun around, transporting me from a library to a bat cave. Glamorous didn't exist in her office. There was no cool, no badass, no invincible. There was only real and unreal, and what I believed didn't necessarily have anything to do with it. I had had many moments—on acid, or just heightened intimacy with a best friend or a lover—when I could see this. I knew, on some basic level, that glamorous and cool and tough didn't exist, just like I knew that beauty was on the inside and that love was the solution to everything and that everything was part of one giant whole, but *really*. I had always had the ability to ignore that knowledge and enjoy fashion magazines, seducing people, and my personal triumphs. At that moment I couldn't. It was very nearly the opposite of that feeling I chased in the dungeons, bedrooms, highways, and hotel rooms that had carried me outside of myself and into the yawning infinity of power and weightlessness. It was not falling, or flying, or evaporating into a dew of consciousness; it was being pinned to one spot, one self, one definition of something that resisted spin, philosophizing, or romance.

When I walked out of there, I didn't know how I felt. It was easy enough to leave our conversation in her office and go on about my usual business. Later on, I felt similar to how I had when I began drinking wheatgrass and going jogging just before getting high. The sense of having done something good for myself increased my license to do what I suspected might not be so good. I was *working on it*.

But I kept working on it. I stopped trying to quit the dungeon and went about my usual routine. Every week I returned to that office overlooking 16th Street and went through the painstaking process of describing my work to someone for whom it didn't connote status, romance, or power.

# 32

WHEN I APPLIED for an extra student loan, I wasn't thinking any further ahead than that. I was curious what it would be like to subtract the financial factor. Perhaps if I relieved that pressure I would be able to see more clearly. Money obscured things, I knew, but never how much.

When the loan was approved, I didn't do anything. I went to class, work, meetings, and therapy as usual for two weeks. Work got harder, though. Fiona was angry at all the sessions I wasn't taking. "Tell him I'm booked," I said, "tell him I went home sick," as if my clients were boyfriends I didn't have the heart to dump. I had disturbing moments of objectivity while working, flashes of disgust and anxiety as my sessions momentarily transformed, the way pornography does after orgasm—its emptiness and desperation no longer obscured by desire.

The last client I ever saw at the dungeon was Jack. This time, instead of sorority girl Margie, he wanted to be "Little Margie," her child incarnation. We had conducted this scene many times before. Instead of sorority girls, Little Margie's antagonist was, of course,

Mean Mommy. Mean Mommy role-plays had always made for some of my favorite sessions, as soon as I found the confidence to pull them off. Jack's topping from the bottom annoyed me, but it had improved since I stopped capitulating to it so much. When Jack pulled a crumpled sheet of paper from his pocket and started to brief me on the intricacies of the scene, I gritted my teeth; he didn't like the sneering to begin *before* the scene did, in keeping with the typical topper from the bottom. I gently tugged the paper from his hands.

"I know what the scene is, Jack. We've done it before."

"Yes, but I, I made some changes to the, the original script? I'd really like you to incorporate a more *sadistic* tone of voice when you find me in the bathroom, and if you could pull my panties down *first*, before my—"

I reached out my finger, as if to press it against his lips, but stopped short.

"Shh! I will look this over," I shook the limp paper, "and be sure to work in any revisions. Okay?"

"Well, okay. If you could just—"

"Good-bye, Jack. I'll be back in five. You should be changed by then." I quickly stepped out of the Red Room and closed the door behind me. Alone in the dim hallway, I sighed long, feeling my shoulders slump. An hour with him was going to ruin my day; I could already tell. My process of slipping in and out of character had only been getting messier. My clients couldn't usually tell, but from the inside the veil of my persona had grown opaque; I could see too much through it. I felt too awake. Many sessions had started to feel like surgery without adequate anesthesia. Walking to the dressing room to put on my business suit, I felt tired, the kind of tired that sleep or a vacation wouldn't remedy.

The scene began with me getting home from work. I strode into the room, sighed theatrically, and then very slowly removed my stockings. Little Margie hid behind the bathroom door, spying on me. As I unclipped my garter, I could hear him wheezing and fidgeting and shivering with a wave of disgust.

Then I answered the phone.

"Hello? Oh, hello, Ms. Jenson, I hope everything is all right at school. Has Margie been behaving herself?" I paused to allow for the fictional teacher to respond. "You don't say." My tone darkened. "Well, rest assured I'll take great pains to make sure that this doesn't happen again." I glowered in the general direction of the bathroom. "Yes, well, thank you, Ms. Jenson. Bye-bye now." I slammed the phone down, and then the scene really got rolling.

Ms. Jenson usually informed me that Little Margie had been caught touching herself in the girls' room. With this information, I stormed the bathroom and dragged Little Margie out by the hair of her wig (not an easy thing to accomplish). Berating her all the way, I forced her to show me exactly what she had been caught doing in the girls' room. Following this humiliation, I beat her with a riding crop. The corporal punishment part of the scene always segued into the finale, wherein I decided to "teach her a real lesson." Using a giant pink dildo, I gave Little Margie a taste of what she had coming to her.

It should have been a cakewalk.

Objectively, it was a disturbing scene. Early on, twisted sessions like this had given me a kind of satisfaction; during them I felt I most deeply plumbed the anthropological depths of my job. Imagine my own depths, to have witnessed, *participated* in, such perversions! Experiencing the reality of obsessions like this made me feel unique, and powerful for having faced their hideousness. They rarely horrified me. After the first year, repetition robbed them of all novelty and they became, while still among my favorites, rote and unmemorable. Jack's fantasy was unexceptional, a stock role-play.

In this session with him, however, I felt smothered. Not explicitly horrified but as if his presence, the story we spun, and even the sound of my own voice were a sealed surface under which I was being snuffed out.

When the session ended, I walked Jack out and returned to the dressing room. My shift ended in half an hour. I peeled off my pencil skirt and pulled on my jeans. Padding down the hallway in bare feet, I opened the supply closet where the huge yellow depository for all our session trash was kept. Under the familiar buzz of the overhead light, I inhaled that old sickening smell of Lysol and latex and pulled a couple of garbage bags from the box on the shelf.

As I transferred the contents of my locker into the bags, my heart began pounding. I decided to leave a few items: pairs of torn stockings, all the shoes that hurt to stand in, hot pants with shot elastic, an ugly silk negligee. I didn't want to look like I was cleaning the locker out, not to mention how difficult it was already going to be to carry just the quality stuff. I had thousands of dollars' worth in clothes, shoes, lingerie, uniforms, wigs, and equipment.

"What are you doing Justine?" asked Camille, who was on the couch painting her toenails.

"I have a photo shoot this weekend." I tried not to visibly hurry and suppressed the insane fear that someone would try to prevent me from leaving. No one did. In the elevator I clutched those garbage bags, their necks sweaty from my nervous hands, and eyed the camera in the corner. It was just before five on a spring afternoon with summer heat. I burst out onto the sidewalk into a stream of tourists and rush-hour commuters. Weaving my way down the block toward the subway, I found myself grinning like a kid on a homeward school bus, infected with the smell of pollen and freedom.

"I quit!" I adjusted the phone against my ear and waited for my mother to respond.

"That's great," she said, hesitantly. I could picture her expression exactly, the hesitation drawn in her delicate features. "That's what you wanted, right?"

"Yeah, for a while now, I—" I stopped myself. "Yeah, I've been ready to leave for a while." Talking with her about it never stopped being difficult, even with news I knew she wanted to hear. I always felt myself scraping up against something painful and backed out of conversations on the topic. She never seemed interested in prolonging them, either. There was less unspoken between us than there had been in a long time, and so it stood out, the rawness, our unreadiness to reveal how we felt about it, and to hear each other.

I knew she underestimated the extent of my using—I let her—but our relationship had changed since I'd gotten sober. On the surface, our interactions remained much the same, but I was less afraid of her, of what she'd see in me, or not see. I began to realize how much more *interesting* relationships became when they weren't so restricted by omissions and half-truths, though harder in some ways. But it didn't feel hard anymore, to keep up with our friendship; I didn't have to work so hard to modulate what information I leaked. It's difficult to feel known when you hide so much; advice becomes meaningless; assumptions about your identity or character, unbelievable. For a long time, our relationship had been haunted by the sadness I felt in her believing that she fully knew me and my knowing that she didn't. The more I revealed, the more I could breathe.

"I'm really happy for you," she said, and I knew she meant it.

I've never quit anything all at once, though, and I didn't this. I kept seeing my private clients: Albert, Tony, Billy, Jeremiah, and a few others. After a few weeks, I had whittled it down to Jeremiah and Tony. The money made it easy to hang on to Jeremiah, and Tony was simply more persistent than the others; he refused to accept my retirement. He called and e-mailed multiple times per week. For every ten or twenty of his entreaties I accepted one. I quit him first. The sense of humiliation that followed his sessions lasted longer than the sticky slicks of lube on my arms and legs; it had only increased over time, and exponentially since I'd quit the dungeon.

I closed my work e-mail account. Mistressjustine@gmail.com no longer existed, and I hoped Tony himself would disappear so easily. He didn't. When I first began taking private sessions, I had naïvely given my phone number to a few of those first clients, including Tony. When his e-mails began bouncing back, he started calling. I kept all my clients in my phone book under "S," for "Slave" Albert, "Slave" Jeremiah, "Slave" Tony. The appearance of his name on that little screen soon prompted the same stomach lurch that my old drug dealer's number had when I first got clean. The dealer stopped calling eventually, I told myself, and Tony would, too.

He probably would have been more inclined to stop calling if I didn't pick up every once in while. It became a cycle that mimicked my early sobriety in a number of ways. When I got clean, it was partly due to a system of postponement; I would pick a day, next Thursday, say, and plan on getting high that day. When Thursday rolled around, I would get scared, go to a meeting, and decide on another day to get high. In this way, I made appointments with Tony for a week or two in advance, feeling confident that I would be able to handle it. I just needed some extra cash to feel financially secure, I thought. As the day of our appointment neared, my anxiety would loom, a mountain on the horizon that I was speeding toward. My anxiety never felt directly related to the session; like the melancholy of my childhood, it would seep into everything. My schoolwork, meetings, even the industrial Brooklyn landscape would seem waterlogged with dread, all that gray concrete dense with portent, the threat of something terrible: a failure, incurable loneliness and fear.

A day or two before the session, I would call my therapist and leave a frantic message. "Something is wrong!" I'd say to her answering machine, and then insist that she not call me back. I had learned in meetings that inditing fears had a special power. There was clarity on the other side of putting things to words. I still didn't *feel* a connection between my dread and the session, but I had a reference for this sort of dissociation, in lying about being clean, and knew that the two could still be related. So I'd cancel at the last minute, and just like that my dread would leave, a swept cloud cover.

The same process applied to Jeremiah—I became anxious and doubtful in the days leading up to our appointment—though I still went through with it and saw him and Eva every couple months.

"Why is it so hard?" I asked my therapist, hoping for a prescriptive answer, something to *do*. Getting sober required a lot of action: list making, reading, going to meetings, helping people, visiting psych wards and rehabs, little exercises to trick me into looking at myself. I wanted this from her, but she resisted. She never gave homework.

"You're still attached to it. Why do you think? What do you get out of it?"

"I don't know. Money. It's really hard to not have a lot of extra money. I've gotten so used to that."

She looked at me, skeptical.

"I mean, it still feels exciting in some way, getting dressed up and going over to that fancy apartment, leaving with all that money. A part of me still feels satisfied, on a kind of power trip, when it's over."

"But during?"

"During, I pretty much am waiting for it to be over. With those two anyway."

"The way you have described it, it sounds more uncomfortable than that."

"Yeah, it's terrible. It didn't used to be, though."

"You are *feeling* more."

"Yeah. I mean I felt things before, not like this. I felt strong. And sexy."

"Feeling powerful made you feel sexy?"

"Yes! Of course it did. Everyone likes to feel powerful, don't they? I mean, wouldn't everyone like to feel more powerful?" My question was meant rhetorically.

"I don't necessarily think so."

"Really?"

"Really."

# 33

WHEN I STOPPED COMPLETELY, I didn't crave sessions the way I had drugs, but my subconscious remained obviously preoccupied with them. I dreamt about domming every night, the way I had about drugs when I first got clean. I craved sessions in dreams, and in dreams they were more vividly sexual and more grotesque than I remembered them. In my dreams, the dungeon's gilded mirrors and wall sconces were replaced by soiled basements and condemned motel rooms, my shame translated into literal filth and disintegration.

Leaving the dungeon left a hole in my life. I struggled with the few sessions I still took and never intended to set foot in that place again, but I had gotten used to the experience of being *wanted*. Over my three years there, I had come to rely on the daily dose of male attention. Never in my life had I needed it less than when I worked at the dungeon—my craving to be desired was as close to satisfied as it had ever been, though it was an empty kind of full, a numb satisfaction. Getting hit on by men on the street didn't quite compare to having them pay to be in the same room as me. I decided to join an online dating site. My profile was a finely cut gem. I honed exactly the right spectrum of authors (Cormac McCarthy to Daniel Clowes), musicians (Coltrane to Aesop Rock), and interests (writing to bondage). After the initial few dates, I realized how many I might need to go on before I met someone eligible. I learned to forgo the lengthy e-mail-courtship process in favor of a short interview over coffee. I began scheduling fifteen-minute "dates" between my other activities. After ten or so of these and a great many other correspondences that never made it to a coffee shop, I found someone who interested me.

He was attractive in enough pictures for it to not be a fluke of light and angling, employed by a worthy nonprofit, and had the right taste in all things. There was also some quality beyond the sum of these parts, difficult to pinpoint, that attracted me. He was *good*; my attraction to him didn't have to do with my identity as it related to domming or to my drug history. He was a match for my self that existed apart from those things. I contacted him first—not my standard practice. After reading my immaculate profile, he backed away. "You're into bondage?" he wrote. I explained that I was a dominatrix, sensing the need to downplay this fact. It was part-time, I said, I was really on my way out of the business. "You seem cool, but I just know I couldn't deal with that," he insisted. So I gave him my best lines on it, the ones that showcased my lack of desire and the pathetic nature of my clients. No, no, I assured him, it's not like that. I'm not really into that stuff; it was just a *job*. "Sorry," he said. "Not for me, nothing personal." But nothing was more personal. He must not have understood, I told myself. I just didn't explain it the right way. I found myself rehearsing explanations to him while walking down the street, telling him off in my head as I watched the city through taxi windows. His rejection clung to me, a shadow. That deeper part of me, who existed before and beneath Justine, desired someone who did not want Justine. What did that mean? I changed the wording of my profile, but the sting of his rejection kept me away from dating for a while.

. . .

"Why should I have a special interest in power, in feeling power-ful?" I asked my therapist. "Isn't it simply human to resent the basic powerlessness of our condition? It's a scary thing! I mean, isn't that why people want to believe in God, why faith is useful to us, be-cause it allays the anxiety of our own powerlessness?"

"Sure, I think that's part of it."

"But no, you're saying, I don't just have this because I am a hu-man being."

"No, I don't think so."

"Okay, when I was younger I felt more vulnerable or sensitive than other people did, but doesn't every kid feel that way?"

"I don't think every kid feels that way."

"In any event, I don't feel that way anymore, so sensitive. I mean, look at what I do! Nothing shocks me. Nothing has for a long time, before I ever worked at the dungeon. For all of my adult life I've felt pretty unshockable." I sighed, scanning across the familiar objects on her desk. "Sometimes, when I am witnessing something I know should be shocking, or would be to someone else, I imagine show-ing a glimpse of it to my younger self."

"How do you mean?"

"When I was a kid I used to wish that I could see what my life would be like in my twenties. I'd fantasize that I could flash for-ward to see what I'd look like, who my friends would be, what be-ing a famous writer looked like."

We both laugh.

"So you imagine showing her, that child you, what you see in sessions?"

"Well, not a child really, more of an adolescent." Spoken aloud, this practice suddenly sounded bizarre. "I mean, not just sessions, necessarily. Anything spectacular and shocking in some way."

"You want to shock her. That younger, more sensitive and vul-nerable you."

"No! I mean, I don't know." I frowned. "That sounds terrible."

"Not terrible."

"Then what does it sound like?"

"It sounds like someone who has been so shocked, or disempowered, that she is determined to never let it happen again. It sounds like someone who wants to destroy her innocence, who fears and feels contempt for her innocence."

I sat with that, watching the morning sunlight soak into the rug between us. Her explanation resounded like a long lovely note expanding into the silence that follows it. Unexpected truth does this, and I recognized it immediately, even if I didn't understand it.

"But why?" I heard the note of distress in my voice before I felt it in my chest.

"I'm not sure."

"I know . . . I know that I have the pathology of someone who is, who has been . . . *traumatized* by something. I have known that for a long time. I used to wonder if I blocked out some abuse from my childhood or something. So many of the people I've become close to in my life have been traumatized. I've surrounded myself with addicts and sex workers, for God's sake. Even my addiction itself! It all adds up like an equation, but the answer is wrong. I'm not like them! I wish I was; it would make more sense."

"Not like whom?"

"The women I worked with at the dungeon, my clients, all the best friends I've ever had who confided their abuse and rape stories to me."

"You feel you don't deserve your own experiences, the domming and addiction, because they are a symptom of something you haven't suffered?"

"God, that sounds so reductive. But yeah, I guess I do. The same way I used to feel that I didn't deserve to be an addict—my childhood hadn't been fucked up enough."

"And you've never been traumatized?"

"Not the way I'm talking about, not the kind that alters the course of your life so drastically, that dictates all your future relationships, your self-esteem and everything. Real trauma is like a giant hunk of scar tissue that the rest of your life accommodates, grows around. It changes the shape of you, of everything that happens after it."

"Some people say the same thing of love."

"They do, don't they? I guess love is a kind of trauma. It definitely reshapes you."

"And you've had nothing like that?"

"What, my parents' divorce? My dad's always going away on his ship? My neighbor who used to spit on me at the bus stop? Growing boobs before everyone else in fourth grade? Cry me a river. That's just normal shit. Basically everyone I know is a child of divorce."

"Maybe, but that's relative. There was a time when divorce was rare and the children of divorced parents were hugely pitied for its effect on them."

"So, just because something happens to everyone doesn't mean it doesn't traumatize everyone?"

"No. But I don't like using the word 'traumatize'; it connotes such a negative value. Because what does it really mean? Something painful and shocking that, as you said, alters the course of your life. It is something that changes you."

"Well then, the whole course of human existence is like one endless series of traumas! I find American consumerism painful and shocking both to behold and to participate in, and the corruption of government, not to mention the meat industry!"

She laughed. "Well, all those things do form our lives and identities; we grow to accommodate them in one way or another, be it by conformation or defiance. But different things, and different combinations of things, affect people in different ways."

"Right, as in some people who were molested go on to be serial killers and others just drink or don't communicate well?"

"Sure."

"So do you think I really was a uniquely sensitive and vulnerable kid?"

"Maybe, but that's not what I am implying. I don't think your experiences are comparable to the symptoms of an illness, or brokenness, or *trauma* as you refer to it—like an unrecoverable handicap."

# 34

I HAD PLENTY OF REASONS for breaking up with Dylan that had nothing to do with my job. But all my choices during my years as a domme were influenced by it, by my need to protect it, including my choice of lovers.

In this way, I was at a loss in my search for a new partner. My primary criterion had been abolished, and I hadn't yet replaced it. I no longer needed someone to cosign my work, to not ask questions or get jealous. I didn't know what I needed. At first I resorted to the conventions of my adolescence—unavailability, in its various permutations. Thankfully, that didn't last long. These men felt like clothes I'd outgrown: misfit, tight in the wrong places. There were a few brief swooning crushes, followed by disappointing sexual encounters. Winded and done with avoiding figuring out what I wanted, I went back online.

Hope sprang forth again with Brian, the architect. In pictures he was lovely, with angles odd enough to avoid too closely resembling a movie star. He spoke easily on the telephone—unlike 99 percent of the heterosexual men I'd known—and told me he'd booked a reservation; all I had to do was show up. The restaurant was perfect, as promised, and he was even more uncommonly beautiful in person. *This is what dates are supposed to be like,* I thought as he smiled admiringly at me across the candlelit table and explained the cheese menu. He gave compliments easily and perhaps I was rusty at judging, but they sounded sincere enough. As we bantered over olive oil–drenched bruschetta and tiny saucers of slippery, piquant olives, I thought of Rick. This was different in obvious ways, though I still noted the common denominators: older man, admiring looks, expensive salty food, and a sense of veiled negotiation. Obviously all dates are on some level a negotiation—based on a trade of information and potential interest. I'd known this before, but still it hadn't seemed so calculated, the social mechanics so thinly veiled. Did it seem too careful to me because of my experience? Had the overt business of seduction undressed it of all mystery? Being a dominatrix had required that I examine the intuitive mechanics of seduction, dissect, refine, and execute them in the absence of desire. Had my perception so fundamentally changed, the way a surgeon must see the body differently—less miracle than mechanical? The date was thrilling, but there was an emptiness to it. Perhaps my expectations had been too high. Perhaps I had succeeded at annihilating my innocence in more ways than intended. Nonetheless, I was still hopeful.

We meandered through a dozen small courses for three hours— this being the sort of place whose prices justify any length of stay— our conversation winding easily through childhood, college, favorite books, and the constant evolution of New York, until we had steeped long enough in the tacit sexiness to graduate to more personal topics, such as former relationships, and thus the implication of other proclivities. He wasted no time.

"I believe in being forthright," he said. "My last relationship began as a business arrangement, became a love affair, and graduated to great friendship. She was a professional dominatrix, though we shared that role pretty equally." He gave an earnest smile across the table. "I am really a bottom at heart, though." I bit off the end of a biscotti and smiled back, wondering if he'd still pay for my cab home if he wasn't in it.


"Can you believe it?" I asked my therapist.

"You lost interest when he said that?"

"Of course!"

"Why 'of course'? He doesn't seem like an eligible partner for you?"

I gaped; did she mean to be obtuse?

"He became pathetic to you."

"Yes, he was just another client, in disguise."

"You felt he disguised himself? That the desire to be dominated negated all those positive qualities you'd first seen in him?"

"Yes, I guess so. That fact just overwhelmed everything else: his career, likes and dislikes, looks, intelligence. I mean, I suppose he didn't exactly disguise it. He even said that he believed in being forthright before he told me."

"So why did you suddenly find him pathetic?"

"Because I know how those desires are. They can consume you. My clients, some of my clients, had all that other stuff, too, the social assets, but that desire was the most important one—even if only I knew it—everything else was on some level a cover for that secret."

"What if it wasn't a secret?"

"I don't know; it always was with them. I mean, let's also not forget that these were grown men who wanted to talk in baby voices and wear diapers. It really is pathetic."

"Why?"

"Why? I mean, grow up, man!" I laughed at the carpet. "Besides, isn't there something essentially immature about imbalanced power dynamics? They mimic parent-child relationships, not adult-adult relationships."

"Yes, but does that dynamic have to permeate every aspect of the relationship, for people who desire it sexually?"

"I don't know," I sighed, a little lost and suddenly tired.

"How did he even know to broach the subject?" she asked.

"I mentioned it in my profile. As a precaution really. I said *former* dominatrix. To discourage people who would be too freaked out or turned on by it."

She gave me the look that said she wasn't buying my reasoning. "Maybe you wanted to alert potential suitors about something else."

"What? That that's my main skill set?"

"No."

"Let me guess, you think I've internalized the demoralization of that role and I still think it's all I have to offer. Is that it?"

She chuckled. "No."

"Then what, what am I trying to tell them?" We stared at each other for a few seconds. "Are you suggesting that I'm actually *into* it?" I asked, in honest surprise. Her nod belied how patient she had been with me on this point.

Anyone who has ever had a good therapist knows the feeling when an obvious truth that you have been committed to not seeing is so neatly pointed out to you. You see, even after four consecutive years of participating in dominant and submissive sexual practices, whether for money or not, I was still telling myself that I wasn't *really* into it. It was for the money. I did it for anthropological interests. I did it for the ego trip. I did it to feel desired, to be bad, to rebel. These reasons were true, but they were not my only reasons, and even if they had been, would they not qualify me as sufficiently interested, as *into* it? I still badly needed to feel separate from my clients, to scapegoat them with my own shame and secrecy. It has been my experience that the people I judge most harshly are the ones in whom I recognize some part of myself.

Shame has rarely been a feeling that I've experienced consciously. My shame in my own desire to dominate and submit to men sexually (and otherwise) did not manifest as a dirty or guilty feeling but as a denial of it. I was not like them! And if my date thought I was like *him*, he was wrong and could therefore never know the *real* me, only the charade of the dominatrix. I was judging myself via him. I knew this now and felt the resistance drain from me, though I still argued.

"I don't know. My subconscious waving a flag of surrender to my secret desires? On my online dating profile?"

"But why else even mention it?"

"I mean—it's such a big part of who I am, who I've been."

"Exactly."

After therapy that day I walked through the Union Square farmers' market with the particular lightness of step that I've come to associate with such hard-won revelations. Believing myself apart from the people I dealt with as a domme gave me a sense of safety; it protected me from parts of myself of which—despite my bravery in facing tangible unknowns—I was deeply afraid. Telling the truth to other people, about my job, my addiction, or anything I concealed, had had the same effect, had been followed by the same lightness of step. Honesty brought my double lives together and in doing so made the world a bigger place, in which I could move more freely.

I didn't end up at the dungeon out of financial desperation, nor anthropological curiosity. I was not a tourist but a member of that world, with reasons for being there similar to those of everyone else: an obsession with power, having it and having it taken away from me. These existed long before I ever walked into the dungeon. My experiences at the dungeon were a result of my own desire and pathology, not the other way around. I had been looking, ironically, for a set of boundaries—someone who might give them to me. While I didn't find that at the dungeon, I found a way to give myself permission to admit my own fantasies of powerlessness. Like all truths, it had been there all along, waiting to be seen. There were still questions. Would I continue to want what Larry had given me, in that form? Was its extremity caused by my inability to acknowledge the desire in lesser ways? What traumas had I suffered that led me there? I surmised that it didn't really matter, just as it hadn't mattered why I became an addict, or whether I was born one or not. It just was, and where it would lead now mattered more.

My sessions stopped here. I let them go with relief, like sandbags that had kept me from floating out into sprawling blue of my own desire. My judgments loosened as well; I no longer had to cling so tightly to my superiority over the women I'd worked with, or the men. It felt good to renounce my expertise in judging others' limits; it also made the world bigger, gave it back some of its mystery. Funny, that I had spent so much time trying to shrink the world to a manageable size when that smallness so broke my heart, when the burden of it weighed so heavily. The unknowable *is* frightening and difficult to trust, but what is the alternative?

In the weeks that followed, I filled with a surprising tenderness, for myself, for all of us humans, so much more alike than we thought. I felt the urge to somehow make amends for my ignorance, my small-mindedness. It never ceases to amaze me, the conservatism that those who consider themselves liberal are capable of, myself a case in point. Scary, how easy it was to judge and belittle those around me, even while I shared their experience. In my meetings, people talked about those who were constitutionally incapable of looking at themselves with honesty. Honesty had turned out to be something I grew into. Some truths are too much for some constitutions, though I have seen my constitution change more than once.

But whom did I have to make amends to? Calling old clients was out of the question. It wasn't about apologizing to anyone or even articulating my new awareness to another person; I wanted to simply exist in honesty about my current constitution in the presence of someone who might understand. But who? Autumn was still my closest friend, but I didn't know the particulars of how she and her therapist handled the subject; besides, instinct told me she wasn't the person for this. I needed to call Jacob.

# 35

I PARKED MYSELF on a bench outside the health food market across the street from our warehouse building. We called it the Snatch, partly a play on the actual name, Brooklyn's *Nat*ural, and partly because it snatched so much of our money away, with its monopoly on soy milk and vegan cookies in the industrial wasteland of our neighborhood.

I have always been fetishistic about preparation and the minute circumstances surrounding activities both pleasurable and not. For instance, I could never smoke while dirty (I had to shower first) or while walking a dog. I didn't like to mix pleasure with duty and enjoyed prolonging the anticipation of pleasure. To call Jacob (an experience both pleasurable and anxiety producing), I armed myself with a fresh pack of cigarettes, a five-dollar iced tea, and freshly shaved legs. Late May, and the heat already lubricated the inside of my thighs under my cotton dress. I shifted to separate them and lit a cigarette. I had quit and then begun again after leaving the dungeon. I still spoke to Jacob occasionally. I usually called him. I knew that he couldn't refuse my calls or even articulate why he should. Although I privately knew his guilt over our continued contact was in some way justified, the pang of my own misgiving when I dialed his number was manageable, and whatever still drew me to him I didn't resist.

"Hi!" That stagy quality his voice always had was still there—a symptom I think of his internal reaction to me: a simultaneous push and pull, an urge to give in and to resist, to expose and to hide; his words fell somewhere between these dual urges and thus always seemed a little false.

"Hi!" I smiled for the pause that followed, our mutual knowledge of each other pooling like water into its shallow basin. This was why I still called. "What are you doing?"

"Well, I am sitting on my couch with Barrett."

"Oh!"

Barrett was one of Jacob's three best friends; they had interned together during college, and been close ever since. When I first began dating and Jacob and I still got together for an occasional meal, I had asked him for boyfriend recommendations, half-kidding, knowing it was a little bit cruel, but still hurt that he had abandoned our friendship for a girlfriend. Jacob had recommended Barrett. "He's tall and lanky, just your type," Jacob had said, implicitly self-deprecating. "Give him my number," I'd said, and he had claimed to. Barrett never called, Jacob said because he was going through an ugly divorce and off making documentaries in Latin America to escape it.

"So, what are you guys doing?"

"Talking. Hanging out."

"Yeah?"

"Yup."

"Huh. Why don't you ask him if he wants to go out with me sometime?"

"Why don't you ask him yourself?"

I'm not certain what prompted me to do this, and I didn't even wonder then. Historically, this was the spastic approach I usually took when it came to matters of dating and sex; many of my first kisses were initiated by a non sequitur "wanna make out?" My prospects usually interpreted it as confidence or caprice, which I encouraged, though it was born more from anxiety.

There was a muffled scraping as Jacob passed the phone to Barrett.

"Hello?" There was nervous laughter in his voice, and excitement tickled my diaphragm.

"Barrett?"

"Yes?"

"I was wondering if you wanted to go on a date with me."

I hid behind what little irony this phrase offered; the formality of proper dates was an alien, old-fashioned concept to me and, I assumed, to the rest of my generation.

"Ah, sure." I could hear his smile mirror my own.

"Well, good."

"How about this Friday?" he suggested, and I felt the subtle shift in power between us, his delicately grappling for it. It reminded me of some pre-session consultations, but not in an unpleasant way, as the dynamic with Brian the architect had.

"This Friday, the first of June. Sounds good."

"Okay, I'll call you later this week about the details?"

"I'll talk to you then."

"Okay, I'm going to put Jacob back on now."

"Okay. Bye."

"Bye." The phone shuffled between them again.

"Wow. You don't waste any time, huh?" Jacob was laughing, but his tone had a bitter edge.

"I guess not." I suddenly felt sheepish. "I should let you go."

"Yeah, another time."

"Sure, I'll call you."


Barrett and I met at a vegetarian place outside Washington Square. Though we'd never exchanged photographs (but he'd seen one of mine, in full nurse costume), I recognized him immediately against the brick wall beside the entrance. Lean and long-eyelashed, he tugged his earphones out and smiled at me.

"Hi."

"Hi." We kept smiling at each other and awkwardly shook hands. How do you greet a blind date?

Being a regular, I knew the menu by heart, and suggested the most benign incarnation of pseudochicken. When the apathetic tattooed waiter wandered over I ordered for both Barrett and me. He adjusted his legs under the tiny table. We took turns sharing hunks of information about ourselves until the food arrived. He grew up in Westchester, went to NYU, and just got back from a three-month stint in Mexico, following the Zapatistas around with a video camera.

I talked about writing and sobriety, my family a little. When the food came, Barrett and I ate quickly, sharing bites, half-covering our mouths as we chewed. Eating feels surprisingly vulnerable in situations like this; you are trying to present yourself as fairly immaculate, and feeding is so animal. For me, hunger is a naked state, a symbol of innate need, and desire. The height of vulnerability to me, then and now, is the expression of need and desire. My dependence on being a dominatrix was partly due to the power I felt in my lack of desire, relative to the need of my clients. I'd unearthed my own need beneath that craving for desirelessness and power, but the impulse to reach for the safety of that emptiness was a long time going.

Chemistry is funny. When it's not there, I am never sure and often try to convince myself that it might be. But its presence makes that effort laughable. I'd learned not to wholly trust my instincts, especially when it came to attractions. The craving to get out of my head, out of reality, muddied desire. The knowledge that my desires often hid deeper, truer ones confused things further. Trying to figure it out didn't work. I'd learned to ask for help, to run things by people not influenced by the rationalization machine in my head, the wily, default escapist. But being *in* it, that chemistry, doesn't make you worry about what it means; that's for later.

After paying the check, Barrett and I stood under the awning over the restaurant's entrance and smoked. Dinner had only taken an hour, and I tried to figure out the best way to prolong our date. Then the sky opened up. Torrents of rain pounded the awning above us, and pedestrians ran, shrieking, soaked magazines clutched over their heads. Barrett and I stood close, our shoulders wet, in a tiny room with walls of water. Ludicrously sexy.

"It's early," I said, our bodies so close I could smell his shampoo.

"Yup."

"Do you want to come back to my place and watch a movie?"

"Uh, sure."

"Okay. Good." More smiling.

With subdued giddiness and wet hair we browsed the DVD rental/coffee shop next to the Snatch, cautiously commenting on things we'd already seen and had confident things to say about. In the beginning, there is such a hurry to leak identifying information but also to please and impress; every subject and activity is a nervous opportunity. We settled on the newest Terrence Malick: *The New World*. The symbolism didn't occur to me then, though I sheepishly realize it now.

Before heading back up to my loft, we smoked a cigarette on the loading dock beside my building's door. Swinging our legs, we watched the rain again pelt the parked cars and running bodies so hard that it bounced back off of them in halos.

"So, is it weird for you how we've met?" I asked, in a hurry to get the words out but consciously slowing myself down.

"Well, I thought it might be. Before, I mean. But you aren't what I expected."

"I don't act like a dominatrix?"

"Ha-ha. No, you don't. I mean, you don't act like I would guess someone who used to be a dominatrix would act, if that makes any sense."

"Sure, no, if I had never been one, I probably would be skeptical about going on a date with one. I mean, I wouldn't think they'd necessarily be like me, if I can know with any accuracy what that is." *Ugh.*

"Yeah, you seem really real. And no offense, but I would expect someone like that to be more affected or something."

"Yeah, well, they can be." I resisted the urge to explain that I was different, not really into it. "Is it weird that I was *Jacob's* dominatrix?"

"Well, yeah. But I haven't been thinking about it the whole evening, or picturing anything freaky, like I was afraid of doing."

I laughed. "Well, that's good."

"Yeah."

It was weird, but not too weird to go ahead with. It would be now. In fact, if the opportunity presented itself today, I wouldn't go on the date. Whether Jacob was in a happy relationship now or not, knowing his former feelings for me and the nature of our former relationship would prohibit me from going there. I'm not sure what to make of that, as I can't imagine my life today if my scruples had been then what they are now. But then, would they be what they are now without Barrett's influence? It's unlikely.


We made it about fifteen minutes into the movie before we kissed. It was so easy! That kind of kissing is what it is: like stepping into a sun-warmed pond at dusk. I'll forgo further explanation; if you know what it's like, you know, and if you don't, well, I hope you someday do.

We kissed for two hours. Eventually, I led him into my bedroom and pulled off both of our shirts. He stopped me.

"This might sound weird; it's not typical guy response." I froze, suddenly awkward. "I mean, if I didn't feel the way I do with you I would be all for it, but I kind of think maybe it would be good to wait. I've rushed into sex, and had it be a mistake." He shrugged apologetically. "I mean, if it's safe to assume you are experiencing the same date that I am, then I think we will have time."

I was a little flabbergasted and more than a little embarrassed. How could I explain that the idea sounded like a huge relief to me, that I didn't quite understand where the impulse to start taking my clothes off came from? I had had the same experience. I rarely enjoyed first-time sex with partners, largely because I usually did it before I really knew or trusted them. Here was where the difference between what I knew and did remained wide. The shame I felt wash over me was tinged with that hatred of my own innocence. Was I still so green? So unconfident? Had I gone straight out of the extremity of sex work to the innocence of my adolescence? Where was all my self-knowledge? Still, I was relieved.

"Of course. I agree totally." I clutched my T-shirt to my chest and smiled at him. "And yes, I am on the same date you are on."

"I thought so," he said. "I mean, I don't think you can feel like this when it's not reciprocal."

He left at 2:00 A.M. and called me at 11:00 the next morning to schedule our second date.

# 36

For weeks I lived in a low-level state of delirium, which would have been heaven if I trusted myself more. Don't mistake me; it was wonderful, but thrilling with a nervous edge, as if there might have been an unseen cliff's edge just beyond my sight. It *was* different from the beginnings of past relationships, but I couldn't point to exactly how, other than the strength of my feelings. It really felt like falling—my insides swooping downward while thinking of him on the subway, in the supermarket, during classes—the intensity unnerved me; instincts that strong had to be old, right? My newer instincts tended to be the safer ones. Not that that slowed us down at all.

On our second date, he discovered that I didn't back up my computer regularly, only e-mailed myself drafts of my writing occasionally. On our third date, he gave me an external hard drive. I spent that night at his apartment and backed up the contents of my computer the following afternoon. Two days later, my computer crashed, rendering everything inside of it unrecoverable. I took this as a sign in the parlance of a twenty-first-century cupid. We spent nearly every night together for the next month.

Our first fight happened about six weeks after our first date. An ex-girlfriend of mine whom I'd dated as a teenager and had remained friends with ever since was passing through town and needed a place to stay. I didn't think twice about sharing my bed with her. There hadn't been sexual tension between us in a decade, although that wouldn't have stopped me in the past.

Barrett got quiet when I mentioned it, but didn't comment. I fleetingly remembered that Jacob had described him as the jealous type. "Sarah jealous" was his exact phrase. Sarah, Jacob's girlfriend, was one of the reasons I should have stopped calling him when we stopped doing sessions. Not only had it been sketchy moral terrain to be calling a man known to have had unreturned romantic feelings toward me, but also his girlfriend actually forbade our talking. I thought him an idiot for telling her that I had been his dominatrix in the first place; what girlfriend wouldn't have such a reaction? Still, I knew what "Sarah jealous" implied.

An evening a week or so later, Barrett and I were walking through Madison Square Park, an oasis of benches and sculpted foliage in the middle of the busy intersection just north of the Flatiron Building. I commented on his uncharacteristic quiet.

"Something on your mind?"

He sighed heavily. I sensed his reluctance and felt a pang of both fear and excitement. Any kind of disclosure in the beginning is exciting.

"What?"

"I just feel a little weird about your ex sleeping over. In your *bed*."

I paused at this, unsure of my reaction.

"What's to feel weird about? We have been friends for about a hundred times the length of our romantic relationship. I'm not attracted to her at all; there's *nothing* sexual there *at all.*" I understood needing reassurance in such things and was happy to give it.

"Yeah, you said that before, but it still makes me uncomfortable."

Here I started to feel annoyed.

"Well, why?"

"I know I can be kind of conservative or old-fashioned or something about these kinds of things, and I don't want you to feel accused in any way, because I believe you that nothing happened, or could have happened. . . ."

"But?"

"But it's more the appropriateness of her sleeping in your bed."

"You think it's *inappropriate?*"

"Not because you did anything inappropriate, but more in it's relation to me. I mean, I just wouldn't even consider having an ex-girlfriend sleep in my bed, not because I think there would be even a remote possibility of anything happening, but just out of respect to you."

I simmered. How dare he? I could be friends with whomever I wanted and could invite them to sleep wherever I deemed appropriate! I was a feminist, for crying out loud! He had no right to impose his Waspy values on me! He couldn't tell me what was *appropriate!* I prided myself on the level of physical comfort that such boundaries (or lack thereof) implied. I hadn't been raised to fear sexual connotations, I thought, and believed that this confidence suggested a sophistication that transcended the rote adherence to antiquated social mores and manners. In slightly calmer tones, I told him as much.

"Autumn and I share baths together, for God's sake!" I said. This did not relieve him. I had never seen him look that way before. He was *angry.* As righteous as I felt, there was something that scared me in the tightness of his face. Was he going to hit me? Leave me? Had I fallen in love with a crazy, possessive control freak? It did occur to me that had he done the same, I would have been furious; in fact, hearing him reference such a possibility gave me pangs of jealous outrage. "Okay," I said. "Can we just table this for now? I mean, it only worries me because I am friends with a lot of my exes, and not that they will be all sleeping in my bed, but I do talk to them."

"I understand that," he said. "A lot of people do. I can only speak for myself when I say that, for me, it's not appropriate. I've tried to be friends with exes, and there is always some element left over, something I get out of it that is different than other friendships, and that I don't think is fair to the person I am actually dating."

"Well, that makes sense. I just think differently." And we let it go.

To my surprise, as much as I judged him for those statements and had felt judged, my feelings for him seemed to grow instantly stronger. The sex we had that night was our best yet.

"I mean, that's ridiculous, right?"

My therapist smiled.

"No? You don't think it's totally controlling and possessive."

"I don't."

I threw up my hands. "So am I just totally off the map when it comes to appropriate boundaries in relationships, or what?"

She smiled. "No. . . ."

"But what? I must be."

"No, you don't have a great knowledge of those boundaries, but you do have a desire for them."

"Are you talking about sex here? I told you we have totally normal sex—to both of our surprise, actually, I think."

"No, I'm not talking about sex. I think that your desire for strict boundaries in sex, your desire to be dominated, comes partly from a desire for nonsexual boundaries. Emotional boundaries. Just plain old limits."

There it was again—the reverberation of truth, humming like a tuning fork into the silence. I knew she was right.

"You mean that I *wanted* him to tell me it was inappropriate for my ex to sleep in my bed?"

"And for you to take baths with someone other than him."

"That, too? But I said that to calm him down!"

"I think you said that to provoke him."

I sat back in my chair.


When I examined a list of my exes to whom I still spoke, it was obvious that Barrett was right. Those relationships fed my need to be desired, to feel as if I had more than one pot on the stove, just in case. When I was fearful or bored in a relationship, I started calling them, offering subtle encouragements for them to think that maybe someday we could try again. I started fantasizing about them when angry at my current partners. The ex who had slept in my bed didn't fit that description, but what was the difference in relation to Barrett? What a mundane revelation, that there should be certain courtesies extended to your partner out of consideration or as a simple gesture of commitment. And yet it had never occurred to me. It would have occurred to me when appraising someone else's relationship; I could have prescribed behavior for a friend based on such a belief, but I never practiced it myself.

Only when I stopped did I realize how much energy I put forth in seduction. Everyone I met! I wanted everyone I met to be a little bit in love with me. There was magic in the way that Barrett's setting limits relieved me of this need. It reminded me of when Greta had told me I couldn't lie anymore, that lying needed to be taken off the menu. What a relief! The craving was lifted, just like that. It turned out to be a surrender to values I already had, which had been buried under some more desperate instinct. No one had ever given me a "no" that I believed in. Was that all I was looking for? For someone else to tell me that I wasn't capable of anything, that

I didn't make up all the rules? In a way, it made sense. What a responsibility!

I remember being seventeen years old, living on my own in Boston, fascistically independent. Still, I took the 88 bus to work every day and was quietly amazed that I made it across the city in one piece, that the bus came on time and drivers obeyed traffic laws, that the world managed for one more day not to dissolve into total chaos. I'm not sure where this fundamental suspicion that the world was perpetually on the brink of dissolving originated from. I remember realizing as a child that my parents were fallible, my teachers tired and often misinformed; that the government could not be trusted; that electricity, money, television shows, and the bus came to me from places invented and managed by people; and that people could be wrong, and cruel, and confused. These are also mundane revelations. Most children experience them, but not every child decides they need to play God. For some reason I did. In drugs, in the dungeon, in my relationships, and in my mind, I was always trying to manage the responsibility of keeping everything under control, trying to prove that it was possible, and then trying to find a way out of it. With drugs and with domming, it was always the two extremes: total forfeit of power and annihilation of will or complete control, a godlike power to manage both my internal and external environments. Both were exhausting. I had gone so far as I did to prove that I could survive anything, to allay my fears. I was preparing myself for the imminent dissolution of the world, but I was also looking for permission to stop.

Greta had talked about aligning my will with the will of a higher power, and I realized that I had aligned my behavior with what I believed. I no longer had to think about what that was anymore, I just knew immediately if I acted in some way incongruent with it. Which I still did sometimes. Especially in the first year with Barrett, I would resort to old methods: withholding, willfulness, attempts to claim more than my share of power in the relationship, testing him. Admitting my own desires sometimes made me feel like a panicked animal. But they didn't work anymore. Our dynamic created a paradigm different from any previous relationship I'd had, one in which those methods no longer worked. It only worked in balance; if I tried to take more, I got less. So I stopped trying. Like my cravings for drugs, these impulses petered out until there was only a bare flutter left, little more than a reminder of what I once would have done.

# 37

Do you miss it?" Autumn leaned over the table, one arm wrapped around her pregnant belly, and plucked the last dumpling out of the bamboo steamer. She was also with a new man, one who didn't need her money. Midday at Zen Palate in Union Square was a zoo; frantic servers jostled our table with their hips and the man behind Autumn barked with laughter. At a certain level of noise and crowd, New York's mania can be a comfort, like bobbing on top of a salty wave, everyone shifting in tandem—tightly bound molecules pulled by some greater force, the jumbled twine of our wills somehow unifying into a single tide.

"Sure! Parts of it, anyway. Don't you?"

"I don't miss giving enemas."

"All those hairy asses in panties, ugh."

We laughed, still happy to share this experience and happy to be on the other side of it.

"No, but I miss that feeling, you know?"

"Like you own the world?"

"Yeah, like it's real. Reminds me of the first time I did cocaine."

"Right! So invincible."

We split the check and kissed good-bye before she headed for the train. Her days were then spent studying for anatomy exams and elevating her swollen feet. It's funny but not surprising that she ended up a bona fide nurse. I've known more than one former sex worker who did. Whatever other reasons brought you to it, our work required a patience with the human body—call it nurturance, caretaking, or curiosity—that not all people have and only some can learn. To my surprise, mine dissipated soon after I stopped needing it. I was never particularly squeamish as a child, increasingly less as I got older, and barely flinched at all the bodily grotesqueries during my years at the dungeon but had since become faint at the mention of blood. Cleaning a surface wound on my dog gave me vertigo mere months after I stopped domming. In so many ways, it was a return to more tender states, as if my suppressed innocence had been preserved for all that time.

Barrett and I moved in together after three months, to a leafy neighborhood a few blocks north of Prospect Park. The routine of our life asserted itself quickly, as if it had been waiting to relax into its natural state and was relieved at our readiness finally. I taught, wrote, went to class, and ran in the park with the dog—a big beautiful animal that had been Autumn's, whose needs and neuroticism lent me more patience for my own.

The normality of my life felt sometimes like a huge practical joke. Mostly though, it felt like a blessing, like finally being ready to relax into my own natural state. Barrett never knew me as an active addict, a dominatrix; no one I met then had. They saw me as I was after those things had passed; they saw what those things made me: a sober, moral, responsible woman who laughed easily, was early for everything, and liked to be in bed by 11:00 P.M. Sometimes it felt like a lie, though I knew it wasn't. If anything, I had more conviction and confidence in the way that I lived than most people I knew. I rarely wanted to be anywhere or anyone else. That is the gift of taking the long road; you know you're not missing anything.

I used to think that happiness, like God, was an idea weaker people were sold on, to manage the grief of a world with so much suffering. It is just easier, I thought, to decide that you are doing something wrong and you just need to buy the right thing, read the right book, find the right guru, or pray more to be happy than to accept that life is a great long heartbreak. Happiness is not what I imagined that mirage to be: an unending ecstasy or state of perpetual excitement. Not a high or a mirage, it is just being okay. My happiness is the absence of fear that there won't be enough— enough money, enough power, enough security, enough of a cushion of these things to protect me from the everyday heartbreaks of being human. Heartbreak doesn't kill you. It changes you.

After watching Autumn waddle down the subway stairs, I walked across the park, killing time before I had to head up to school. I *did* miss it sometimes. I still had the dreams—I would for a long time. But I didn't miss the best part—that feeling of pressing up against the barest parts of being human. I'd thought I had to look for it in dark places, that it would be hidden. Turns out it wasn't.

# Acknowledgments

WHILE WRITING A BOOK can be a lonely task, it is not one that can be done alone. Above all, I must thank all the brave and beautiful people I knew during the years that this story takes place, the ones I included, and the ones I didn't. I am enormously grateful to my agent, Scott Hoffman, for asking all the right questions and accepting nothing less than my best, but most of all for his faith and encouragement throughout the painful process of ushering my story into the right hands, and for knowing whose those were. I cannot imagine a more perfect editor to have worked with than Karyn Marcus, whom I trusted instantly for her marvelous vision, understanding, and belief in this book. For their invaluable guidance, I owe more than I can say to Jo Ann Beard, Nick Mills—who suggested I write this, and especially Vijay Seshadri. And thank you to those who helped me maintain my sanity all along the way, among them my first readers: Caitlin Delohery, Susan DeFord, Shelly Oria, Elizabeth Reichert, Jill Jarvis, Alanna Schubach, Shoshana Sklare, Michael Mah, Erin Duff Shanahan, Emily Anderson, Claire Boland Gage, Anne Hall, Laura

Snyder, Jill Stoddard, Jenna Giannasio, Kat Byrne, Beth O'Brien, Laura Schurich, Will Mangum, Nelly Reifler, Joan Silber, Kathleen Hill, Irini Spanidou, Jan Clausen, James Marcus, Seth Colter Walls, William Georgiades, and all my Saturday ladies, who listened. And to Ann Roberts, without whom this book could not have been written. And to my family, for never doubting me. And to Barrett, my happy ending.